By Earl Shorris

OFAY

THE BOOTS OF THE VIRGIN

THE DEATH
OF THE
GREAT SPIRIT

AN ELEGY FOR THE AMERICAN INDIAN

EARL SHORRIS

SIMON AND SCHUSTER · NEW YORK

FIRST PRINTING

SBN 671–20870–5
LIBRARY OF CONGRESS CATALOG CARD NUMBER: 70–139660
DESIGNED BY EVE METZ
MANUFACTURED IN THE UNITED STATES OF AMERICA
BY AMERICAN BOOK–STRATFORD PRESS, NEW YORK

A portion of this book appeared in the Atlantic
Monthly, © *1971. The publishers wish to thank The
University of Chicago Press for permission to reprint
an excerpt appearing on pages 71–72 from* The Savage
Mind, *by Claude Lévi-Strauss, © 1962 by Librairie
Plon, Paris, © 1966 by The University of Chicago
Press.*

FOR MY INTREPID TRAVELING COMPANION,

JAMES SASSON SHORRIS

CONTENTS

PREFACE

THERE is a chapter in this book about the Sun Dance at Pine Ridge, South Dakota that probably should have been longer and even more personal, but I don't generally admire that kind of journalism, and I thought it best to keep the book entirely free of it. The purpose of expanding the chapter would have been to demonstrate the kindness and hospitality of the Oglala Sioux by showing how they treated me and my son, particularly my son. Calvin Jumping Bull taught him Sioux words and signs. The Sons of the Oglalas let him sit with them while they sang and drummed. Gary Tobacco taught him to ride a horse. The rapport was formed almost immediately, and it was never strained. He was eight years old then, and I think it must have been the best week of his life.

I was prepared for something quite different. We were strangers, representatives of the people who had made war on the Indians for three hundred years and now hold them in poverty and subjugation. I could not imagine either their capacity to forgive or their fondness for children. Nor was their warmth toward him shown in an expected way. He was not physically embraced, as in the academies of group joy and therapy. They let him be a human being; they gave him his dignity. And he basked in the safety and comfort of it.

It was less easy to find friends when I traveled alone, for I lack my son's talent in that area; nonetheless, Indian people invited me to their homes, shared their food with me and often told me secrets, not in innocence, but in the hope that something good would come of their revelations.

In some cases, I have chosen not to reveal what was told

9

to me, either because it would have been embarrassing to
the person with whom I talked or because it was not understood at the time of the conversation that it would be
reported in a book. The latter is the case with my friends
Laurie and Donovan Archambault. Much of this book, particularly those parts dealing with urban Indians, has been
influenced by them. It was Donovan who said to me, "I
didn't know whether I should take that job teaching Indian
history. Hell, Indians didn't have any history. I had to start
with 1492." He had looked into his Sioux and Gros Ventre
background to find an idea that had come to Claude Lévi-
Strauss out of a lifetime of study. It ended any doubt I had
about using Lévi-Strauss' thoughts on the "hot" and "cool"
societies as a guide in attempting to understand the circum-
stances of American Indians.

There are places in this book where people whom I have
liked are criticized or shown in an unfavorable light. I think
of such criticism as an act of joining, a consideration of the
people I wrote about as human and worthy of my participation. It is criticism made out of care rather than distance, for
I never found myself able to achieve any great distance from
the people I interviewed; my hopes for objectivity died
early. So to those people who find I have sometimes returned
criticism for frankness, I plead equality, which has made me
incapable of either patronizing or objectifying them.

To avoid duplicating work that has already been done, I
have either left out or only briefly mentioned some important aspects of the problems and successes of American
Indians. Edmund Wilson has written of Mad Bear Anderson
and the Iroquois in *Apologies to the Iroquois*. Stan Steiner
has produced an encomium for Indian activists in *The New
Indians*, and the policies of the Bureau of Indian Affairs are
deservedly castigated in *Our Brother's Keeper*, edited by
Edgar S. Cahn.

The Rough Rock Demonstration School, which seems to

me to be the most promising of Indian efforts toward self-determination, is mentioned only briefly here. The school has published several books explaining its educational and community programs, and more will be published soon. Navaho histories, biographies, myths and stories are also being prepared for publication by the staff at Rough Rock. A documentary film about the school has been produced by the National Educational Television Network and numerous articles about it have appeared in journals of education.

Historical and anthropological works about American Indians are available in any bookstore or library. Each of them has a bibliography that lists most of the others.

Four books by Lévi-Strauss and a book of *Conversations with Claude Lévi-Strauss* by Georges Charbonnier, which is an excellent general introduction, have now been published in English. They are indispensable to anyone who is interested in the human mind and the societies that have been constructed by it.

To Mrs. Mifaunway Hines, Woodrow Sneed, Alexander Ami and perhaps a hundred others who took the time to talk with me, often when it was not convenient for them, and now do not find themselves mentioned in the text, I apologize. When it came time to begin the writing, I had gathered over a thousand pages of notes, and I had to choose, sometimes simply for reasons of length, what would be reported directly and what would be included only as part of the general observations and conclusions.

Many people have been helpful to me in writing this book. I would like particularly to thank Herbert Gold, Anita Gross, Tony Lehman, Lynn Nesbit and Tom Hedley. Most of all, I would like to thank Sylvia Sasson Shorris, my wife and my friend, who endured my many trips, listened to endless hours of conversation about the people and the ideas, made suggestions about the manuscript after each reading, and did it all with wit and reason.

A warrior
I have been.
Now
It is all over.
A hard time
I have.

—The last song of Sitting Bull,
translated by Frances Densmore

When the Indian has forgotten the music of his fore-fathers, when the sound of the tomtom is no more, when noisy jazz has drowned the melody of the flute, he will be a dead Indian. When from him has been taken all that is his, all that he has visioned in nature, all that has come to him from infinite sources, he then, truly, will be a dead Indian. His spirit will be gone, and though he walk crowded streets, he will, in truth, be—dead!

—STANDING BEAR

1 THE SIOUX AND THE CZAR

You SHOULDN'T HAVE taken advantage of me, Injun Charley; not then, when I was five and you were a hundred and five. You shouldn't have taken advantage of me when my child's mind was naked and you had such luxuriant swaddles to offer: heroic gore, John Locke, the sound of bugles, glory in the God of your fathers. They were naked too, Charley; you told me so yourself. You said they wore nothing but paint and feathers.

The afternoons belonged to you. In the evenings, my grandfather told of Cossacks in Russian streets, beasts on horseback, the Czar's own devils. The Cossacks drove him to walk for seven months until he reached Constantinople, and the memory of Cossacks sent him across Europe in a traveling tailor's wagon, with crusts of bread to eat and lice to fight for the sanctity of his body. I gloried in his pioneer spirit, wept for his suffering, and wondered to God that there had been no Injun Charley to protect my grandfather from the Cossacks.

The lobby of the hotel was quiet while you talked. It was before Muzak, before barbers had electric clippers. Even the buzz of the switchboard faded rounding the corner into that three-sided room of rough fabrics and pipe smoke. Your hair was yellow again with age, and scant, spilled down your neck, chopped off reaching for your shoulders. There were tobacco stains in your mustache. You had never become used to those gold-rimmed spectacles, forever consigning

15

them to the hard blue case that closed with a clap. You wore a cavalryman's boots and liar's galluses, and I think you must have been the tallest man in that part of Illinois.

"I knew Bill Cody," you said, after I had seen the movie. "Showfolk. I seen Colonel Custer too in my time. Betrayed by Injun scouts. It cost us one of the smartest outfits in the United States Cavalry. The Sioux had to have some sort of sneak advantage the way they did over Custer, or they couldn't fight." Then you fell asleep, your hands folded over your belly and a tear running from each eye, as if for fallen comrades.

The sleeps were frequent, but short. When your eyes teared and your head fell, I was afraid you were dying, because the elevator man had said you were the oldest person in the world. But you always came back, as long as I knew you, and every time it was as if you had been with them out there on the Great Plains, galloping through oceans of grass, badlands, great stands of cottonwood and pine. You never came back smelling of blood, though I knew they shot arrows at you in your sleeps. "We seen a raiding party from a train one time," you said upon returning, "a big party with their tipis and pony drags. The captain stopped the train right there, and we took the horses down. While we were saddling up, they were taking down their tipis. It was a race to see who could get moving faster. We had good Army discipline, that's how we won the race."

"And what happened then?"

"Injun fighting," you said, smiling, drawing yourself up in the chair, searching for the old bearing.

"Did you get one?"

"Two or three that time. But the number is no matter, son; only a savage counts how many he kills."

"Did the Indian ladies cry?"

"You got to understand, son, Injun women aren't like your mom or your grandma; they're savages. They hack a body to pieces. They do the worst kind of torture, worse than the men. No, Injun women are just as savage as the men, especially among the Sioux. You can't trust a Sioux, not a brave or a squaw or even a Sioux baby. That's how ornery they are." You slept again, the tears ran from your eyes. I saw you as you were then, blue trousers with a yellow stripe tucked into those boots you could not abandon, a kerchief around your neck, a white campaign hat covering your yellow hair. You smelled of sage, you smelled of pine. Mountains rose behind you. Injuns fell at your feet. I loved you, Injun Charley. I loved you because you made me safe in America, you conquered the Cossacks.

Now you are dust, Charley, your boots are dust; and I am not so naked anymore. I know you. I know your real history. At Mystic River you smelled the Pequot flesh burning. You saw five hundred Wampanoags in slave chains shipped out of Plymouth. Dressed in trapper's gear, you touched off the cannon at Santa Rita del Cobre. Resplendent in blue again, you saw the pubic hair of the women scalped at Sand Creek. You rode with Custer at the Washita. You, Injun Charley, cut off the breasts of Navaho women and used them like baseballs. You played kickball in the streets of New Amsterdam with the heads of the Wappingers. At Wounded Knee, you manned a Hotchkiss gun and dug a common grave.

There were 840,000 of them when you waded ashore, Charley, and when you put away your sword there were 250,000. Was there no other way? Did you have to be the Cossack? Damn you, Injun Charley; you told me you were God's own man.

2 THE CHILDREN OF DECREPITUDE AND THE YOUTH OF THE WORLD

THEY DRESSED THEMSELVES in splendid rags, animal hides, beads, bells and feathers. Their hair was long, tied with shreds of cloth and thongs, and they were barefoot. They organized themselves into a tribe, these seekers of God, believers in magic, worshippers of Nature, and they left their place in the West, moving across the deserts and awesome canyons to the high mesas of Northern Arizona. When they arrived at the Hopis Reservation, they emerged from their Volkswagen buses and declared themselves the spiritual brothers of the Hopi.

The children of the rich in the world had come to seek salvation from the rich in spirit. They were not invited, but no one is invited to salvation. They were refugees, escaping the last moments of a decayed civilization, able to carry with them only a few charms; a magical acid, a substance that could change the tempo of inner worlds, a cushion of grass. Mystics, visionaries; victims of progress, history, objectivity, these people who saw in themselves the hope of the world sought to learn from the Hopi the secret of the inner peace that manifests itself in perfect passivity.

Instead, they saw land too poor to cover its nakedness, and they met a people whose immutable world-concept had been shattered by pickup trucks, bureaucrats and Christ. But the problems of the Hopis did not deter them from their mission; they took what they could. They followed the Hopis into the fields, watched them pray before shrines buried there to mark the boundaries of the clan holdings. They learned that the shrines had been buried in those fields for more than a thousand years, since the Hopis had come, barefoot and with long hair, out of the West. They watched and waited, patient seekers. And when the opportunity came, they dug up the shrines and carried them off.

The shrines had survived conquistadors, missionaries, native marauders, the Bureau of Indian Affairs and Ruth Benedict, but there is no defense against a disappointed disciple. The Hopis could not deliver what the hippies needed; the life of the noble savage was not free of everything but satori. Instead of meditation and obvious joy, the hippies found people with rough hands and expectations for their children. The sons of the priests of the kivas were university students. No one seriously denied the merits of electricity or running water. The spokesman for the radical traditional group on the reservation was also the head of a two-car family.

The religious rites coveted by the hippies do exist, but they were not available to them. The ceremonies are conducted in the Ute-Aztecan language of the Hopi, and they are, with a few exceptions, private, the privilege only of those who have been initiated into the tribe. They are also complex and exotic, the product of a vision of the world so alien to Western man that he can grasp it only through the remarkable abstractions of Claude Lévi-Strauss.

For the benighted hippie, the Indian offers a dimly perceived model of an alternative to the society he finds unbearable. Drugs that distort or destroy the mind are to him more efficacious. But the hippie is not alone in seeking an alternative to the artificial life of technological society. The cultural dissidents in America are not all pathetic children. They have a long history, begun in the writings of Rousseau, whose theories about "primitive peoples" have been misinterpreted for so many generations that his great work on "the origin of inequality" now goes unread, having been replaced by the crude thinking of the cultural evolutionists and other cultural elitists. Working with very limited ethnographic data, and without computers, knowledge of structural linguistics or even field experience, Rousseau was able to reach these conclusions about "primitive men" in their passage out of the state of nature:

> . . . though men had become less patient, and their natural compassion had already suffered some diminution, this period of expansion of the human faculties, keeping a just mean between the indolence of the primitive state and the petulant activity of our egoism, must have been the happiest and most stable of epochs. The more we reflect on it, the more we shall find that this state was the least subject to revolutions, and altogether the very best man could experience; so that he can have departed from it only through some fatal accident, which, for the public good, should never have happened. The example of savages, most of whom have been found in this state, seems to prove that men were meant to remain in it, that it is the real youth of the world, and that all subsequent advances have been apparently so many steps towards the perfection of the individual, but in reality towards the decrepitude of the species.*

The cultural dissidents now recognize the signs of that decrepitude which Rousseau foresaw in 1753: pollution is destroying the symbiotic balance necessary to continuing life on the planet, war and revolution are the works of every generation, the great corporations devour men, loneliness is epidemic, technology has failed to produce social justice; wherever man turns he is unable to find limits, everything is

* Rousseau, J. J., A Discourse on the Origin of Inequality, etc., in *The Social Contract*, New York, Carlton House, n.d., p. 200.

possible, nothing is complete; the quality of life is malaise, the fear of the known is unconquerable.

For many of those who have abandoned hope in the direction of Western Civilization, salvation lies in returning to the life of neolithic man, the savage described by Rousseau. Theodore Roszak, at the conclusion of his work on the "counter culture," advises us to emulate a Pawnee shaman in choosing a life-style. After twenty-five centuries of Western Civilization, a return to neolithic wisdom is the best advice of a scholar who represents the thinking of a significant part of America. The antithesis of Injun Charley is arrived, bearing in some secret genetic memory the chthonian myth that will replace Darwin.

But the return to "the happiest and most stable of epochs" is not easy. The hippies, failing in their attempts to learn the Hopi religion, had to be content with stealing the shrines; it was all they could get, as their more sophisticated brethren will get only slick-paper reproductions of paintings and painstakingly inept translations of songs. It is a difference, as Lévi-Strauss has pointed out, between the hot and the cool. The progressive, historical man cannot enter the crystallized, immutable world of neolithic thought, for his very entrance into that world shatters it. The construction of that closed world in which everything is explained is so delicate that it can be hypothesized that the Indian culture was destroyed when the first white man arrived in the Western Hemisphere and demonstrated that he was not a god. Lévi-Strauss did not choose the image casually, crystal is not malleable, nor can history, once begun, be terminated except by the termination of the species.

The Navahos, knowing that horses were brought to America by the Spaniards, are publishing a history of their tribe in which the introduction of the horse will be attributed to the act of a supernatural being. It is an attempt to maintain the world-view which was held by their pre-lite-rate forebears in a book compiled by Navahos and whites for the use of Navaho children. Several white historians who worked on the book have asked that their names be removed from the title page because of the section on the origin of the horse in America. The two realities cannot be merged; a man who sees a different world with each eye is paralyzed. Western Civilization will have to proceed in its own direction, depending upon objective reality, systematic logic, art and laughter to find a life-style in which joy and technology are compatible. The Pawnee shaman will offer some advice, though his magic is of another world. The Hopi shrines, interred again in some corner of a Volkswagen bus, will reveal nothing.

If we can assume that time is irreversible, and that white men will not become Indians, the question that remains is whether time, once begun, can be stopped, and the synchronic world of neolithic man be retained, so that Indians do not become white men.

3 HALFMOON FIRE PLACE

SHE HAS PEYOTE EYES and gypsy hair. Her words come in the drawl of Oklahoma, Appalachia, diction out of the dust bowl, tone from the massacre at Wounded Knee. She is lean and she should be tired. There are eight children to care for, and a house as naked as a barracks. But somehow her face is unlined, and the skin is tight to shining across her cheekbones. She is a missionary of the embodiment of God, the Great Mystery, in the dried button top of the peyote cactus.

Her eyes are black and staring, open to the round. They are the eyes of a priestess of the revivalist's tent. Her intensity is gathered in them, projected, seeking in everything the incomprehensible communion by which she is sustained. She is an instiller, a maker of faith in the face of temptation. A thousand times she has heard the water drum and the rattle, a thousand times she has taken the medicine and been transported.

And her anger has not slowed: "We pray all through the night that even if we're poor we can still live in this world."

There are two chairs and three cots in the front room of her house. The floor is covered with unmatched patches of linoleum. She grinds out cigarettes on the round iron stove in the center of the floor. In the room, there are no cupboards, shelves or chests. The bedclothes have faded to pastels; salmon, green and plaid. Under one of the beds a pair of glittering, gold-colored pumps are sprawled.

In the cracking mud forecourt of her house a garish rented car has been parked. She demands with the missing button at the waist of her dress and the tension of her jaw that there be an apology for the wasteful opulence of this car that has followed the muddy ruts to her house. She demands. It is her due for being made to live in this house of thin walls that is in the night as lonely as an island. The white man is indebted to her. He has taken everything palpable, and he now comes for her spirit.

There is nothing to give. It is an anthropologist's moment. The inquisitor has come, like Sartre assassinating Genet, to ask, to note, to clean the life from her like mud from a nugget. A descendant of Plato, he has come to reduce her to a form, to hack away the uniqueness of her face and dry up her sweat, making the deadly mutation that will make her immutable. She, as a woman, a dreamer and wailer of her Lakota songs, must stop, disappear. The very subjectivity that makes her an Indian must become an object. The investigator, acknowledging his cultural superiority by the act of investigating, freezes the instant of her and her people, a euphemism for the murder of the spirit that Western men work so well.

Mrs. Bernard Red Cloud of the Halfmoon Fire Place of the Native American Church is already a victim of the anthropologist and the missionary; the church itself is ushering the Indian into the house of his conqueror.

The Indian rejected Christianity at first. The suffering figure upon the cross held out nothing that he wanted. A leaf, a sleek animal, a bird in flight would have seduced him more easily. Now the people of the Native American Church call Christ their brother. They pray to Jesus. They celebrate Easter. In the genesis of the Church, as Mrs. Red Cloud tells it, one can see its appeal to a person living in a log house on a polluted river, a wrecked car, like a monument to his condition, rusting in the front yard: "They said an Indian woman and her two children were in the desert lost from their tribe. They got hungry and thirsty and fell asleep. And they had a dream in which they were told to take a green herb and they wouldn't be hungry and thirsty any more. When she awoke she saw the peyote sitting there and they took it and they weren't hungry or thirsty any more. So they brought it back to the tribe."

About a quarter of a million American Indians belong to the Church. Mrs. Red Cloud said, "If it's possible, I'd like for my children to grow up in the Native American Church, because you get good understandings from it and you try to better yourself. Our oldest boy and a daughter go to the Native American Church. They came by themselves. We don't try to boss 'em into going; the children see that we're doin' good through the Church."

"Doin' good" in Mrs. Red Cloud's lexicon refers to economics. It is a tenet of the Church that those who do well in terms of material goods are good people, for had they not been good, they would not have been rewarded. This apotheosis of materialism may seem peculiarly American, but it is not Indian: the law of inheritance among the Sioux was that nothing could be inherited that could be lessened by division. A man achieved honor by giving away his possessions, not by acquiring them.

"We pray the way our heart tells us to pray," Mrs. Red Cloud said, and so she must, for the institutionalization of dreams is impossible. The external structure of a Native American Church service is simple: a tipi, a crescent or Cheyenne Moon made of sand, a fire built of sticks in the shape of a right angle, the drum, the gourd rattle, the fan of feathers and the four shapes made of ashes by the Fire Chief during the night. "We hold service on Saturday night because that's when a lot of temptation is out. We pray instead of goin' into temptation." During the service each person sings his own songs, accompanied by a drummer. The progress of the service is marked by the displays of the Fire Chief:

"The first is a triangle. That stands for 'In God we trust.'" At midnight, he puts out a heart: we should all have brotherly love, like it was meant to be. Around 2 or 3 A.M. he puts out the Morning Star. That represents the Lord—He said, 'I am the Morning Star, anything you ask at this time, it shall be granted unto you.' Before the service is over, he puts out a waterbird. That represents an eagle. The eagle is king of all our feathered friends, so in the morning he's the first to be awake, and when he whistles, all wild life wake up and go for water."

Prayer meetings are often recorded on tape cartridges, which are exchanged among the various Fire Places of the Church. Mrs. Red Cloud played a tape on which part of the service was sung in English:

> Jesus, our commander, watch over our soldier boys.
> Jesus, our commander, watch over my son-in-law.

The English song was over after a repetition of the lines, and she turned off the machine. "They're singin' in Indian now," she said.

It is not easy to belong to the Native American Church at Pine Ridge. Neighbors complain of the drumming; they find a strangeness about the peyotists. The "medicine," as Mrs. Red Cloud prefers to call peyote, has become expensive; they are now forced to travel from South Dakota to the Mexican border to harvest the buttons. The Native American Church is also caught in the round of church affiliations in which the Sioux participate, the newest mission usually being the one most generous with its larder and consequently having the most adherents.

Mrs. Red Cloud is a besieged woman, but she is also laying siege to her enemies. When the drum is for her song and the Morning Star is out, she speaks to the Great Mystery, the First Grandfather. There *are* Thunderbirds and a White Buffalo Woman; the pipe that was carried on the shoulders of the Woman of the West still exists on earth and is the connection with Wakan-tanka. And now there is Jesus too. Her song is born in mystic communion with them all. Understanding is hers. She wears the eyes of invincibility. Her siege is of the spirit, her weapons are incomprehensible. She has consumed the embodiment of God.

"There's a new church here called The Body of Christ, and it took all the members away. But they'll come back. And it seems if people stay away a long time, they come back with a better understanding." The rattle and the water drum are ready, there is medicine enough in the sack for all; she awaits them; she has seen their returning.

The church of Mrs. Red Cloud has been so invaded by anthropologists that when asked how the church had spread to the Navaho Reservation, the national president of the Native American Church refuses to answer for fear that his information is erroneous. "According to Dr. Stewart," he says, "boys that were in the Army learned from other tribes, and that's how it was introduced to the Navaho Tribe." The monographs on the "peyote cult" pile up, the chemical analysis of peyote is common knowledge, the paraphernalia of the prayer meetings have been diagramed and photographed, the split between the Ute, Winnebago and Navaho factions is documented, the legal history is recorded in the archives of the United States Senate, but the Native American Church is not discussed for its theology, nor are its adherents given their moment of glory in the possibility for survival that has come to them through the church.

It is a church of the poor and the wounded, the church of the last resort. In the prayer meetings, the members pray and comfort each other, telling of their miseries past and of their earthly salvation through divine communication. For Mrs. Philip Jackson, a Navaho, the church is the center of life. "For almost two years I went because my husband wanted to do better and have a better life. Then I had the experience. The peyote makes you see yourself. I had this complex about being an orphan, people were saying things about me. My grandmothers and my aunts and uncles spoiled me when I was a little girl, but I always felt alone. I didn't know why my parents died, or why my firstborn died. Then I had the experience: it seems like He was talking to me, and He said, 'I am your Father, the Earth is your Mother. You can call me Mother. You can call me Father. Your firstborn died, but you have two sons in her place.' You see, if we didn't use peyote, if we didn't go to Native American Church, we wouldn't be able to find ourselves."

Mrs. Jackson is the secretary of the Native American Church of California. Her husband is the president. They live in an industrial town near San Francisco, and hold their meetings in a hogan in the redwoods when the weather is good. They also go to meetings in Southern California, Nevada, and on the reservation. The Fire Place to which the Jacksons belong is small; there are only twenty members and their children, all of them Navahos but for one family, which is Winnebago. The membership is like the extended family of the reservation. Whenever one of them is ill or depressed or in trouble, they hold a meeting and pray for him. "They had a meeting for my husband," Mrs. Jackson said. "He was tired and didn't have pep. They told him, 'We need you. We wouldn't even have this church, this hogan if it wasn't for you.' That's how we are. We help one another. This weekend, we're going to the reservation, to a meeting for my brother. He was the biggest drunk there ever was for fourteen years, and then he took peyote and he gave it up. Now his wife left him, and they're putting up a meeting for him."

For her, the eclecticism of the church is obvious. She was

raised a Presbyterian who believed in traditional Navaho medicine. She understands and uses the tools of group therapy in the role of support. She believes that Native American Church services can cure physical ailments, though she also sees the value of a meeting in preparing a patient for treatment in a hospital. She accepts everything that contributes to a better life, for she, like most Indians, was in communion with despair long before she heard the voice of God, and though God has spoken to her, there is not an "experience" for her in every meeting, and she knows that despair does not vanish, but merely recedes to a lower level of consciousness to await the inevitable moment of weakness, the breach in the good life that will allow it to dominate again.

For Mrs. Jackson, Mrs. Red Cloud, and thousands of other Indians in Arizona, New Mexico, Oklahoma, California, Nevada and the Dakotas, the ritual of peyote, if not the drug itself, is survival in a world of alkali water, dry grass, soil erosion, unemployment, alcoholism, disease and early death; for many years they were arrested for using or transporting the drug, which they prefer to call medicine or a sacred herb. The man who led the long fight to legalize peyote for American Indians is the only hero in the Native American Church. In his role as president of the church, he corresponds with United States Senators, attends important conferences, lectures at universities, and appears as an expert witness in the highest courts. It was he, Frank Takes Gun, who offered the resolution at a meeting in Oklahoma in 1944 that "a national intertribal organization of the peyote church be formed to protect the state, tribal and local organizations." The resolution resulted in the founding of the Native American Church.

In his office in Albuquerque, Frank Takes Gun quietly accepts the gratitude of the thirty-five thousand Navahos who are no longer persecuted for their religious practices because he fought for them and won. He is venerated, mysterious powers are ascribed to him, his name is spoken carefully. But Frank Takes Gun is not a Navaho; he is a Crow, and he must sometimes go home, back to Montana, to his family and his land and his cattle. And when he is at home, the hero of Albuquerque is an outcast.

They whisper about Frank Takes Gun on the Crow. There are rumors, cruel, contradictory stories about his past, many of them centering on the amputated finger on his right hand. The rumors are old now, distorted by time and retelling. It is impossible to sort them out, to discover the ancient wounds and secret jealousies that gave rise to them. Only one thing is sure; almost forty years ago he suffered a terrible beating. His hand was crushed, gangrene set in, and the finger was amputated.

His lower teeth are missing but for one straggler on the right side and a molar or two on the left. He pushes his food far into the left corner of his mouth to find a place where his teeth meet in a bite. They even accuse him of drinking, though he speaks against alcohol with such fervor it would seem impossible. The sight of an Indian boy staggering on a side street in Hardin, Montana, on a Saturday afternoon appalls him. His soft voice catches, rises, hardens with zeal; a boy who could communicate with God is looking for a handle on a brick wall, stumbling over nothing, and the power of God, the gritty, foul-tasting passport to the good life, is resting in plastic sacks, waiting for that boy.

They call him Frank Takes uh Gun on the Crow, which is the way he speaks his name, adding the unclear article, but they do not speak of him often; even the members of his own family avoid him. He, the president of the largest pan-Indian organization in the thirty- or forty-thousand-year history of man in America, ran for vice-president of his tribe, and for his humility, he won less than 10 per cent of the vote. He passed part of his life lobbying in the Montana Legislature for the legalization of peyote in that state. And he won, but

he is not invited to prayer meetings on the Crow Reservation. It is the Winnebago version of the peyote church that is
popular on the reservation now, and its members say their
church is more generous, less concerned with material
goods, not acquisitive, but giving. And perhaps it is so. The
Crows are not rich, but their land is better than that on
many reservations; there are jobs nearby and Federal antipoverty programs are putting money into the reservation.

The Native American Church of Frank Takes Gun belongs to the deserts and log houses, not to the neat bunga-
lows and white fences of the more affluent Crow. His is the
church of a life so hard it is nearly unendurable. It is the
church of the alternative to suicide or starvation, a comfort
on hard ground, looking inward for fertility. Perhaps the
Crows have become too sophisticated for the church of
Frank Takes Gun. "In our church," he said, "every man
prays in his own native language. He doesn't read out of a
book. He says things he understands. In something so important as divine communication, a man should say only what
he understands.

"Sometimes a song will be given to a man. Sometimes he'll
learn a song. The old people, sometimes they sing and it's
not words. You can't understand what they're saying. It
sounds like humming, but it's their song. They know."

Frank Takes Gun himself reads slowly and with effort,
saying the words softly as he reads them, a man still of the
oral tradition, wearing bifocals, sitting in his dusty car off
the main street of Hardin, the town that was built to sell
liquor and cars to the Crow and Northern Cheyenne. He
wears Levi's and a ten-gallon hat. His brown-and-beige-check
cowboy shirt is fading, and his pinstripe suitcoat with the
pointed western-style yoke is worn as if it were denim. He
produces copies of letters from senators and Department of
the Interior officials, unfolding them slowly, thick fingers
and blunt, heavy nails examining treasures. He had been on

horseback for twelve hours the previous day, herding his cattle back after they had broken through a fence. He is sixty-two years old, getting tired. A waxy roundness is forming over his cheekbones, and his hair is graying. He is a man of average height, broad across the back and chest, but small for a Crow, the *beaux hommes*. He walks with the straddling gait of the full blood Crow men. He leaves the spoon in the cup while he drinks his coffee, the campfire etiquette too deep to have been lost in the statehouses and Senate hearing rooms.

His grandfather was a medicine man. His father took him to his first tipi meeting when he was thirteen years old, though the elders were opposed to having children attend. He ate peyote in that first meeting, and became a believer: "It gave me a feeling after I absorbed divine communication; I felt a gaining of strength. I felt reborn into a new world. I felt I was only human. I felt it was my duty to worship and adore God for my future good."

He speaks slowly, with a great formality about his words. When he speaks of communion with God, he raises his hands before him, the left before the right, the palms open and parallel, and he lifts his face upward, looking in the direction marked by his hands. In a café of plastics, speaking over the sound of the jukebox and the waitress calling out orders, the gesture is so Indian that an atavistic aura envelops the conversation. The mystic sensibility prevails; in a romantic instant, the youth of the world returns.

"Some people talk about their divine communication. It's a private thing, but sometimes they tell a close friend. Some people have told me their communication." His voice falls to a whisper. He raises his hands again, and looks beyond his listener. "They say they have seen pictures. Pictures of God Almighty." He stops, awed by what he has revealed. The jukebox continues. The waitress calls out to him, asking if he wants more coffee, but he does not hear. "The greatest thing that God gave to man is the mind. The mind has the power of God Almighty in it. The mind can communicate with God. In divine communication, man receives the power of God."

He wishes no competition between churches, though he remembers the persecutions by missionaries and the Women's Christian Temperance Union. To define the place of the Native American Church, he draws three places with the side of his hand; on the outsides are the Christian churches, "a religion that was imported to the shores of this continent," and Indian medicine; in the center is the peyote church. "Take the Sun Dance," he said. "They go without food and water. Take a man that goes out in the country all alone to be in pain, to be in sorrow, to be pitied—cuts a finger off. The fasting, the suffering, seeking visions, as they are called. It is nothing other than divine communications. So when members of the Native American Church say that they have visions, they are also divine communications. The dictates of your conscience is what it amounts to."

He calls the members of the Native American Church "good Christians," but he operates with a special definition. "When they believe in God, we feel they are good Christian people. Good Christian means people that goes to Church. The Indian was always aware that there's a divine power behind Mother Earth. All of God's gifts are from Mother Earth. The older people have reservoirs of religious belief; the Indian is a believer in divine power."

Frank Takes Gun has not seen God or Christ. "I don't have to," he says. "I know God is there. I felt as a young man that the people should and must begin to learn the truth. Then, in 1933, the Secretary of the Interior, Harold Ickes spoke over the radio. He said, 'The policy of the Department of the Interior and the Bureau of Indian Affairs shall be: we want the Indian to live his own life in his own way. We want to preserve the cultural values of these people. We want the white neighbors of these original Americans to learn and respect their religions. We want both races to live together in mutual tolerance and understanding in this country.' From there, I felt a gaining of strength. The only way that could be accomplished was to organize the Indian intertribally to preserve their God-given right."

So he fought for religious freedom, and unlike that of the Europeans who came to settle in America for that purpose, his belief in that freedom extended into the reality of his life. He organized the Native American Church to protect its members, and he asked no more of them than the opportunity to do that. "If they get in trouble, we go in and help them," he said. "That's the only authority we have over any group. We're not the boss. We do not try to curb religious activity on anybody." He realizes that it is in the structure of the meeting that the "experiences" are born, and he understands the concept Carlos Castaneda has called "special consensus," although he would not use it as a tool of the church. There is no Bible, there are no rules, the church has no hierarchy to provide a source of consensus which may be withheld in case of disobedience. The phonograph records of peyote songs that fill the store windows in Gallup, New Mexico, are unofficial. The beaded gourd rattles that cost $60 in Gallup or $20 in Rapid City, South Dakota are not blessed by the church. "Special consensus" is limited to the group within the tipi or hogan, though it is not limited to hallucinogenic experience. Unlike Castaneda's sorcerer, the members of the Native American Church operate as a group, and one very much influenced by American Christian concepts. Instead of visions of flying or a meeting with supernatural figures, the peyote church member experiences the Protestant Ethic. They do not know his name but it is John Calvin rather than Jesus Christ who appears before them.

God may change the peyotist, but the peyotist, like the Calvinist, has no hope of changing God. "When my daddy died," said Frank Takes Gun, "I prayed for him. But he had to go. God sets a time for men and they have to go then. Nothing can change that. My daddy had to go. We don't pray to change what God sets down. We pray for a good life, a good home, a good family. We pray for the good things; we can't change what God does."

The special consensus of the church limits the peyote experience in the same way that Castaneda's Don Juan expanded his experience. Church members who have heard of hippies are astonished by the reports of their psychedelic experiences; they have experienced nothing so spectacular. And so long as the church maintains its ties with the Protestant Ethic, they will see nothing spectacular, for the mystical psychedelic experience is tightly harnessed for social purposes; the sufferer of poverty in the midst of affluence does not have the leisure to do otherwise.

Perhaps because it is a church of inhibition and prohibition, the Native American Church has won its case for the legalization of the use of peyote by the American Indians. Perhaps it is only a case of justice being done. The reason for his success is of little consequence to Frank Takes Gun; he has succeeded. He no longer feels a need to talk about peyote or his church. The time for publicity is over. He would be satisfied, comfortable, if he could be at home among the Crow. Instead, he complains of the people who want to use the church for political purposes: "When we needed help, there was none. Now that we can worship God Almighty without a shadow of fear, they realize this is a big group of Indians, and they're joining." In anger against the people who keep him out of the church on his own reservation, he points to his own accomplishments: "There's a lot of work there, a lot of work." Surely they know; his tormentors, the ones who cast him out, must know of his work; he must have told them, showed them his letters, offered them a share in his victories.

It seems to make no difference, though, for on Saturday night, when the drum is going down near Yellowtail Dam, Frank Takes Gun has gone to Billings to stay in his room in the Stardust Motel. The leader of 225,000 peyotists chats with the owners of the motel before he goes to a high school basketball game. The conversation is friendly. They like him. "He's very clean," they say, "a smart man. And he's said he won't bring any more Indians into the motel." By midnight, when the peyotists are taking their first sip of water, Frank Takes Gun has gone to his room to lie in his rented bed and listen to the echoing booms of empty freight cars connecting in the switching yard beyond the grain elevators.

The church that Frank Takes Gun founded on the strength of a radio broadcast crosses the lines made by generations and languages. It is the church of a Navaho girl who also belongs to the Third World Liberation Front at Berkeley. It is the church of a Grand Knight of the Knights of Columbus. It is one of the most important political issues for the 118,000 members of the Navaho Tribe. Raymond Nakai became chairman of the tribal council through the support of the peyotists, then refused to recognize them. The Legal Services Program of the Federal Government represented the peyotists in their struggle with Nakai to legalize the Native American Church on the reservation. It was, for the most part, an academic battle; more than thirty thousand Navahos had joined the church before it became legalized. They risked arrest, fines and jail sentences to find the good life.

Traditional Navaho medicine men have cut their hair and given up their colorful headbands for the white cloth and stiff triangular folds of the peyote church. The sacred gatherings of a lifetime—bluebird and eagle feathers, turquoise, coal, exotic herbs—are exchanged for the staff, the rattle and the drum. The lure of the church is almost irresistible: a loving, supportive family gathered around every member in intimate communication; the promise by example of a life richer in material goods, the reward of the sober and industrious man; and the expectation of communion with a half-breed God, whose parents are nature and success. Through poverty, the Indian begins to understand Christ. The missionary could not convince him, but soil erosion, overpopulation, disease and despair bring the nearly naked suffering figure closer to them. Memories of better days have been buried, become fabled days; it is more real to identify with a God for fry bread and drought. It is better than believing that God has abandoned man, easier; the responsibilities are lighter, less faith is required. The victims of Western Civilization pray for each other, the thin Jew upon the cross and the weary Indian in the tipi.

A bridge into the white world is created at the deepest level. Indians are united in the most successful pan-Indian movement in history. But the victory of unity is a failure of identity. The man who called himself Absarokee or Lakota or Dine becomes Indian, peyotist, red man. The descendants of separate civilizations are defined by their conqueror, like the young Crows who no longer call themselves Absarokee, but use the word meaning "our side," a word that they apply to any Indian of any tribe. The process is understood even by some missionaries; peyote meetings have been held on church grounds with priests and nuns in attendance. The missionary is an opportunist: the theft of the spirit is his work. He has learned subtlety since his predecessors were roasted alive and eaten by the Iroquois. He accepts the Native American Church as an earthly step for man on the way to his destiny.

But the missionaries have not been wholly successful; the crystal is shattered, not obliterated. Shards remain. The Native American Church is an accommodation, less than surrender. There is an effort to keep the languages, though that too is failing; portions of the ceremonies and the confessions are translated for the young. The God of the peyotist is constantly redefined, and his dictates, which rise from the mind of the listener, are amended by every experience of the believer. But there is no element of existentialism in the Native American Church; the Indian has no interest in the philosophy of the affluent. The struggle to survive has been excitement enough for him. He seeks a preceding essence in the form of a promise of the good life, the old God of hard times.

Apologists for peyotism say, "It is the only thing we have left that is Indian." But what is Indian? Before the whites came there was no drug culture in America north of Mexico.* The Iroquois studied dreams, the medicine men of the Southwest could and still can bring about the complete remission of some forms of psychosis, the Plains Indians sweated and fasted and prayed for their visions, the Salish-speaking Indians of the Northwest dived into rivers from great heights to bring about visions. Contact with the Great Spirit or the Great Mystery or the One-Whose-House-Is-the Sun was made through acts of discipline. Visions came but few times in a man's life, if at all. The medicine man was an artist, the culture-bearing gene of his people; his was a life of ascension to knowledge. After conquest and poverty, there is a button, and the only necessary discipline is the ability to stomach it long enough to enjoy its effects.

The vision that made Crazy Horse reckless in war, or the vision that caused Chief Seattle to refuse to fight the whites is degenerated into a vision every Saturday night. Iroquois psychotherapy, which antedated Freud, and the complex ceremonies of the psyche of the Navaho are reduced to a

---

* An exception is the use of Jimson weed (*datura*) by the Indians of California and possibly some of the Pueblos. Tobacco and Black Drink, an emetic, were also used. However, the use of peyote did not become widespread until the end of the nineteenth century.

handful of symbols with interpretations plagiarized from the face of a coin.

If the Native American Church is a church of Indians, how can it not be Indian? A paradox is not proposed. It is as Indian as a Navaho's pickup truck or a wrecked car beside a Pomo's house or the suicide of a Quinnalt boy. The peyote church is a gift of conquest, the specimen wriggling to take on the form of the beholder. The attempt at transformation results in transmogrification.

4 AN AX OF STONE,
AN AX OF STEEL

I

ONLY A FEW MILES from the Halfmoon Fire Place,
off a rutted street in a camp crowded with mongrel dogs and
ragged children, in a house behind a house lives an old man
called Fools Crow. He is a Uwipi, a medicine man and prac-
titioner of the traditional vision quest, and there is not a
Sioux Indian within two hundred miles of Pine Ridge who
does not regard him with a certain amount of awe. He is in
contact with the mysteries, and he has given evidence of
that contact too often for them to doubt him. Some Indians
believe that peyotists can find lost objects or identify a thief
while influenced by the drug, but the Uwipi are thought to
have more powerful medicine. The healer and diviner is
also a witch; he can cause illness and even death.

So Fools Crow is venerated. Some do it secretly; they are
the God-fearing, educated Indians trapped between indoor
toilets and the transmundane contacts of the Uwipi. They
have scoffed, good Catholics or Baptists, champions of sewer
systems and sociology, but he has answers for them, con-
firmations of beliefs buried at the level of dreams. He tells
the leader of an urban reconstruction group, "At midnight,
you will hear a bird calling." She laughs, but that night, in
dreams and the immense darkness of the prairie, Fools Crow
triumphs: belief rises in her consciousness, and she is
awakened by the sound of a bird. She does not abandon the

reconstruction project, nor does she cease to participate in the sociological arguments between the Indians and the government of Rapid City, but she accepts empirical proof of mystical truth. She sends a small gift to Fools Crow, and speaks of him softly, no longer amused by an old man who feasts on boiled dog and converses with little stones beside a stream.

For others, he is more than medicine; he is a delicious anachronism, proof that there was a time before conquest. He is the validation of the fathers, and therefore the validation of the sons, antidote to the Ford with a broken axle, the reservoir of a language before English, confirmation that life is a circle—men feed upon the buffalo, men die and are fed upon by the grass, buffalo feed upon the grass—the whites conquered the Indians, the Indians will conquer the whites. Vain hope, perhaps, but sustenance, the Ghost Dance prophecies recalled, the possibility of plenty enabling them to endure the reality of poverty.

At the War Eagle Dance Club Powwow, dressed in feathers and bells, the paling of age hidden under red paint, a pipe in one hand, a fan of feathers in the other, dressed in the old way before the beaded harness, dressed as if the hostiles had not yet surrendered, dancing round after round to the rhythm of six mallets on a drum and a thousand tiny bells, Fools Crow *is* another time, but he is one of the last remaining instances of it, and he has chosen no successor.

He is a flash of history standing on a street in Rapid City, pointing at a thundercloud piling up to the south, and saying through his interpreter, "The Uwipi starts from there. It comes down from Crazy Horse time."

The epitome of *wakan* (magic, mystery, supernatural power) for the Oglala Sioux of Pine Ridge was in Crazy Horse, the son of a medicine man, a warrior who led "the greatest light cavalry in history," according to one of the United States Army generals who fought against him, the

possessor of seven powers, a gallery of totems—and a completely unselfish leader. He was preternatural man, a tragic
hero in the classical sense, and that was but the reality of his
life. For the Sioux, there are more important meanings; he is
proof of the power of the Indian in communion with the
greatest power as defined in that world before history. They
point to several unusual aspects of Crazy Horse in the historical world to demonstrate the supernatural aspect: he is
the only Sioux leader of that time of whom there are no
sketches or photographs in existence; after he was murdered,
his parents took his body out onto the prairie to bury him,
but his bones have never been located; attempts to paint
pictures or make statues of him have always met with bad
luck. The Catholic Church recognizes the importance of his
memory to the Sioux, for they have sent out a priest to find
the bones, giving him $30,000 to support his work. It is a
sixteenth-century tactic, proved in the destruction of a dozen
civilizations: new legends are more easily accepted after the
old ones are destroyed. The secularization of Crazy Horse
precedes the sanctification of Father Smith.

The powers of Crazy Horse rest now with a few old men,
the Uwipi; the burden of the culture has been left to them.
At evening, they put small stones on the bank of a stream,
marking the places where the stones were positioned,
demonstrating to their audience of skeptics the end of human participation. In the morning, leading their herd of
unbelievers, they return. The stones have moved. They have
gone to the water to drink, say the Uwipi, and who can
doubt them? The positions of the stones had been marked.
There were witnesses.

They await their opportunities to demonstrate the inabil-
ities of the Public Health Service, watching for the cases
declared hopeless by the corps of internes and residents who
attend to the Indians. Then the Uwipi bring out the dish
with the figure of a man cut into the bottom, rolling a fluid

around in the bottom of the dish until it fills in the man-shaped depression, always finding a spot in the figure that has not been filled in, identifying it as the place of the ill-ness. After the divination, they go to pray for the patient, perhaps administering herbs before they leave. They take a great risk; it does not take a great physician to recognize the signs of imminent death. But to go against the odds is their only opportunity, and they succeed often enough to main-tain an undercurrent of credibility in their manipulation of supernatural powers.

When it comes time for Fools Crow to practice his priest-hood in its highest form—the purification of himself and the seeking of visions in which divine power is communicated to him—he goes alone to Bear Butte, where he builds a sweat-house and fasts. For four days and four nights he cleanses himself and "gives thanks." Amos Lone Hill, his son-in-law and interpreter, explains, "That's how he gains understand-ing." Perhaps he speaks of giving thanks because Fools Crow became a Uwipi out of gratitude. "In the time of the horse and wagon," Lone Hill says, "he was very sick, and a doctor told him he wasn't going to live for twenty-four hours. He made a promise that if he lived, he would fast. He had to find a medicine man to help him perform, and that is how he became Uwipi." The son-in-law, dressed like the old man, his lips and the upper part of his face painted red, cools himself with his feather fan, looks over at the old man, and then up at the thundercloud. He lights a cigarette, and shakes his head—there is a rustling of feathers and the bells hanging from his waist sound softly. "He is the last Uwipi on this part of Pine Ridge. My kids, the young ones don't even speak Lakota. He is looking for someone to teach, but he didn't find him yet. Maybe the kids will want to be Indian again someday. Whatever they see, they want. Now the girls want to wear miniskirts. Maybe if they see you, they'll want to grow beards." He laughed. The old man laughed too. He could not have understood the joke, but it was a politeness, and Indians like to laugh; the put-on is their favorite kind of joke, and they are expert at it. Teasing is so important in the Indian social structure that it is institutionalized in some tribes, and the pun is the delight of Indians speaking their own languages, though it is not yet often found in their use of English.

After the joke, more cigarettes were lit, Fools Crow and Lone Hill both taking care to keep the long braids of their wigs away from the flame. The old man indicated that he was anxious to get back to the dancing, but he waited while his son-in-law spoke of him again: "It's not easy to be a Uwipi; he can't drink, he can't get mad, and he can't make faces at people."

They went inside the building again, the gymnasium floor of a public building of Rapid City, South Dakota standing in for Mother Earth, the smell of popcorn mixing with that of sage; Mexican shawls, Davy Crockett hats, and tennis shoes with beadwork sewn over the toes mixing with painted faces, buckskin and quill work. The master of ceremonies shouts, "Hoka-hey!" into the microphone, the drunks share a pint bottle of bad whiskey in the foyer, and Fools Crow, who took up the practice of Uwipi medicine in the time before the automobile, dances round after round, crouching, sweating, carrying his pipe and medicine bag—heel and toe, hips still, working his knees—the honorary president of the War Eagle Dance Club and the last of the Uwipi in his district of the Great Sioux Nation.

II

The Navahos were among the last Indians to arrive in America, say the anthropologists. They are quite certain about that, though they would be more comfortable if some

definite linguistic link could be shown between the Athabas-
can language and that of the Siberian tribes. They also say
that the Navahos reached the Southwest only five or six
hundred years ago in the last migration southward of Indian
tribes. It is all meaningless to the Navahos, who believe they
emerged from a lower world through a lake in Colorado.

Wherever their language originated, if their chthonian
myth must be denied, must have been a quiet and easy
place, for the language is in its glottal stops, its almost
imperceptibly differentiated sounds and its tonality the most
subtle language known to man.

The people do not call themselves *Navaho,* but *Dine,*
which means "the people." The Spaniards called them
"*Apache de Nabajo,*" *Apache* being the Zuni word for enemy
and *Nabajo* a Spanish word which may have meant a knife
or a piece of useless land. There is speculation among
anthropologists that "Navaho" may be derived from a Tewa
word, but the Navahos themselves are agreed on the Spanish
derivation.

It is not unreasonable to think of them as latecomers, for
who else would have settled upon such unwelcoming land
but a small band, split off from a larger unit, weary of dissension or war or famine or all three, seeking a place where
they could be in peace, if only because the land was too
poor to engender covetousness in other, stronger bands. The
Apaches must have chosen the mountains (the Navahos call
them Mountain Top People), while the Navahos settled in
the foothills, which are mostly below the tree line. The land
was better then; erosion had not stripped the topsoil away
and the rivers had not been dammed. There was timber
enough for the building of hogans, good land for gardens,
and game enough to round out their diet.

They were organized into bands, each with its headmen,
medicine men, warriors, and ordinary citizens. Some bands
were more warlike than others, raiding the various pueblos

in the area, but they were not ferocious people, like the Toltecs or the Iroquois. They undoubtedly mixed with the pueblo peoples in trade or marriage or through the exchange of captives, or in all three ways, for there are undeniable similarities in the cultures.

Since 1868, when the Navahos were returned home from captivity at Fort Sumner after enduring murder, rape, starvation and total destruction of their homes, flocks and crops by the United States Cavalry, the size of the tribe has increased tenfold and more. It is a mark of their astonishing vitality, for during that period of increase, they were exposed to disease, alcohol, poverty, Christianity and the Bureau of Indian Affairs.

The size and vitality of the tribe and the reservation (fourteen and a half million acres) have allowed the Navahos to fend off the intrusion of Western Civilization until very recently. It was the young men returning from World War II who brought an end to their insularity. Like the hero of Iwo Jima, Ira Hayes, they could no longer live with the horse and wagon, herding sheep, telling stories, dancing and believing. As the Pima world of Ira Hayes was shattered, so was the world of his Navaho counterparts. Alcoholism and venereal disease haunted them. In the city of Gallup, at the eastern edge of the Navaho Reservation, there are drunks on the street before ten o'clock in the morning, and the rate of venereal infection is fifteen times the national average.

Still, there are thousands of Navahos who cannot or will not speak English; some people continue to prefer the hogan as a dwelling; and despite the incursion of the peyote church, traditional Navaho medicine, with its basis in belief in the harmony of the world, endures, and the people endure with it, because of it. Medicine brings no light to the darkness; it is the result of darkness, the institutionalization of darkness, a host to anxiety. But it is also the explainer of darkness, the path through a world where the naked, red

ribs of the earth rise up out of the desert. It explains the
frying air of summer and the impenetrable snows of winter.
It gives hope that the dry grass will be enough for the cattle,
and lets a man be easy with the trader who keeps his
account, doling out his money, deducting the sacks of salt
and flour and penny candies from the arbitrary sum paid for
all the wool he could shear from his flock. If the price of lard
is not fair, then will the trader suffer, for there are forces
greater than men to insure the order of the world. Because
of medicine, men may fear lightning, sacred trees and walking over the places of the dead rather than hunger or disease. The real dangers are made pale before the darkness.
Despair is defeated by fear. The world is programed, and
one has his place within the program; it is impossible to be
alone.

There is witchcraft among the Navahos; they do not deny
the existence of evil, but it is medicine as the healing explanation that is most often practiced, and its approach to
darkness is unexpected, for mysticism as a normal part of life
is utterly unlike mysticism as it is known in Western societies, where it is an aberration.

Near Rough Rock, in the afternoon shadow of Black
Mountain, on the east-central part of the Navaho Reservation, a man with a twisted face gave a feast of mutton shank,
fry bread and tea in preparation for the Apache Way Ceremony, which he hoped would cure the distortion of his
features. The feast was made in a hogan that had been
loaned to the patient by a relative who had also assigned
two of his three wives (three sisters) to the ceremony as
silent hostesses.

A doctor from the Public Health Service at Crownpoint
had diagnosed the man's illness as Bell's Palsy. He had said
that the partial paralysis of one side of the patient's face was
due to pressure on a nerve in the neck, almost certainly

caused by an abscess. If the abscess were lanced, the doctor said, there would be a quick, if not an immediate, remission of the symptoms. Although he expressed little hope that the medicine man would be able to effect a remission of the paralysis, the doctor was careful to say that he believed the paralysis might be psychosomatic. The possibility of the medicine man's curing a physical ailment was thus eliminated, though this *a priori* assignment of malpractice was not communicated to him or the patient.

The doctor and two other whites were permitted to witness the ceremony and to ask questions about the singing and the ritual, but the condition was made that they were not to bring tape recorders or cameras into the hogan, nor were they to make notes during the ceremony. Any questions would be answered by John Dick of the Rough Rock Demonstration School and his interpreter and assistant, Wilbert Begay.

The meal was eaten slowly, chunks of mutton cut from the bone with a butcher knife, pieces of fry bread torn from the flat, doughy loaf, tea or coffee washing the grease away. Lard and lamb fat: the incidence of gall-bladder disease on the Navaho Reservation is extraordinary, the sickness of fats flourishing beside the sicknesses of hunger. In the hogan of prehistoric gods, the dishes were put into a chipped enamel basin filled with water, and a nationally advertised detergent was poured into the basin.

Outside, it was forty degrees and clear, but snow clouds were moving down out of Colorado, pushed by a cold wind. In the hogan, a stove made of half an oil drum kept the tea and coffee hot and warmed the low round room. A tin flue carried the smoke up through a large hole in the roof, which also served to light the interior of the hogan. When it snows, the heat of the stove melts the flakes, which fall upon the metal, turn to steam and rise up out of the hole. Thus the

problem of having no windows is solved by an understanding of convection currents.

Wood is put into the stove through a hole cut in the side
of the oil drum. One of the wives of the owner of the hogan
stokes the fire, pulling the hot steel covering away with her
fingertips. There are no handles, and she must touch the
metal that contains the fire, but she is deft, and her hands
are horny with years of work; she makes no miracles. After
stoking the fire, the woman goes back to her place on the far
side of the room to sit beside a tiny white metal table. Beside
her are shelves of dishes, metal cups, salt, sugar, coffee and
tea. A sack of Bluebird Flour slumps on the floor. She is as
shapeless as the flour sack, hidden behind the thick skirts of
her traditional Navaho dress. It is a costume copied from
the officers' wives at Fort Sumner during the Navahos' in-
ternment there. The middle of the nineteenth century is
decorated with horned moons of silver and ovals of polished
turquoise. Below the skirt, which reaches almost to the floor,
are small feet encased in red canvas shoes.

She is old or she is not. Her hair is black, but her face is
tired. A baby sleeps beside her, her child or her grandchild.
There is a coyness about her, in the delicacy of her ges-
tures, the quickness of her eyes when she looks at the men
on the other side of the room. She is so ready to laugh. When
the baby awakens, she is gentle with it, refreshed by cooing,
as if in awakening the child were newborn.

It is a room without secrets, built of logs and mud, the
lower part of the interior walls covered with black tarpaper,
the upper part narrowing slightly, a dome of logs. The
patient reclines upon a mattress, the medicine men sit on
sheepskins, the observers sit on wooden chairs. There are
suitcases piled against the walls; a saddle hangs from a peg
driven between the cribbed logs. There are rolls of toilet
paper and rolls of paper towels. Cigarette butts are thrown

against the stove and left to burn out on the hard packed red
sand floor.

The medicine man has come a long way for the ceremony.
He is one of the practitioners of the Apache Way and an
uncle of the patient, as well; no man could be better qualified. Beyond that, his record is excellent; he claims never to
have failed to cure a patient. Perhaps the claim is an exag-
geration; there are no statisticians among shamans. The
medicine man talks of his record of successes while unwrap-
ping his paraphernalia—the stones, feathers, rattles, quills,
hoops, herbs, plants and corn pollen he has brought with
him in buckskin wrappings and sacks. He is seventy-three
years old, and his knees creak and pop when he rises from
the cross-legged position. He laughs about it, talking of age.
Then he turns his age into wonder as he tells of the eagle
feathers he will use in the ceremony. He was riding a white
horse, high in the mountains, when he saw the eagle. He
threw a rope at it, hooking himself up to the eagle's talons.
The old man and the eagle struggled, the bird screaming,
swooping down to tear at the old man's flesh, the old man
pulling on the rope, playing the bird like a great fish of the
air. After an hour, he subdued the eagle, holding it until he
had plucked its long tailfeathers; then he let it go.

The story is told casually, with smiles, mixed with joking
references to his age, halted while he lights a cigarette or
withdraws the feathered skin of a bluebird from a pouch.
Everyone may listen, but it is told for the man with the
twisted face, who watches the ease of his physician, making
grotesque smiles at the proper times, responding, learning to
believe, prepared with sweatbaths and emetics, focusing on
the moment when order will be restored to him.

They are blood relatives, the doctor and the patient, but
two men could not be more different. The patient is fat, his
eyes are dull, his hair is cut so short his scalp shows through
it, and he is listless, clumsy—sentient clay, no more than

that, and sick, for he has walked over a place where a long
dead enemy is buried. The medicine man is as lean as the
land, possessed of the same masculine elegance. His face is
marked with the dry riverbeds and canyons of seventy-three
years. He wears a plaid cowboy shirt, Levi's and work shoes.
His hair is long, gathered in back, folded once, and wrapped
with white cord. He wears a red headband tied with a flat
knot over one ear. His features are different from those of
the other men in the room, sterner, more carefully made. His
face deserves the word visage; it could serve a Caesar. The
room belongs to him; he is the keeper of the point at which
parallel lines converge. And he is at ease with his centrality,
Moses gossiping, tucking the tablets under his arm while
lighting a Camel. The patient watches him, a fat man
peering at a rich coin.

The second medicine man, the assistant and observer, is
from the Rough Rock area. He is small, dark, a man more of
secrets than of power. He is seventy-eight years old, but his
face is that of a man of fifty. He shakes a rattle and chants
while the medicine man from Navaho Dam and the patient
begin to prepare the materials of the ceremony.

A blanket is spread over the dirt floor, and the medicine
man and the patient sit at opposite ends of it, beginning the
ceremony, making a gentle entrance with soft singing and
the preparing of the ceremonial objects. There are four
hoops to be colored with paint made by grinding turquoise
and coal on a trapezoidal piece of limestone. The patient
does the work, making small piles of fine dust on the stone,
then wetting the dust with drops of water and using the
paint to color the small hoops. When the hoops are colored,
they are laid out on a blanket beside bluebird, sparrow and
hawk feathers. The two medicine men chant together while
the patient works. A hawk feather is tied to each of the
hoops and wound four times with fiber stripped from a
Yucca leaf. On his first try, the patient places the feather on

the wrong side of the hoop and begins to wind the fiber around it. Both medicine men stop chanting and point out his error. He makes his crooked smile, unwinds the fiber, and begins the process again with the feather on the right side of the hoop.

When the hoops are completed, the medicine man produces a strange plant for which Wilbert Begay, the translator, knows no English name. The spongy leaf top is half the size of a man's head and rests upon a thick stalk. The medicine man inserts four feathers in the center of the plant, then places a hoop over each of the feathers and anchors it in the spongy material below, dividing the plant into four circular areas, each marked by a feathered hoop with a larger vertically placed feather at the top. After the preparation of the plant is completed, the medicine man puts it off to one side, and returns to his buckskin bags, removing more equipment: quills, a knife, and several small bags. The rattle and the chanting continue. The words are spoken so quickly, so distorted by the rhythm that the interpreter cannot follow them. A beat is missed now and then while the medicine man clears his throat and spits neatly against the stove. Not until everything is prepared does the chanting stop. Then the medicine man lights a cigarette, unfolds his legs, and makes a joke.

The Indians laugh. Even the patient is amused to animation, momentarily losing his selfconsciousness about his palsy. The interpreter explains: "He wants to know why you ask so many questions. Do you plan to do this ceremony when you get home to San Francisco?" The observer laughs, and the Indians join him. The put-on is good humored; the interest is neither unnoticed nor unappreciated.

A blanket full of sand is poured onto the center of the dirt floor and made into a large circular mesa by the medicine man. While he smooths and shapes the low mesa, the patient sits on the mattress to remove his clothing, and the woman puts more wood on the fire. Almost immediately, the room becomes hot, and there is a moment of confusion while the observers shuffle their chairs and remove their jackets. The patient watches the medicine man and the observers, his eyes jumping from one to the other, a fat and naked sparrow, his modesty in a breechclout of raw cloth tied below his belly with a string.

The second wife enters, carrying a wedding basket that has been soaked in water to expand the fibers until every opening is closed and the basket has become a waterproof vessel. She is slimmer than the first wife, a quick woman, wearing an irritated mien, the sister of earthly efficiencies. Her eyes do not stray from her work. She pours water into the wedding basket, produces a piece of Yucca root, and begins to knead the root in the water, creating thick white suds. Meanwhile, the medicine man marks the sand mesa with corn pollen, letting it pour through an opening between his thumb and forefinger. First, he draws a circle; then he divides it into quadrants with perpendicular diameters. Then he makes an inverted "V" in each of the quadrants, the closed end pointing outward. The chanting and the rhythmic shaking of the rattle continue. In the brief intermissions between the parts of the ceremony, the medicine men and the other Indians converse, discussing the ceremony. They are more akin to Talmudic scholars than to savages, aged exegetes conferring over the language that leads to earthly salvation, believers in the exorability of evil, men of the Word placing their faith in the elemental ingredient of civilization.

The chanting and the rattle resume when the woman has finished preparing the suds. The patient stands before her while she lifts handfuls of suds to wash his hair, his face and all the exposed parts of his body, even the bottoms of his feet. Then the patient kneels upon the sand mesa, facing east. He puts one hand in each of the eastern quadrants, raises himself into a squatting position, and places one foot in each of the western quadrants. The medicine man sings over him, completing the song by trailing off the last word into a sigh. At the end of that part of the ceremony, the medicine man draws a circle with corn pollen on the surface of the thick suds in the wedding basket, and divides it into quadrants, but does not make the inverted "V" in each of the quadrants, as he had done on the sand. The woman comes forward to wash the patient again, but lightly, merely touching him with corn pollen and suds.

The patient then retires to his mattress to watch, while the woman brings a blanket and a spade without a handle, shovels the sand into the blanket, and carries it outside. After a few moments, she returns with a shovelful of dry sand to cover the muddy spots and slight depressions in the floor. It is an extraordinarily efficient sort of housecleaning: whenever the floor is unclean, it is removed and a new floor is put in its place.

During this *entr'acte,* the second wife leaves, having spoken not a word. There is conversation again between the Indians, while the medicine man sharpens a quill, stretches his legs, grinds coal and turquoise into dust on the trapezoidal stone. The patient is not included in the conversation, but it is intended for him: the medicine man speaks of his successes and of the eagle. As before, as always, it is easy conversation, loose accompaniment to the rigidity of the songs and the ritual. There is a feeling of camaraderie and concern for the patient, an air of optimism. He will be cured; it is the wish of everyone in the room, the central thought, after which all other thoughts evanesce.

Through the medicine man the attention of the room is turned to the patient; the man of the dreary edge becomes the center. He is made aware, reached through his consciousness. There is no magical abreaction. Trances are not expected. Demons are not summoned. The man is out of order, nothing more; the result of the ceremony will be entopic rather than extraordinary, harmony is perfection, wisdom is knowledge of the order of nature, the pantheon pales before the rising of the sun and the changing of the seasons, every leaf is holy, no grain of sand exists without place and purpose, out of one miracle there are endless miracles. The restoration of one man is a contribution to the perfection of the world; he cannot be alone in his will to health. It is sung to him and symbolized for him, wished upon him. He is loved.

The medicine man turns to the observer, "Do you want to mark him?" He offers the quill. There is laughter again. The observer declines, suggesting that he is in need of further study. More laughter. It is called witchcraft, magic, sorcery, and it is a time of love and laughter, as if these men are comfortable with their gods, suffering human anxiety before them, but expecting the gift of ataraxy from them. Men disturb harmony, causing their own suffering; then they implore the gods to return them to the beautiful state. There are echoes of Homer in the room, of the moment before prosperity visited unbalanced minds to breed sin; it is the paradise envisioned by Theognis and Solon, the dream of Rousseau—man standing between savagery and science. To the cultural evolutionists it is the last moment of darkness before civilization; to Rousseau and Lévi-Strauss it is the civilization for which man was destined, the state of grace from which he moved by mere accident into history and progress.

But it is less than pure in the hogan; the accident cannot be undone. The patient moves from the mattress to the blanket. The medicine man sits before him. They sit with their legs crossed, the man in the breechclout and the sorcerer in cowboy clothes. The medicine man dips his finger into a bowl of water, letting drops fall on the coal and turquoise dust, making his paints. He raises his quill pen, then puts it down, pausing in the work to reach into his shirt pocket for his bifocals.

When he is ready to begin the painting, he rises to his knees and takes up the chanting. The drawing begins in the center of the patient's chest, and proceeds outward. A slim, one-dimensional figure is painted in black. It is in the Navaho style, but the body is not so elongated as usual, and, the relative length of the legs and the torso is more realistic. Out of the headpiece of the figure two lines are drawn, extending across the patient's chest parallel to his shoulders and then down his arms to his wrists.

The patient turns around, and a figure is begun on his back, painted in turquoise. Again, the figure is begun in the center and drawn outward. This painting is in the more familiar Navaho style, with short legs and elongated body, a feather rising in the center of the head. An arc is drawn at each side of the figure with lines extending from the top of the arcs up the patient's back to his shoulders, across his shoulders and part of the way down his arms. The black and turquoise lines meet just above the elbow.

It is a long process, though the drawing is done without an error. The quill holds but little of the dust-and-water mixture, and several times during the painting, the medicine man must stop to grind more coal or turquoise. After each grinding, he dips water from the bowl with his finger, letting the drops fall in precise measure. The singing is continuous, beginning to take on an insistent character.

After the painting is completed, the stone, the pieces of coal and turquoise, the quill and the water are carefully removed. There is some tension, for the culmination of Apache Way is coming, everything must be correct. The medicine man takes up the spongy plant prepared with hoops and feathers, kneels before the patient, and begins again to sing. The rattle is quiet. The other medicine man does not join in the singing now. The baby cries and is hushed by the first wife.

The medicine man raises the prepared plant before the patient, singing, now with urgency in his voice. He touches the plant to the patient's body, beginning at the feet; then he touches the knees, hands, breast, shoulders and head. At each touch his song is interrupted with a hoarse cry. It is a burst of sound, an outpouring seemingly generated by a contraction of the entirety of the man, and it is this sound which is said to make the ceremony holy. After all the words and the carefully made symbols, holiness itself is ineffable, without even a recognizable phoneme. Language is the limit of man; holiness is beyond.

At the conclusion of each pass up the patient's body, always beginning with the soles of the feet and culminating at the head, the medicine man takes the patient's face in his hands and pushes it back into its proper shape, illustrating to gods and man alike the shape of harmony. There are four repetitions of the song and the touching, as there are four directions to describe the world. In the number four is completeness, the sense of the existence of a whole which man may contemplate though he is only a part of it. And in that whole is the concept of an ordering force beyond the gods, a force before which the pantheon is no more than a host of angels, the ineffable First Cause, an understanding perhaps more elemental than monotheism, belief in something utterly without anthropomorphic qualities, for the order of nature has neither the personality of the God of Moses or the God of Christ; it is pure.

The singing ends in a sigh, and the spongy plant is put away. Silver and turquoise bracelets and a necklace are brought out, placed in the suds in the wedding basket, blessed, dried with a paper towel by the first wife, and given to the patient, who will wear them for four days. The wedding basket is then emptied and given to the medicine man as part of the payment for his work. Apache Way is completed; it will be followed, like most ceremonies, with a Blessing Way song.

The patient is sent outside to walk around the hogan. When he returns, the door is bolted behind him, for no one may enter or leave the hogan during Blessing Way. The ceremony is brief, the medicine man and the patient in the center of the room, the light falling upon them, the fire cooling, the baby quiet. There is a litter of cigarette butts around the stove. The dregs have gone cold in the enameled metal coffee cups. The medicine man stands over his patient and recites the words of the Blessing Way, each phrase repeated by the patient. During the responsive saying of the song, the patient is fed a mixture of corn pollen and water, which is also tasted by the medicine man.

A translation of one of the Navaho Blessing Way or *hozhonji* songs was published in 1897 by Washington Matthews. The translation also appears in N. Scott Momaday's Pulitzer Prize novel, *House Made of Dawn*,

> Tségihi
> *House made of dawn.*
> *House made of evening light.*
> *House made of dark cloud.*
> *House made of male rain.*
> *House made of dark mist.*
> *House made of female rain.*
> *House made of pollen.*
> *House made of grasshoppers.*
> *Dark cloud is at the door.*
> *The trail out of it is dark cloud.*
> *The zigzag lightning stands high upon it.*
> *Male Deity!*
> *Your offering I make.*

I have prepared a smoke for you.
Restore my feet for me.
Restore my legs for me.
Restore my body for me.
Restore my mind for me.
This very day take out your spell for me.
Your spell remove for me.
You have taken it away for me.
Far off it has gone.
Happily I recover.
Happily my interior becomes cool.
Happily I go forth.
My interior feeling cool, may I walk.
No longer sore, may I walk.
Impervious to pain, may I walk.
With lively feelings, may I walk.
As it used to be long ago, may I walk.
Happily may I walk.
Happily, with abundant dark clouds, may I walk.
Happily, with abundant showers, may I walk.
Happily, with abundant plants, may I walk.
Happily, on a trail of pollen, may I walk.
Happily may I walk.
Being as it used to be long ago, may I walk.
May it be beautiful before me.
May it be beautiful behind me.
May it be beautiful below me.
May it be beautiful above me.
May it be beautiful all around me.
In beauty it is finished.

At the conclusion of the ceremony, the patient dresses, putting on new clothes, even new moccasins. The medicine man sits again on his sheepskin at the northern extremity of the room. The work is done: he is smiling, confident that it will succeed. He lights a Camel and begins the long process of wrapping his materials in buckskin, putting them away carefully, attentive to the order. The other medicine man leaves quickly, going home to prepare his own materials, for that night he will begin a four day sing.

The patient will spend four days in prayer and meditation. At the end of that time, he will be cured; his uncle, the medicine man from Navaho Dam, has told him so. And he was right, his confidence was justified. A week after the ceremony, John Dick and several other members of the National Institute of Mental Health Project at the Rough Rock Demonstration School saw the patient: there had been a complete remission of symptoms.

It is, of course, wholly unacceptable to the rational mind that a man can be cured of a physical ailment by an Indian medicine man. It is unacceptable to the experienced doctors in the Public Health Service hospitals on the Navaho Reservation, too, but when a Navaho is brought in and he is Lightning Way (schizophrenic), the doctors at times advise the relatives of the schizophrenic to take him to a Navaho medicine man; the Public Health Service can hardly be expected to deal with a case of Lightning Way schizophrenia, and the Shooting Way Ceremony was designed for it.

Still, there are possible explanations for a primitive cure of schizophrenia. It is more difficult to account for the cure of the small child who stands beside Fools Crow at the Sun Dance. The Public Health Service doctors had said that that child would not survive some sort of pulmonary infection; Fools Crow had said he could save him. The former "terminal case" danced for three or four hours a day during the four days of the Sun Dance.

Indians report cures of migraine headaches, dizzy spells, rattlesnake bite, heart disease, various kinds of paralysis and problems of childbirth and infancy. The Sioux use a boiled weed as a birth control device. The Navahos even claim to be able to cure tuberculosis with a combination of herbs and prayers.

A senior staff member at the Rough Rock School, the son of a distinguished scholar and himself an anthropologist, is moved to astonished belief by the case of his mother-in-law. In the early stages of her last pregnancy, the Public Health Service Doctors had wanted to perform an abortion. They had studied x-rays of her chest which showed her to have such an advanced case of tuberculosis that they thought it impossible for either her or the child to survive the pregnancy. She decided to have the baby in spite of their predictions, putting her faith in Navaho medicine rather than in the white doctors. The treatment lasted all through the pregnancy, her husband bringing her herbs even when she was in the hospital to give birth to the child. After the baby was born, a second set of x-rays was made. Her lungs looked clear; most of the scar tissue was gone. The doctors refused to believe it, insisting that the second set of x-rays were those of a different woman, perhaps a sister of the first woman. The anthropologist is careful not to draw any conclusions from the case, though he makes it quite clear that during those nine months he had but one pregnant mother-in-law.

Milton Bluehouse, a Navaho student at Arizona State University, went back to the reservation during the winter to participate in the Yeibichai Dance. "I just went out of curiosity," he said, but it becomes obvious as he talks about the dance that it is more than a curiosity for him. "You put on a mask," he said, "and inside it are the constellations. But before you look through the mask, you have to put it on four times in four ceremonies; otherwise, when you look through it, you'll go blind."

Bluehouse, who is thirty-two years old, acts as surrogate father for the young Navaho students at Arizona State. It is not an official responsibility—it fell upon him because the boys wanted it that way. He studies in the library so they can use his room as a dayroom and meeting place. He has taught them to cook their own food to stretch the paltry allowance of a tribal scholarship. When it seems important, his pickup truck and the money he has saved are theirs.

He is a gentle, supportive counselor. Do not be lonely, he tells them, arranging a birthday celebration, buying the beer, providing the buoyant structure in which they may find the strength to eat another tin of hash cooked on a hotplate or endure another of the poisonous words or glances that send Indian students into flight from education. "Hey, Chief," or a few words in the style of the Lone Ranger's faithful Indian companion can destroy a man's hope, for the implication of cultural evolution is there—the Indian becomes the missing cultural link between the ape and man; what chimpanzee can expect to survive in a university? To his beleaguered wards, Bluehouse administers identity and hope: "When *the bomb* is dropped and the white man is lost without his cities, we will walk back to the reservation and live as we have always lived." The destruction of the world is not enough to frighten him; the Navahos have survived the end of previous worlds. By the light of the flickering television screen in his room, he tells the students of the white ways that there are also Navaho ways; the constellations inside the mask of the Yeibichai dancer have meaning:

When the Hero Twins arrived in the house of God, which is the sun, they saw four doors. Because they had come to complain about the hardships on Earth, God opened each of the doors for them, and offered to them whatever they saw beyond the doors. The first three doors opened onto vistas of material wealth, each of which they rejected. When the fourth door was opened, they looked out upon the constellations, and God told them, "That is knowledge, and I will give it to you, but you must understand that knowledge has no end." And that was the gift they chose.

It is Bluehouse's own version of the legend, bowdlerized to be meaningful to a young engineering student, a product of mission schools who can find no end to the problems of calculus. It is an Indian view of knowledge, finite even though it is beyond the grasp of any man; the created world exists, and one may know it but he may not change it, as no man may disturb the stars. He shuts the open end of Western thought; the stars have no history and make no progress beyond the circle of the seasons and the passage of the night. He teaches them this perfection while the stench of the slaughterhouse lies heavy in the air of Tempe, Arizona, and men walk in the dust of the moon. He saves some, he loses most. Each failure is saddening, but no failure is irreversible: Bluehouse has tried before to earn a college degree; if he fails this time he will try again.

Indian mysticism is so thorough it infects anyone who has extended contact with Indians. The snake is a devil, the owl is bad luck, to look at your mother-in-law brings blindness, telling a story to the end means the death of the storyteller is imminent. Everything is explained; for every effect there is a cause, though the relationship between cause and effect may be entirely illogical. A man who cuts down a piñon tree for a Christmas decoration suffers abdominal pains, for he has unknowingly cut down a holy tree. Such beliefs do not survive analysis, but Indians are not analytical. Everything is real, exactly as it seems to the beholder. There is no magic, nothing is supernatural; nature encompasses everything. Wakan-tanka is atop every hill. If the white man takes the land of one who was faithful to the Great Holy, there will be a Dust Bowl. And indeed the Dust Bowl has come. The laws of physics are learned for every occasion, and there is no mathematics beyond arithmetic. The language is oral, words in context. One may learn; one cannot be taught. Laughter is becoming, gossip enlivens the day, there is a place for wailing, harmony is a goal, leaders are chosen by those they lead and become their servants, grossness is intolerable, selfishness is unacceptable within the clan, humans differ from animals but are no greater. Time is counted in nature. There are powers beyond comprehension: all things live and die, there is a Direction, man is not alone.

III

In 1637, the Hurons were infected with a "pestilence," apparently smallpox. They had no immunity to the virus, which had been newly introduced to the Western Hemisphere, and many of them died soon after the symptoms appeared. In one of the Huron villages, a group of Jesuit missionaries vied with the Huron medicine men to see who could most help the suffering people. Francis Parkman described one of those contests in *The Jesuits in North America:*

> One of these magician-doctors, who was nearly blind, made for himself a kennel at the end of his house, where he fasted for seven days. On the sixth day the spirits appeared, and, among other revelations, told him that the disease could be frightened away by means of images of straw, like scarecrows, placed on the tops of the houses. Within forty-eight hours after this announcement, the roofs of Onnentisati and the neighboring villages were covered with an army of these effigies. The Indians tried to persuade the Jesuits to put them on the mission-house; but the priests replied, that the cross before their door was a better protector; and, for further security, they set another on their roof, declaring that they would rely on it to save them from infection.*

* Parkman, Francis, *The Jesuits in North America*, in *Works*, Pt. 2. Boston, Little, Brown & Company, 1899, p. 182.

Throughout the long work, Parkman makes the same kind of comparison between Indian medicine and the prayers of the Jesuits, writing of Chaumonot, the priest who cured his headache by putting a religious medal into his mouth, and Brebeuf, who cured a squaw of protracted labor pains by allowing her to touch a relic of St. Ignatius. To Parkman, who believed in rationality as if it were a religion, the differences between the Jesuits and the Indians became blurred at the most basic level, the reason for the success of the French missionaries among the Indians was that blurring, and the answer to both failures of thought was the scientific approach to the great philosophical questions prevalent in New England intellectual circles during the second half of the nineteenth century.

As Parkman failed to see clearly the differences between the Indians and the Europeans, others saw differences that did not exist. To Henry Rowe Schoolcraft, the Indians "constitute a branch of the human race whose history is lost in the early and wild mutations of men." Neither Schoolcraft nor Parkman would concede the Indian the possibility of leaving his "primitive" state. The only differences between most nineteenth-century thinkers on the problems of American Indians were over the cause of their condemnation: were they to remain barbaric because of their habits or because of their genes?

Out of Spencer and Darwin came a variation: Darwin's concept of evolution and Spencer's "survival of the fittest" created an option: either the Indian evolved or he would not survive, and his survival was not considered a good bet. There was never any question as to the direction of the evolution. Even Franz Boas compared European and Indian societies by referring to the Europeans as "the higher civilization." In 1968, Peter Farb was still making the same point. Western man, the objective thinker, suffers no attacks upon his superiority. He has conquered the known world, even China has succumbed to the religion which is history, man progresses toward perfection through science. All other possibilities have been eliminated by destruction. The vision of Western man—seeing himself in the central role— might have been considered solipsistic only two hundred years ago, for the Earth was not yet in his possession; but now it is changed from vision to fact. Western man's erroneous conclusions about other ways of life are now of only academic interest. Because Columbus thought the people of the Americas were Indians, they will be called Indians, even though every schoolchild knows the name is a misnomer, for it is tedious to change the nomenclature now, and there is no use in doing so. A pratfall on the way to heaven is acceptable, and in many instances pratfalls have aided the progress toward heaven, serving as propaganda, motivating the invincible army of the West.

Since 1755, when his *Discourse on the Origin and Foundation of Inequality among Men* was published, the chief disputant of the theory of Western perfection has been Rousseau. There have been others, kind hearts and committees, but about their utterances there has been a tone much like that of the antivivisectionists: all living things must be loved and protected. There is little in their work that speaks any more for the humanity of the Indians than does Schoolcraft. There is also an element of Spencer's notion of charity about them: charity is good for the character of the charitable—they learn altruism. The unfit may therefore be preserved a while longer without any great damage to the general society.

Descartes' idea that ". . . all those who have attitudes very different from our own are not for that reason barbarians or savages but are as rational or more so than ourselves . . ." found no adherents beyond Rousseau, and even Rousseau speaks of "the development and advance of the mind" of Western man, though he believed Diogenes could not find his man, because he was seeking a man of an earlier period. It was the social organization of the man who lived in the state between savagery and civilization that excited Rousseau. He defined that man by his use of language, but he thought of him as using his body to its fullest extent rather than his mind. More than anything Rousseau admired the savage for his freedom: ". . . when I behold numbers of naked savages, that despise European pleasures, braving hunger, fire, the sword and death, to preserve nothing but their independence, I feel that it is not for slaves to argue about liberty."

It is perhaps a flaw in the consistency of his argument that he has compared their response to that of ". . . free-born animals dash [ing] their brains out against the bars of their cage, from an innate impatience of captivity . . . " Perhaps it was only an unfortunate choice of analogue, but it is certain that, for all his celebration of "the youth of the world," Rousseau had some misgivings about the equality on a human level of the savage and the European.

The idea of the "noble savage"—Diderot's idea, though it is usually connected with Rousseau in the common misunderstanding of his work—has remained popular, but it is used more often to set up a contrast with modern society than as a description of the American Indian. James Fenimore Cooper had a bit of the noble savage in his heroes, Melville attacked Indian-hating and gave positive values to his "savage" characters, Andrew Jackson saw a noble side to the people he destroyed, but the major thrust of Western thought was in the opposite direction.

> Santayana: . . . while delight in drums and eagle's feathers is perfectly genuine and has no cause to blush for itself, it cannot be compared in scope or representative value with delight in a symphony or an epic.

> Kant: We become cultivated through art and science, we become civilized to a variety of social graces and refinements.
>
> Ortega y Gasset: Uncultured life is barbarism . . .
>
> Cassirer: Human culture taken as a whole may be described as the process of man's progressive self-liberation. Language, art, religion, science are various phases in this process.

Franz Boas was able to write: "There is no fundamental difference in the ways of thinking of primitive and civilized man." He was strong enough to attack the notions of primitive culture as psychotic, and he could deny that the primitive mind was comparable to that of a child or a feeble-minded person. But even Boas, with his obvious sympathy for primitive people, carefully concluded:

> It should be emphasized again that we can never be sure whether the mental character of a primitive tribe is the cause of its low culture so that under favorable conditions it could not attain a more advanced cultural life, or whether its mental character is the effect of its low culture and would change with advancing culture.

The generous but unsystematic mind of Boas suffered at the brink of a new concept of primitive man; the able ethnographer who broke the link between race and culture could not escape from the value judgment. He had been trained as a scientist, and his devotion to science barred him from applying scientific thought in the fullest measure to his work. Boas allowed the primitive man possibility, but he could not admit the achievement of Neolithic man, perhaps because he was not able to see that achievement.

The very word *culture* provides a barrier to the admission of the equality of primitive man. It comes from the Latin *cultura,* from the verb *colere,* which means "to tend" or "to cultivate." That is the earliest idea of "civilization." Later, meanings having to do with husbandry or tilling were attached to the word *culture* (silk culture, bee culture, agriculture). After that, the word becomes attached to the training of the mind. But this notion, growing out of the activities of sedentary societies, was inappropriate when applied to nomadic societies and to all hunting and gathering societies, even if they were sedentary. Neolithic man was held to be savage, barbaric, because he had no "culture"; by definition he was excluded from humanity and cast with the animals.

Anthropology has since progressed to admit of the culture of all human societies, but a Germanic distinction between culture and civilization remains and is apparent in such works as Farb's *Man's Rise to Civilization,* published in 1968, indicating in that distinction a notion of civilization as material or scientific, an amusing antithesis to the Germanic distinction of an earlier period between culture and civilization. And also indicating a failure to understand the structural concepts of anthropology. The application of the concepts of Sumner and Darwin to human thought and society still persist; survival is still the criterion of the value judgment. And even that criterion is questionable, for the duration of Western man has been so brief, and the possibility of his further survival is so precarious that an objective comparison of the duration of Western man and Neolithic man would lead one either to inconclusion or to a conclusion opposite to that of the cultural evolutionists. Only the egotism of the conqueror allows him to judge the past by his own unduly optimistic speculations on the future.

It was Rousseau again who adumbrated the work that has led anthropology into a new phase when he wrote of "the vast space which must lie between a pure state of nature and that in which languages had become necessary."* It was

---

* Rousseau, J. J., op. cit., p. 178.

Rousseau who first saw the connections between thought, language and socialization that brought men out of the state of nature, out of savagery into the "youth of the world," as he called that Neolithic state in which the Indians existed when they first were confronted with Europeans.

Two hundred years elapsed before Rousseau's thesis was restated by Claude Lévi-Strauss: "Whoever says 'Man', says 'Language,' and whoever says 'Language,' says 'Society.'"* And where others had stopped, either fearful or unable to devise a systematic approach that would allow them to comfortably speak their conclusions, Lévi-Strauss moved ahead, applying the systematic approach that had been developed in structural linguistics to the study of man. Out of it emerged a new view of primitive man. He is no longer seen as simple-minded or psychotic; the lack of progress for which he had come to be damned by Western man suddenly appears as purposeful:

> . . . the clumsy distinction between "peoples without history" and others could with advantage be replaced by a distinction between what for convenience I called "cold" and "hot" societies: the former seeking, by the institutions they give themselves, to annul the possible effects of historical factors on their equilibrium and continuity in a quasi-automatic fashion; the latter resolutely internalizing the historical process and making it the moving power of their development. Others (which we call primitive for this reason) want to deny it [history and change] and try, with a dexterity we underestimate, to make the states of their development which they consider "prior" as permanent as possible. It is not sufficient, in order that they should succeed, that their institutions should exercise a regulating action on the recurrent sequences by limiting the in-

* Lévi-Strauss, C., *Tristes Tropiques*, New York, Atheneum, 1961, p. 389.

cidence of demographic factors, smoothing down antagonisms which manifest themselves within the group or between groups and perpetuating the framework in which individuals and collective activities take place. It is also necessary that these non-recurrent chains of events, whose effects accumulate to produce economic and social upheavals, should be broken as soon as they form, or that the society should have an effective procedure to prevent their formation. We are acquainted with this procedure, which consists not in denying the historical process but in admitting it as a form without content. There is indeed a before and an after, but their sole significance lies in reflecting each other.*

The evidence for this statement and Lévi-Strauss' analysis of the evidence are incontrovertible: it is not a question of the species evolving toward one predestined goal which is Western society; there is an alternative. Of the thousands of societies that reached the Neolithic stage, only one chose history and "progress"; Lévi-Strauss concludes with Rousseau that it must have been an accident.

In his comparison of "cool" and "hot" societies, Lévi-Strauss achieves a level of scientific detachment beyond that of any of his predecessors:

> This thirst for objective knowledge is one of the most neglected aspects of the thought of people we call "primitive." Even if it is rarely directed towards facts of the same level as those with which modern science is concerned, it implies comparable intellectual application and methods of observation. In both cases the universe is an object of thought at least as much as it is a means of satisfying needs.
>
> Every civilization tends to overestimate the objective

* Lévi-Strauss, C., *The Savage Mind*, Chicago, The University of Chicago Press, 1966, p. 233–5.

orientation of its thought, and this tendency is never absent. When we make the mistake of thinking that the Savage is governed solely by organic or economic needs, we forget that he levels the same reproach at us, and that to him his own desire for knowledge seems more balanced than ours . . .

The capabilities of the primitive mind are everywhere evident to Lévi-Strauss. He lists the abilities of some peoples to recognize vast numbers of flora: two hundred and fifty are recognized by a single Seminole, three hundred and fifty by the Hopi, and more than five hundred by a Navaho. He finds the Navahos able to recognize fifteen different parts of a stalk of corn; and with amusement he tells of the anthropologist who could not learn a certain aboriginal language because the people attempted to teach her the names of the various plants they recognized, and while she was able to repeat their words, her powers of observation were not sufficiently acute to differentiate among the various plants.

In his analysis of myth Lévi-Strauss explains the role of the trickster, the coyote or the raven, as mediator, a part of the direction of mythical thought which proceeds from the awareness of oppositions to their resolution: the carrion-eater stands between the killer and the producer, for it eats flesh but it does not kill what it eats. The place of the trickster is therefore between life and death; and the inconsistencies of the trickster, which have caused anthropologists to comment upon the lack of organization in primitive thought, are thus shown as among the more interesting conceptions of man.*

It is the same everywhere for him; magical and rational thought are both forms imposed upon content: One system is no less than the other, one mind no greater than the other:

* Lévi-Strauss, C., *Structural Anthropology*, New York, Basic Books, p. 224-5.

What makes a steel ax superior to a stone ax is not that
the first one is better made than the second. They are
equally well made, but steel is quite different from
stone. In the same way we may be able to show that
the same logical processes operate in myth as in science, and that man has always been thinking equally
well; the improvement lies, not in an alleged progress
of man's mind, but in the discovery of new areas to
which it may apply its unchanged and unchanging
powers.*

The qualities of mind that differentiate "primitive" men
from rational men have yet to be fully explored, for the uses
of the mind by men who have neither science nor complex
tools may be more extraordinary than we have so far come to
understand. The doctor, using science and such tools as
modern surgery may require, can easily cure the patient of
Bell's Palsy; the medicine man, if we assume the Indian
pantheon to be an invention of man, has only the mind.
Though there is not enough data available to prove the
theory, it is not absurd to think that the human mind may
function at a higher level in the absence of science.

Perhaps it is a futile argument, like comparing the relative
intellectual powers of chemists and poets, but there is a
fascination in the question. Most of the world has now
chosen history or succumbed to it; progress and science are
the accepted measure of man. Yet Lévi-Strauss, whose intellectual qualifications are indisputable, leans ever more heav-
ily in the opposite direction, finding in the "primitive" society the more humane of the two parallel systems of life
and thought. Perhaps there is a further clue in the comparison of the Navaho devotion to harmony and the classic
definition of civilization offered by Toynbee in *The Legacy
of Greece:*

* Op. cit., p. 227.

There are two constant factors in social life—the spirit of man and its environment. Social life is the relation between them, and life only rises to the height of civilization when the spirit of man is the dominant partner in the relationship—when instead of being moulded by the environment (as it is in the tropical forests of Central Africa and Brazil), or simply holding its own against the environment in a kind of equilibrium (as it does on the steppes of Central Asia or Arabia, among the nomads), it moulds the environment to its own purpose, or 'expresses' itself by 'impressing' itself upon the world. Now you will see why I have suggested that the study of a civilization is not different in kind from the study of a literature. In both cases one is studying a creation of the spirit of man, or, in more familiar terms, a work of art.*

The end of harmony then is the beginning of civilization. And as harmony is synchronic, disharmony is progressive. Toynbee sees the progress of the progressive society in an analogy: "I cannot describe it better than by calling it a tragedy with a plot, and history is the plot of the tragedy of civilization." The synchronic society, like nature, is infinite; the Sioux describe it as a circle, realizing that it is continuous, without a midpoint or an endpoint, believing that the beginning is the creation of the circle. Western society, the "hot" society in Lévi-Strauss' analogy, is progressive, and therefore historical and irreversible. But it is not infinite, either to Lévi-Strauss or Toynbee, and therefore it is tragic.

As in every well constructed tragedy, there is a flaw that brings about the "peripety." In Western Civilization the flaw is property. Whether one looks to Rousseau or Toynbee, to the proponent of the hot or the cool society, the flaw is the same, and the resultant injustice, strife and dissolution of the

* Toynbee, A. J., "History" in *The Legacy of Greece,* ed. by R. W. Livingstone, Oxford, Clarendon Press, 1921.

civilization are envisioned by both men. "What can be thought of a relation," asks Rousseau, "in which the interest of every individual dictates rules directly opposite to those that public reason dictates to the community in general—in which every man finds his profit in the misfortunes of his neighbor?"*

But similar problems must also exist wherever man exists, for we are aware now of the territorial instinct and the instinctive aggression of all vertebrates, including man. How then can man exist without the tragic flaw in one form or another? Rousseau answers for man living in harmony with nature; in that symbiotic situation there is room and there is abundance: a man dispossessed moves to another place; the situation does not necessarily become critical; a study of the language families of American Indians indicates that whenever situations leading to strife arose, the bands split apart and formed new bands, moving into new territories. In Rousseau's vision, man living with abundant space in a contra-historical society was not destined for tragedy. The "cool" world he described was idyllic, because even Rousseau could not foresee the problem of population expansion. The inhabitable areas of the earth being finite and the increase of man being infinite, the notion of property is inevitable. Man has no natural enemy but man; the Navahos attack the Hopis, the Iroquois destroy the Hurons, the Toltecs invade the Yucatan peninsula. Harmony is a matter of balance and the preternatural creature inevitably destroys that balance. Thus the cool societies, though their duration is far greater than that of the hot, are also destined for tragedy.

Meanwhile, the Indian continues to exist in America, the man of the cool persuasion in the hottest society in history. Before the white man invaded the Americas, the Indian had language, society, customs, objective as well as subjective

* Rousseau, op. cit., Appendix, p. 225.

thought; he had imposed form upon existence, he had a life-style, but the life is almost gone now; only the essence re-mains. He is a frail island, consigned to the care of a thousand bureaucrats. He is a problem, and he will continue to be a problem until he ceases to be an Indian. Still, he is luckier than most conquered peoples, for the administrators of his captivity are generous, offering him two choices: poverty or the melting pot.

5 THE THREE HUNDRED YEARS' WAR

THE SUPPRESSION of the true history of America is one of the more exquisite works of human society; the suppressed information is easily available to every citizen, yet few are even aware of its existence. Injun Charley, the long retired hero, is America's leading historian, a pragmatic editor of his experience, delivering to his audience the only story it will hear. He is the man described by de Tocqueville—both the slave and the master, the victim and the victimizer of democracy; Quintessential Charley, long-lived, has his eye on a place down the road, and he aims to get there comfortably, kith and kin beside him, his guiding horde.

But Charley's interest in history must not be mistaken for weakness. He is no bespectacled academic in a shiny blue suit. If Nikita Khrushchev had told Injun Charley that Abe Lincoln was a non-person, Charley would have headed straight for his Winchester; nobody lies to a free man and tells him to believe it; Charley knows who freed the slaves. It is not 1984 in the nation hewed out of the wilderness by such men as Charley, nothing so crude as Orwell's nightmare could succeed in America. Charley is his own despot, the creator of a history of pragmatic ignorance without which the nation could not survive.

It is, in its pragmatism, a changeable history kept in a looseleaf binder: if the blacks are loud in their protest, they will appear in the history as scientists and statesmen, rhythmless captains of industry; if the Chicanos become enraged, peons will be described as princes of Spain; and with the growth of an Indian protest movement, it will be discovered that Athens thrived in Arizona in the fourteenth century. The goal of popular history in America is not truth but the preservation of the state; what de Tocqueville called the "tyranny of the majority" is also the supportive therapy of the majority, while truth, in this instance, is a precursor of anarchy and madness.*

The Indian must suffer, because the nation must survive; his history lies so close to the foundation of the state that it could endanger the entire structure. So the history of the Indian is not suppressed, but it is not known. The Indian is of little use to the nation. He is an embarrassment. He does not exist, except in those places where he is useful: Custer the brave, who wept whenever he left his mother, was "massacred" at the Little Big Horn, but Custer fought a brave battle against the Cheyenne women and children at the Washita. It is the only possible history; Injun Charley knows that what is good is what is good for him. It is not difficult to understand why such a philosophy was conceived in America. Tyrants may be evil, but if a democracy practices genocide, who will be called the villain? If there can be

---

* Popular history would appear to have some of the aspects of myth. The variations on the structure are, of course, much more complex in historical societies than in those contra-historical societies which Lévi-Strauss and others have used in developing a structure of myth, but the great difference between true history and popular history in "free" societies would indicate that popular history may be a function of the human mind separate from objective reality, and not influenced in terms of structure by it. If that is the case, the opening sentence of this chapter would have to be revised, for the suppression of the true history of America would be no more "exquisite" an activity of human society than the storytelling of the Bororos, and the pragmatism of which I have spoken will prove to have been nothing more than an inexorable manifestation of the structure of the human mind. The popular history would then be the "natural" as opposed to the objective history of a society.

no history of goodness, there must be no history, for ignorance is better than a history of evil.

The sacrifice of the Indian to the state has been one of the basic tenets of American political philosophy; it was at the core of expansionism, it is one of the fires under the melting-pot theory, and it plays a significant role in the useful history of the nation. To establish the nation under that philosophy, it was necessary to consider the Indian as less than human. That is the first precept of genocide—an attitude different from that of nations at war, for men may be incited to attack other men for reasons of self-defense or the conquest of evil, but genocide demands the debasement of the victim prior to the act.

There are some discomforting parallels between America during its three hundred years of war against the Indians and Nazi Germany in its war against the Jews. If one considers each tribe as a nation having its own territory, language and culture, the act of genocide was committed many times, for there are nations that no longer exist, languages lost, cultures destroyed, lands completely usurped. With few exceptions, there are survivors; the genes exist, but their existence indicates only the imperfection of the act, not the failure of it. However, the odious comparison with Nazi Germany is not entirely valid; statistics alone are insufficient evidence for such a harsh judgment. It was rarely the aim of the whites to exterminate the Indians: acculturation was almost always an option. The matter of choice is the essential difference between Nazi and Christian genocide: The Nazis were mad, while the conquerors of America were pragmatic, and pragmatism implies a sense of limits in that one need go no further than achieving that which is good for oneself. Surrender, cession of territory and acculturation are as acceptable to the pragmatist as extermination.

The war between the conquerors of the territory that is now the United States of America and the native population began in 1589 or 1590 on Roanoke Island with the end of the English colony there. By the time Raleigh's privateers arrived in August, 1590 to determine the progress of the colony, there was no one left alive; the invaders had either been starved out or killed by the Indians. The war came to an end at Wounded Knee, South Dakota, on December 28, 1890 with the slaughter of three hundred Sioux men, women and children. The bodies of the Sioux men at Wounded Knee were found in a group; those of the women and children were scattered for two miles, indicating that they had been murdered while trying to escape. The massacre was considered a victory for the cavalry, and the investigation of it by the military and the Commissioner of Indian Affairs was limited to determining how the Indians had started the fighting. There is no record of reprimands given to officers or enlisted men of the Seventh Cavalry for the murder of two hundred women and children.

Between Roanoke and Wounded Knee there were dozens, perhaps hundreds, of slaughters of Indians. The Cherokee Removal by Andrew Jackson in defiance of a Supreme Court order is comparable to the Bataan Death March; one fourth of the entire Cherokee nation died on the trip from North Carolina to Oklahoma. In 1637, a Pequot town was burned. The Governor of Plymouth said, "It was a fearful sight to see them frying in the fire . . ." but he called the massacre "a sweet sacrifice," and gave praise to God for it. The sacrifices of similar sweetness that were made at Auschwitz are thought to be the most horrible crime in the history of man. The Pequots who were burned at Mystic River (Connecticut) are not part of the useful history of America; their deaths are all but forgotten.

Can the attorney who defends the men accused of massacring Vietnamese at My Lai find the case law of massacre in the war against the Indians? Wounded Knee alone would appear to be an adequate defense. The victory over the

Indians at Sand Creek is somewhat different; children whose mothers were slain there were paid for their suffering. But it was strange payment: they were each given 160 acres of land, the very land on which those Indians had lived for several thousand years.

The National Commission on the Causes and Prevention of Violence said, "It is arguable . . . that the brutalizing traditions associated with the Indian Wars have left their callous imprint on our national character . . ."

The effect of the Three-Hundred-Years' War upon the national character is impossible to determine. Jung thought every American he treated was part Indian in his outlook; the history might be said to indicate that every American is also part beast. Neither view can be confirmed. The descendants of twentieth century immigrants can hardly have been influenced by Indians except as they are portrayed in movies—a portrayal which bears little resemblance to real Indians; the history thesis fails because the history is non-existent, an unheard wailing.

The extent to which history is made comfortable in America is indicated by the national response to the publication of details of the recent My Lai massacre: *Time* took a national poll which revealed that Americans were more disturbed by the publicizing of the incident than they were by the murders. "Incidents such as this are bound to happen in a war," people told the magazine's interviewers. It is an idea born out of Calvin, on whose moral authority tens of thousands of Indians have been killed. Of course it was "bound to happen." Calvin has told us of predestination, and how "eternal life is foreordained for some and eternal damnation for others." And he tells us also that everything God wills is fair and just for the reason that He wills it; thus the terrible fate of the non-elect is not a violation of the principle of justice. Obviously, one cannot change the course of God's will, nor can one even question it, for Calvin has said,

"To be ignorant of things which it is neither possible nor lawful to know is to be learned; an eagerness to know such things is a species of madness."

God was not ready to give eternal life to those Vietnamese, just as he had no good in store for the Indians. Camus became an atheist because he could not bear the thought of a God who willed massacres of innocents, an immoral God. The Puritans and pioneers took Calvin at his word and became the conquerors of a continent. They had no time for the subtle arguments in Calvin's writings. Predestination was the salient idea; relief from responsibility for one's actions opened the way for immorality without guilt. The Pequots of Mystic River were born to be burned to ashes, the Sioux were born to be slaughtered at Wounded Knee, and the incident at My Lai was "bound to happen." That the phrase "manifest destiny" should have become the rallying cry of expansionism is not an accident of language on the part of the editor of the *Democratic Review;* the conquest, the massacres, the war, all were unavoidable and completely just, since man is but the instrument of God's will. It is a part of the useful philosophy that helped to create a nation. At its most efficient level, it allowed the British General Sir Jeffrey Amherst to write the following during the war against Pontiac in 1763: "Could it not be contrived to send the smallpox among the disaffected tribes of Indians? We must on this occasion use every stratagem in our power to reduce them. You will do well to try to inoculate the Indians by means of blankets, as well as to try every other method that can serve to extirpate this execrable race."

After two and a half centuries of continuous war against the Indians, Col. William Gilpin, an expansionist from Missouri, wrote, "National wars stimulate progress . . ." and went on to explain how each successive Indian war brought new men into the military, men who went on to open new territories, causing new wars in a cycle that moved the nation westward toward final conquest of the continent. He had Calvin and then Spencer to support him. Spencer's idea of the "survival of the fittest" being the best argument for the murder of Indians since the Presbyterians defended the perpetrators of the Connestoga massacre by saying that the Indians were the Canaanites whom God had commanded them to destroy.

Few Americans were untouched by the war. Andrew Jackson fought the Creeks and Seminoles and betrayed the Cherokees. In 1832 Abraham Lincoln participated as a company commander in an expedition against the Sauk and Fox of Blackhawk that culminated in a massacre. Theodore Roosevelt stirred up anti-Indian sentiments with his *Winning of the West,* in which he called the Plains Indians "cruel beyond belief"; when Helen Hunt Jackson tried to come to the aid of the Indians with her tract *A Century of Dishonor,* Roosevelt said the work was "beneath criticism."

War and slaughter were the way of the nation for three centuries, the crude tools of conquest, of the making of a nation. The history of practicality romanticizes the war, fostering the love of country that allows future wars, creating a chauvinism of assassination, an essence. The anthropologist who visited the Sioux and called them "warriors without weapons," laying the blame for the depressed conditions of the men living on the reservations on their lack of opportunity for war, made no attempt to compare his own culture with that of the Sioux. War for the Plains Indians had been ritualistic, a game with unreasonably high stakes, but a game with limits. The Sioux were appalled by the white enemy who fought to conquer. They were dumbfounded by his cruelties: hanging, imprisonment, the beating of his own children. Yet the anthropologist manages to look upon the Indians as if he were a man from a society of peace and reason straining to see downward to understand the plight of the abruptly pacified warriors.

The Indian emerged from the war stripped of his land, his social organization and his means of survival. The white conqueror meeting tribes that were organized into bands demanded that they be organized into chiefdoms, a structure that reflected his own, as authoritative as the cavalry and as easily manageable from above. Thus the pyramid of Western civilization was thrust upon the Indian, forcing him into conflict with his own people to insure compliance with the demands of his conquerors. Kit Carson, that folk hero, destroyed the flocks and fields of the Navahos to bring them to subjugation. The buffalo were slaughtered for sport as well as for their hides and tongues, causing the species to come very close to extinction. The forests were cleared for farms, and the irrigation water of the dry-farming Indians of the Southwest was locked away in dams. The fisher Indians of the Northwest were barred from the salmon streams that had made them rich to corruption. It was total war, efficient, a war from which the loser could not recover, the first work of the scientific barbarian.

Out of the war came the "pioneer," one of the great euphemisms of history. Caesar and Alexander are thought of as conquerors, the Spaniards who came to the Americas were called *conquistadores,* Hitler invaded Poland, but the people who moved westward across America, taking everything, slaughtering and imprisoning the native population as they went, are said to be "pioneers." And so they were, for the word comes from the Old French *peonier,* which meant foot soldier, the one who went first into the bloody battles of ancient wars. But the practical history of America the nation builder gave a new meaning to the word: the sense of being first remained, but the notion of war disappeared. The pioneer became one who advanced the highest aspects of Western Civilization, the leader in art and science. Washed clean of gore and dressed in a costume of thought, the ignorant usurper becomes the harbinger of utopia.

Western Civilization was brought to America on the sword—the pioneers are guilty of that brutality which considers property more important than people—but America was hardly Paradise before the white man arrived. The tribes of the Iroquois Confederation tortured prisoners. A form of slavery existed in the Pacific Northwest. Raiding parties, territorial displacements, cannibalism, polygamy and conspicuous consumption in its purest form were all part of Indian America. But the single aspect of his life-style that most clearly made the Indian a savage in the eyes of the Europeans was his relationship to the land. Indians made no attempt to conquer Nature, they considered themselves a part of it; therefore they were neither civilized nor completely human.

The rationalization for usurping the Indians' lands was found in John Locke:

> As much land as a man tills, plants, improves, cultivates, and can use the product of, so much is his property. He by his labor does as it were enclose it from the common. . . . God, when He gave the world in common to all mankind, commanded man also to labor, and the penury of his condition required it of him. God and his reason commanded him to subdue the earth, i.e. improve it for the benefit of life, and therein lay out something upon it that was his own, his labor.

And speaking of a man eating apples that had fallen on the ground, Locke asks;

> Was it a robbery thus to assume to himself what belonged to all in common? If such a consent as that was necessary, man had starved, notwithstanding the plenty God had given him. . . . Whatsoever, then, he removes out of the state that nature hath provided and left it in, he hath mixed his labor with it, and joined to

it something that is his own, and thereby makes it his property.*

The interpretation was an easy one for the European: if an Indian picked berries and hunted deer on the land, the berries and the deer were his, but when the European plowed the land, it became his, for he was the first to attach his labor to the common land. When it came time to take the land of the agricultural Indians or to slaughter the sheep of the herders, or to bar the fisher Indians from their streams, there was no need to apply the economic reasonings of Locke or the arguments of Divine Will of the Rev. John Cotton; the Indian had by then lost his humanity in the eyes of the whites, for the early lovers who called him a noble savage had made their pleas and lost. Nothing more than a beast, a sub-human at best, was now to be dispossessed.

If we can look beyond the romanticism of the conquest of America and see the Puritan as he truly was—the bastard offspring of Christ and avarice—the Puritan's attitude toward the Indian is consistent with the philosophy of conquest, intolerance, and joyless acquisitiveness which he brought with him to the New World. A tribal foraging heathen was sub-human, without rights, evil, and as such liable not only for his real sins, but also, like the witches whom the good people of the Colonies burned in their towns, guilty of innumerable sins that existed solely in the grim fancy of his white adversaries.

The nobility of the savage was inexpedient; the bestial savage merited the treatment he received, therefore he was a beast. It is a necessary quality of conquerors that they be able to believe in the goodness of their work.

The proof of the efficacy of this belief is in its demise, which came with the end of the Indian Wars and the completion of conquest. As the last hostile Indians surrendered or were killed, the voices of the lovers emerged. Shortly after

* Locke, John: *Of Civil Government*, Chapter 5 "Of Property."

his death, Tecumseh was praised for his attempt to unify his people. Chief Joseph of the Nez Percés was praised in the East even before his surrender, for the West had been won, and his war of desperation could be allowed nobility.

It would be vain history to speak of the attitudes of the conquerors if they had not been the progenitors of the lovers, whose works are the acts of conquerors in disguise, and whose genes carry, however subtly, the necessary attitudes of conquerors. Moreover, when there is economic justification, the atavistic attitudes prevail.

With land growing scarce in the United States, there is increasing pressure to terminate the Federal Government's trust relationship with Indian lands. "It will bring the Indians into the mainstream," cry the legislators from the Western states, knowing that termination always results in the sale of Indian lands to whites. It is a Puritan cry, the same one that calls for logging the remaining virgin forests. Christ, epitomizing the conquered, is the banner of conquerors. The convolutions of the Western mind are miraculous; it is no wonder that an Indian woman, forcibly baptized when she was a child, now says, "I can't understand Christianity; how can I know if I am a Christian?"

The lovers, the helpful but iron-willed occupation troops, have nearly completed their work with the savages. Even in Hollywood movies it is now permissible for Indians to closely approximate human beings. Star politicians visit Indian reservations and weep their findings to the world. Complete empathy is not far away; the work of the Founding Fathers will be fulfilled tomorrow or the day after.

And suddenly the vestigial savage chooses to rebel. It is as if culture is animate, and will not let go its life without a final convulsive effort. Four and a half centuries after Columbus had certified his doom, the native American is looking for his identity in a pre-Columbian life-style; men are eroded that slowly.

If he staves off extinction momentarily with his new traditionalism, what will the Indian elicit from the people he calls the dominant society? The answer lies in whether economic and social necessity will permit a pluralistic society, and in the time of technology that seems doubtful. It is more likely that the Indian's traditionalism will bestir the conqueror once again, and even that will happen only if in dying the Indian is reckless enough to try to live by assumption of his old ways.

The three hundred years of war is long over now; the Indian child found at Wounded Knee beside its dead mother, its head covered with a leather cap on which an American flag had been made with beads, is dead now or surrounded by great-grandchildren. There are now as many Indians as there were when the colony was lost at Roanoke, if there are any Indians at all. There will be no more Indian wars. What remains is a nation conceived in the longest war in history, and within it, a powerless minority, the descendants of the dispossessed, the victims of love.

Time continues to move away from Indian America; moments past are lost, except as they are carried in the minds and the chemistry of men. History exists as it is needed, but men are inescapably defined by their becoming, the act of delusion as much a cause as any other. With the end of immigration, the pioneer mentality grows again in the nation; a ghost of Spencer appears. Injun Charley lives in the unconscious mind of the nation he helped to create. But there is no more open land, neither are there buffalo or Indians to shoot, and with the dismissal of the myth of an omnipotent God, the moral authority of Christianity is dissolved; yet Charley cannot put away the Winchester. The tragic plot of another progressive, historical civilization begins to emerge: if he can find no other use for the Winchester, Charley must turn it on himself.

6 BIG DADDY WHITE EYES

I. Love's Bureaucracy

THE ACCOMPLISHMENT of genocide through violence is apparently impossible; it lacks subtlety. Recognizing it, we give it repulsive names. We are horrified by it. But the other form of genocide, the form in which the spirit is murdered, elicits a different reaction: we are pleased to be able to bring civilization to barbarians and heathens; God glories in such work. For those who doubt God, cultural genocide is the prerequisite for entering the paradise of the machine age, now the technological society. Obviously, lovers make the best assassins.

Thus, the history of the natives of the Americas and the people the Apaches called *white eyes:* Western man, a sword in one hand and a cross in the other, wades into the world, secure in the superiority of his God and his machines. Speaking on his behalf is General Philip Henry Sheridan, patron of Col. Custer: "The only good Indians I ever saw were dead." Thomas Jefferson took another view: "The ultimate point of rest and happiness for them is to let our settlements and theirs meet and blend together, to intermix, and become one people." It is unfortunate that Mr. Jefferson chose to use the euphemism "intermix," for he did not, at least in those of his writings that have been preserved, ever contemplate the wearing of feathers. The summing up of both positions was made by Abraham Lincoln: ". . . the time will come when they will be either civilized or extinct."

The failure of the butchers was abysmal; even with the help of tuberculosis, smallpox and the repeating rifle, they never succeeded in reducing the native population by much more than two thirds. It was not for lack of will or wherewithal that the butchers failed. Western men suffer from empathy: we can destroy only lesser beings. As the life of the Indian declined, the will of the white man also declined. There were too many who saw the Indian, particularly in defeat, as a potential Christian, and they sabotaged the work of the Sheridans and the Custers. They called for the Allotment Act, which they believed would help to civilize the Indian by forcing him into sedentary agriculture and nascent capitalism. They pushed the Bureau of Indian Affairs out of the War Department and into the Department of the Interior. Knowing the limits of their empathy, they sought to make the Indian over in their image, for they were good and loving people, and they desperately wanted to love the Indian. They strove to become God, and as their first act on the path to Divinity, they recreated these subhumans. The apprentice gods nominated Indian agents, and sent missionaries. They told the Apaches that their Holy Mother Earth was truly the Virgin Mary, and replaced the Indian pantheon with hosts of angels.

> It is unnecessary to mention the power which schools would have over the rising generation of Indians [wrote John Wesley Powell, founder of the Bureau of American Ethnology of the Smithsonian Institution]. Next to teaching them to work, the most important thing is to teach them the English language. Into their own language there is woven so much mythology and sorcery that a new one is needed in order to aid them in advancing beyond their baneful superstitions; and the ideas and thoughts of civilized life cannot be communicated to them in their own tongues.

That statement, made in 1874, could have been the credo of the Bureau of Indian Affairs then. Emasculated into the language of the bureaucrat, Mr. Powell's statement could serve the BIA now. And it is not entirely the fault of the Bureau that it still takes this position; the Indian land base, reduced by 90 million acres between 1886 and 1934, is no longer sufficient to support the growing Indian population, unless the Indian gives up his traditional way of life.

The possibility of living in the traditional way declined with the wild life population, but even the herders, like the Navahos, can no longer support themselves entirely from the land. The end of Indian life in America was ordained in Greece, for the real powers of the rational man are greater than the supernatural powers of the mystic.

In 1824, the powers of the Indian's conquerors were concentrated in a Bureau of Indian Affairs. The Indians were to become wards of the Federal Government, in much the same way that inmates of Federal prisons are wards. The power of the Bureau over Indians was absolute. It was as if Lord Acton's maxim were being put to the test; corruption in that first federal welfare project was so monstrous it is now generally conceded to have been the primary cause of the Indian Wars of the last half of the nineteenth century.

Out of these ignominious beginnings, the Bureau of Indian Affairs has tried, with less than complete success, to love the Indians to death. The cause of its failure lies in the ambivalence of the lovers; Indians are not yet enough like their captors to elicit the fullness of their empathy. It is not unlike the relationship of the rich whites and the poor whites; if the poor had gone to Yale, they would be so much easier to love and help. The interchangeable aspects of men, which are the basis of empathy, have little impact on the relationship between beggars and kings.

The lovers tried: they banned many Indian religious ceremonies, they took Indian children off to boarding schools where it was forbidden to speak in any language but English, they baptized thousands, they made church attendance compulsory, they refused to feed "bad" Indians. Over the entrance to the Ganado Mission School on the Navaho Reservation there was a sign that expressed the attitude of the lovers: "Tradition is the enemy of progress."

But the reservation system itself prevented a quick victory. Indians were separated from the rest of society. Few of them had any idea of the growing material wealth and ease of the outside world. The Jesus Road, as Indian traditionalists still call it, meant little to them, for the acts of Christians, from the corporal punishment of children to the time clock, were appalling to Indians.

Yet, aided by poverty, disease, and a piece of harness loaded with lead, the lovers made progress. Indian languages began to be used less; people suffering from tuberculosis and gastrointestinal disorders looked to the BIA clinics for help; the hungry sought jobs and favors from BIA administrators. Slowly, the white man's view began to prevail: the Indian saw himself from outside, his own life force failing, no longer sufficient to provide a reference point from which to meet the world. The very self upon which his life was founded had been shattered and was invaded from outside—he was entered by his enemy.

He lost his name, even that. *Iroquois* is French. *Apache* is a Zuni word for *enemy,* pressed upon the Apaches by their conquerors. *Sioux* is a French corruption of a Chippewa word; the "Sioux" called themselves *Lakota, Nakota* or *Dakota. Navaho* is Spanish; the Navahos called themselves *Dine;* there is not even a "v" sound in their language.

Love conquers all, yes, but no love could be less generous, more devouring.

The BIA demands obedience, or it will, like a vicious mother, withhold its love. When Alan Aleck, Chairman of the Pyramid Lake (Nevada) Paiute Tribe, spoke out against the Bureau, his father, who worked as a ditch rider for the BIA, resigned his job. There is a regulation dealing with employees of the BIA and politics. When Lehman Brightman, a graduate student at UC Berkeley, began to speak out against Bureau policies, his sister, he said, was interrogated by a member of the Bureau, and his own family asked him to stay away from the reservation for fear of reprisal by the BIA.

Whether all the fear of the Bureau is justified is unimportant; the fear exists, and the Indians live under it. There is no necessity to exercise absolute power to benefit by it; mutual awareness of the power is all that is needed to produce control and dependence. The objectified Indian, powerless, and so poor he is often forced to live on welfare, ceases to exist except as he is defined by his captors.

He is told that he may have a tribal council, but in most cases the tribal council is so thoroughly dominated by the BIA that it is a charade. The chairman is like the high school student who sits in the Mayor's chair for an hour while his picture is taken for the local newspaper. When the BIA services to the Klamath Indians were terminated, the tribe simply fell apart, for there was no real structure beyond the Bureau. The Klamaths sold their land as Indians did under the Allotment Act, spent their money, and soon found themselves broke and begging their relatives for a place to stay.

The BIA is an indispensable monster with which the Indian must deal as long as he lives on the reservation; the lover is so in need of an object for his love that he does not want to destroy it by raising it up so high as to make the Indian truly his brother. Instead of freedom, the lover gives charity; instead of self-determination, he gives dependence, for the strong are not so easy to love and the free may choose another lover. Thus, the bureaucracy of lovers perpetuates itself, because it is a jealous lover.

Yet, the BIA is by no means evil, for evil is conscious

malevolence, and there is probably not a man or woman in the Bureau who does not love Indians and want to help them. The evil of the Bureau is the soul of conquest. It is unavoidable evil. It cannot be ended until the Indian is free, and the Indian cannot be free until the Bureau is ended. Justice lies within the paradox. If the problem is to be solved, the Indian will have to solve it himself, for the Bureau of Indian Affairs has not found the proper solution to any problem since it was founded in 1824.

There is probably no other area of Federal Government that has suffered as much justifiable abuse as the BIA. Its schools have achieved a 50 per cent dropout rate. Last year, the Bureau again spent over four million dollars on road maintenance, but the roads on Indian reservations remain among the worst in the world. Indian grazing lands are leased out through the Bureau at as little as one-tenth the going rate. Half of the BIA's 16,000 employees are Indians, but only 16 per cent of the teachers in BIA schools are of "one-fourth or more degree Indian blood." It is the avowed policy of the Bureau that Indians should have the right of self-determination, but within Bureau policies and regulations.

The most astonishing example of Federal incompetence in Indian affairs has already been pointed out by Ralph Nader, but it is so revealing the arithmetic needs to be done again: Federal funds spent on Indians who live on reservations add up to about $460 million a year. If the money were distributed in cash payments, it would come to $5,600 for each Indian family, but the average family income of Indians living on reservations is only $1,500 a year.

Love incarnate may appear to be sloppy, but it serves its purpose: the body of the Indian is weak with hunger and disease, and his spirit is irrevocably fragmented. Only greater love can save him now.

II. BOWDLER THE GOOD

Candice Bergen, film star, journalist, daughter of the ventriloquist, lady of good causes, spoke from her heart when she told the press of her feelings about the Indians. She was, at the time of her speech, acting in a film about the massacre at Sand Creek. She explained her interest in Indians, which she said predated her playing the part. Then she told the press that she was glad to be working in a film where the Indians didn't say "How!" It is a noble but ignorant statement, for the loss of that word would deprive the Siouan-speaking Indians of their most common salutation.

Miss Bergen, however, may be the forerunner of a new form of love. She wants only to bowdlerize the Sioux language. Helen Hunt Jackson, a predecessor in the area of liberal sentiment and unabashed love for Indians, had more definite plans for the people she called "wild, warlike Sioux." She wrote: ". . . there is in them a native strength of character, power of endurance, and indomitable courage, which will make of them ultimately a noble and superior race of people, if civilization will only give them time to become civilized, and Christians will leave them time and peace to learn Christianity."

These two are ladies with good intentions, and it is perhaps unfair to make a slightly comic example of them. But they are human and of the historical society—they cannot bear to move without leaving footprints. Everything must *not* be as it was; they are not Indians—they belong to the society of the seekers, the discontented of the world. The mark they leave is a lover's bite gone too deep, turned to poison in the blood. That is what they must do, since change is the only proof of existence for them; their choice is between poison and limbo.

Lévi-Strauss noted the result of the changes wrought by such good people when their goodness is directed at Indians: ". . . our own society is the only one which we can transform and yet not destroy," he said, "since the changes which we should introduce would come from within."*

It is impossible for men of Western culture to help Indians except by destroying them as Indians and resurrecting them in a new culture. The destruction is quick—the crystal is delicate—but the resurrection is slow, for the Indian has seen the options, and chooses, perhaps unconsciously at first, to be shattered rather than obliterated.

III. ROGERS STOPS-AT-PRETTY-PLACES, PROPRIETOR

The Custer Battlefield National Monument is one of the clearest indications of America's attitude toward Indians. There, on a round hill rising up from the Little Big Horn River, are the headstones marking the graves of the men who died in the battle. It is a small park, surrounded by the broken foothill land of the Crow Reservation. It is grassland, unkempt, barely useful for grazing, rising to mountains where great herds of elk still roam. On the highest hill in the immediate area, the place where the egomaniacal general was killed or committed suicide, there is a graceful stone monument to Custer. Below it, the National Parks Department operates a small building displaying artifacts and selling souvenirs. Below that in the only stand of pines for miles around are the neat rows of headstones.

The battle was probably the worst defeat the United

---

* Lévi-Strauss, C., *Tristes Tropiques*, New York, Atheneum, 1961, p. 392.

States Army ever suffered, and it was the result of Custer's arrogance and stupidity matched against the brilliant tactics of Crazy Horse, Gall and Two Moons. Popular history suggests that the odds in the fight were 400 cavalrymen to 3,000 or more Indian warriors. It is doubtful that there were so many Indians, for the Sioux and Cheyenne traveled with their families and their herds of horses. Such an encampment would have covered miles, and the problem of grazing the horses would have been insurmountable. However large the Indian force may have been, it was so inferior in terms of firepower that had Custer been as good a tactician as his Indian counterparts, he would either have defeated the Indians or at least have held them off until the next day when a larger force under orders from General Terry was due to meet him.

But Custer was not only a fool—he was a relatively poor soldier in combat. According to all accounts of the battle, Custer and five companies of cavalry were driven back from the river early in the battle by four Cheyennes. It was a humiliating defeat for the cavalry, and a great victory for the Indians, who were making a stand to keep the territory that had already been guaranteed them in several treaties.

Crow and Arikara scouts died along with Custer. The number of Sioux and Cheyenne who were killed in the battle is unknown, but the wailing of their mourners after the battle was said to be terrible. Yet, there is no monument upon that hill to the Indians, patriots or traitors, who died there. It is as if Custer and his troops were killed by animals or invading aliens, or died of a plague.

Thousands of tourists visit the battlefield every year, passing through the Crow Reservation to get there. They come away, most of them, thinking that it was the Crow who defeated Custer, because the land is surrounded by the Crow Reservation. Perhaps that is the reason why they do not stop in the little reservation town called Crow Agency. Perhaps they are too angry at the people who "massacred" Custer. Some of them think the Crow are still hostile, and consider their trip across the reservation an adventure. Whatever the reason, they do not detour on their way to the battlefield, and Roger Stops is not rich. His nameless café is empty and his laundromat is crumbling. The entrepreneur is behind in his payments, thinking of new schemes.

In midwinter, Crow Agency is a grim town. Dogs gather on the sidewalk, skidding on the thick gray ice. People come in to buy groceries, do their laundry or pick up mail. Kids buy soda pop. The gas station will close at dark. There are no recreation facilities except for a pool table in a café owned by the Mexican. A white woman walks across the snow-covered town square to the post office and general store. She wears a beautiful buckskin jacket. The Indians wear mackinaws and quilted jackets made of cheap synthetic fabrics. The buildings are clapboard and in need of paint, except for the Federal buildings and the church. The weather stains everything; houses, cars, walkways are all dimmed as if seen through unevenly smoked glass.

By 6 P.M. on Saturday night the town is closed but for the two cafés and the laundromat. There is nothing to do but go to Hardin, and there is nothing to do in Hardin but get drunk. The occupations of Indians—making clothing and weapons, education through prayer and storytelling—and the diurnal rhythm of life have disappeared, but the occupations of Western leisure have not yet appeared. The choices of the evening are drunkenness, the peyote church or boredom. Crow Agency, like so many reservation towns, is held in limbo, knowing both poverties, dreaming of both riches.

The emptiness during the process of acculturation, the torpor of a managed life, and the resultant loss of will are perhaps the worst problems of reservation Indians, but they are not problems to which the BIA addressed itself. The symptoms, alcoholism and suicide beginning at the age of twelve or fourteen years, the school dropout, the unwed mother, venereal disease, are of great concern to all the lovers, but the causes, perhaps because they are rooted in the works of the lovers, are ignored.

Yet, many of the people have been to the cities, and like Roger Stops, who has soldiered in Europe and Asia and crossed America a hundred times in the cab of a truck, they have returned to the reservation, driving up out of the boxed valley at Billings, winding around the rocky grade, past scrub trees and a sudden pine, through the anachronism of Hardin, onto the winding road that suddenly breaks into a freeway (a tourist road running as far as the battlefield and Garryowen, then dwindling into two lanes again), and home to Crow Agency, or Lodge Grass, Fort Smith, Yellowtail, Pryor or some nameless place in the Big Horn country, home to captivity to be free. If they are Cheyenne, they turn left at the Custer Battlefield, and go east to Busby and Lame Deer. The boredom of the reservation is better than the loneliness of the city, poor land is better than a tenement, and what man would not rather be pitiable than comic? There is gossip at home, the ongoing saga of the extended family. A man can talk of his ancestors and question the acculturation of his children when he is at home; the city is a clock surrounded by asphalt and concrete, a crowded cage.

The problems of the Indian are the weights and measures of Roger Stops. He fills saucers with cigarette butts while contemplating them. During the day, he stands behind the counter of his café, drinking coffee, playing with his granddaughter, talking to her in Crow. Sometimes he cooks a hamburger or sells bottles of soda pop or shouts to his wife or tells a kid the juke box is broken because he is not yet ready to hear it. The whole of his day is pocked with the problems of washing machines: change is needed, the rinse cycle has failed, a machine has spun itself into collapse, and then there are the dryers and children who make too much noise. Through it all, he smokes and schemes and practices the arts of exegesis and nostalgia on everything that touches his life. If only he had a little capital, enough for this machine, which is certain to . . .

His name is not Stops, but Stops-at-Pretty-Places; and it isn't Roger, either, not his Indian name—he is really Likes-to-Go-on-the-Warpath. He is a member of the Greasy Mouth clan on both sides, which is unusual for a Crow or any Indian, for it defies the function of the clan system. His wife is Mandan and Hidatsa, both of which are Siouan-speaking people, as are the Crow, but since they cannot easily speak to each other, the language in the home is almost always English. So Roger Stops speaks English to his wife and to most of his customers, and Crow to his children and friends.

He is a man of great bulk, more than six feet tall, wide at the shoulder and deep through the chest. After fifty-one years, his belly has begun to dominate—his shirt separates from his trousers when he stretches. He leaves his dapper brown shoes untied. On the Crow, Roger Stops is something of a celebrity because his brother died in combat in France during World War II. Roger believes that he survived Korea as well as World War II because the old men who gathered around to name him Likes-to-Go-on-the-Warpath said he would be safe in combat.

He achieved the rank of master sergeant, fighting without being injured except for his teeth, which were knocked out by a comrade who jumped into his trench feet first. He tells of the incident in the way of apologizing for having no teeth now.

After the Korean War, he decided to stay in the Army until he was able to retire, but he became ill. The Army doctors diagnosed his illness as cancer of the stomach, operated on him to remove the cancer, then discharged him as incurable. He returned to the reservation to die, his body shriveled and weak at 146 pounds. "I came back here and took sweat baths and prayed," he said, "and I cured myself in the Indian way." He keeps a medicine bundle in his house, but he hesitates when asked about it, saying that he is afraid it will only make white men laugh. "The things in a medicine bundle are things we see in visions," he said. "They have the power of God in them. They don't look like much— a stone or a feather or a piece of fur. Whites wouldn't understand."

He is a deacon in the Baptist Church, but he never goes to church. He is an Indian and that is the way he and all Indians really believe, he says, proving his point with an anecdote: "They had a Pentacostal Revival across the river (the Little Big Horn), and they had an Indian woman over there. She was screaming and shouting the way they do, telling the Indians to come and be saved. The next day, she went around asking the people to join. She came into my office and told me about it, what it had done for her. I told her she was spouting off like a dog doing what it was told, and I asked her if she was really an Indian. She told me she was an Indian and that she believed.

"So I asked her if she'd swear on the Bible she'd never committed adultery. She put her hand on the Bible and swore. Then I took down the bayonet from the wall and I asked her to point the knife to the sun and say she never committed adultery and then lick the knife. And she said, 'You're trying to get me killed.'

"Oh, she'd swear on a stack of Bibles, but not in the Indian way."

It is a triumph for him, Christianity outwitted by a Crow. He calls himself a "dumb savage," saying that he never really went to school, that he preferred to stay outside and play with his "bow and arrows." It is a bitterness befitting a man conceived by Dostoyevsky, and in the night, when the café is empty, Roger Stops retreats to his Underground in a laundromat. He locks himself into a storeroom, sitting on a high stool behind a discarded display counter or reclining on a couch of raw board and rags, filling the room with smoke, sweetly stale, suspended on the steam that pours from the washing machines and dryers, and reading Indian history or law.

The room is further decorated with a single shelf of books, a typewriter on a high stand and a calendar. Outside, the washing machines and dryers roar and grind, and children shout over them, playing, aware though unconcerned that Stops is in his office reading Felix Cohen's book on Indian law, battling the Bureau of Indian Affairs with bookmarks and underlining. It is a room adjacent to Hell, and in it, contemplative and powerless, Stops turns the pages with enormous and slow hands, seeking the little victories that allow him another day. It is a terrible battle he fights, matching the little victories of language and wit against the realities of his life that crowd his memory.

"My grandfather was a full blood, a chief, but my father went to Haskell and learned to be a Christian. I remember my grandfather riding an old roan with his felt hat turned up in the front and wearing his braids. We had a farm; my father worked it. One time, my grandfather said to him, 'Hitch up a team and get a sack of spuds and a hind quarter of that beef hanging down by the creek and half the coal and some of the wood you cut, and bring them over to that man's house. He's sick and his family's hungry and cold.'

"There was a big blizzard then and my father didn't want to do it. 'Oh, shit,' he said. But my grandfather told him 'Don't mumble at me. Go do it now.'

"My father used to get drunk and raise hell with the old man, and my grandfather would just sit there and listen and never say anything. Then, the next morning, he would tell him quietly, like he told me, 'You don't eat unless everybody eats, and you don't get warm until all the people are warm. That's our way.'

"But my father, he went on in his way, being a good Christian, until my mother died. Then one day he went up to her grave and cried like an Indian. We do that, we cry and moan, asking the one who's gone to take pity on us. We don't cry for them. We cry for ourselves. Then my father came into the café, and I fixed him a steak, and he said to me, 'Roger, did I do right? I don't think I lived a good way, and now it's too late to do anything about it.'

" 'You done the best you know how,' I told him. 'You thought you were doin' good. That's the best you can do.' "

The declared purpose of Roger Stops' reading, scheming and contemplation is "to help my people," but there would seem to be another purpose, the saving of himself. He works hard, two or three hours a day, on a Crow language project, thinking back on the old words, collecting them from his friends and customers, learning the structure and development of his own language, pleased to understand that the Crow words for dog and horse are actually "my horse" and "my real horse" and that they are linguistic proof of the history of domesticated animals among the Crow. He plans to translate the Bible into Crow, though he is not a Christian. There is no payment for the work, and it takes a subtle mind to understand how such an effort can be of help to his people. Though there is little doubt that Roger Stops is capable of such subtle thinking, it is also clear that the intellectual stimulation is a requisite of his own sanity, the lonely joy that sustains him through another day of overdue payments and lost customers.

He is bitter about the café owned by the Mexican, quick to point out that the Mexican's café is on deeded land rather than tribal land, and that the Mexican is not a Crow or married to a Crow. But the Mexican has the business. Stops does not know why, though he thinks it may have to do with the money owed to him. "I have eight thousand dollars on the books," he said, relating the debts to his business, explaining that people who owed him money did not feel comfortable in his café. But it is more than that: when he ran for tribal office, he got only two hundred votes, a poor showing, but better than his running mate, Henry Old Coyote, who got only thirty-six votes.

Like most contemplative men, Roger Stops is a trouble-maker. The lonely hours of books and mind give rise to a private vision, the synecdochic metaphor is made, and anything that disputes the metaphor must be opposed. There is a strength in it, the power of will, but it also contributes to further loneliness, fewer customers, fewer cronies who will brave the roar of the laundromat to knock on the door of the office and pass an hour in conversation.

In the privacy of his office, Stops has rethought some of the history of his tribe. He does not see the Crow and the Sioux in times past as bitter enemies. Rather, he envisions a purely ritualistic competition between the tribes, one in which honor was of supreme importance. "They used to camp together," he said. "They'd say to each other, 'This man says he took two of your horses and counted coup on one of your warriors around the time of first buffalo calves; is that true?' They compared notes, checked out each other's stories. It wasn't war."

He will not admit that the Indians were conquered. "The land was taken from them in a businesslike way," he said, "by legal treaties. The Government granted them certain privileges in return for the land." He paused over the statement to reflect on his choice of words. "Privileges? I guess I'm just used to thinking of Government that way." It is a strange view of history, but it is not entirely fanciful. The Crows never fought the whites, realizing from the beginning that such a war was hopeless. And if surrender to an invader can be considered as something other than conquest, it is no less practical a view of history than that of Injun Charley;

the conquered are no less in need of comfort than the conquerors. "It was strictly business," he said. "The Indians only wanted to save their people. If we had known what they wanted, we would have given it to them." The neighboring Sioux could easily have answered that question for the Crow; they called the white man He-Takes-Everything. Stops knows that, knows the word and the history, but he is concerned with saving face for his ancestors; if there is to be a resurrection, there must be a nadir, the descent cannot be infinite.

Brooding and hopelessness are the occupations of Indians; the managed life allows little else. An Indian cannot plan his future—the BIA does that; he cannot decide what to do with his land, his crops, or his herd—the BIA has rules for that; he cannot even enjoy the prerogatives of power within his own tribe—the BIA superintendent has veto power. He is neither a free man nor a captive; weeping and dreaming have the same value in his life.

Roger Stops, soldier, truck driver and entrepreneur, rejects the psychology of the managed life in his businesses and in his attitude toward the BIA. But he cannot escape the reality of it: when he argued with a BIA official, complaining about him, demanding of him, the official was not unpleasant to him, nor did he do anything that could be considered a direct reprisal. Instead, the Federal Government quite suddenly purchased 114 washing machines and distributed them to the Crows. "I used to make thirty-five to thirty-seven dollars a day in the laundromat," said Stops, "good money. Now, I can't meet my payments. I don't know what to do. The whole tribe is watching me, waiting to see if I make it."

He refuses to pay his water bill, citing an obscure passage in a treaty as his authority. It may cut back on his expenses for a while, but 114 free washing machines is more than he

can cope with. He is thinking of turning his laundromat into
a recreation center for the young people on the reservation,
something beyond the occasional movies shown by the
churches and the pinball machines and juke box that now
serve that purpose. The problem is that such a place couldn't
support itself.

Then what will he do? A bar? Liquor will soon be made
legal on Indian reservations. "No," he said, "I'd never serve
liquor, even if it was legal. We can't handle it. I can't handle
it myself. I found that out in the Army, where I thought it
was a privilege to be able to belly up to the bar. No, I
wouldn't serve liquor here. Now the kids can stay home with
their mothers while their fathers go to Hardin. If I opened
up a bar here, the kids wouldn't have their mothers either."

So he schemes. He has a plan to make money from selling
a photographic gimmick to tourists. As a start on the scheme
he has built a darkroom in his laundromat. "You wouldn't
think a dumb savage could learn that all by himself," he
said. He smiles proudly and runs his hands through his hair
like huge combs. It is a gesture of concern encroaching on
the pride. Everywhere he turns there are restraining enemies.
"I fight the BIA in my own way," he said. "I don't join any
of those organizations. But it's hard to fight them, because
they can always get you, like the guy with the washing
machines. I made trouble for him, so he ruined my business.
You can't go to the tribal council and complain because the
chairman is in on it. At the tribal fair not one Indian had a
concession. I wanted to run a concession, but they asked me
for a payoff, and I told them I wouldn't do it."

Even when the Federal Government seems to be helping,
the Indians are, in his view, somehow made to suffer. "I
knew a guy in Los Angeles," he said, "who wanted to get
into a relocation program. He went to the Bureau and they
told him he had to go back to the reservation to apply for

relocation in Los Angeles. He didn't go; he couldn't." And then there is the new Boy Scout Camp. The tribe donated a hundred and sixty acres of land, and an Office of Economic Opportunity Community Action Program supplied the money to build a fine camp on the land. Stops describes the camp proudly, giving details of the construction and operation. Then he shakes his head: "The first year it was for Indian kids. Now they say the OEO rules prohibit discrimination because of race. The camp has to be opened up to white kids from Billings. By next summer there won't be room for any Indian kids up there. Another hundred and sixty acres is gone."

When there are visitors to his smoky office, they come with serio-comic deference. Stops once participated in a land-leasing negotiation which raised the rate per acre from ten cents to sixty cents. He once helped to get surplus commodities distributed on the reservation, about which he says, "Our people didn't feel like it was charity. They took it as a victory over the white man. They outsmarted him." Those are his successes; there have also been failures. He is a sorcerer of dubious powers, poring over his ragged books, marking the possibilities, making war on the white man with his own logic.

George Bad Bear, tidy in his windbreaker and cowboy hat in contrast to the thorough deshabille of Stops, takes his wife to the laundromat, visiting in the small office for the duration of one complete washing machine cycle. He and Stops talk over their victory over the state of Montana. Bad Bear had been notified by the state that he had to pay back taxes and interest for three years during which he was employed by the Federal Government on the reservation. The Legal Services office on the reservation told him they could not take his case, because his income was too high for him to qualify under the OEO rules. The lawyer, however, did give him some advice: he told Bad Bear to pay the taxes and penalties, although he admitted that he had no specific information on the subject.

Though he had no knowledge of the law, Bad Bear did not understand why he had been singled out to pay state taxes. He took the problem to Roger Stops, who consulted his books, and determined that an Indian living on a reservation and employed by the Federal Government was not obliged to pay taxes to the state of Montana. They wrote a letter to their United States Representative, who confirmed the opinion. A few weeks later, Bad Bear walked by the Legal Services office. The young lawyer called out to him, "George, about those state taxes, you don't have to pay them. I got the information." Bad Bear said, "Yes, I know. I had them send it to you."

The dissident sorcerer is not the only one who knows, but he is an Indian, he is the one who cares. Where else can those who are governed without their consent turn for help? The enemy of power is surrounded by washing machines and soda-pop bottles. His hair is grown long, reaching for his collar. He has no connections among the college students who conduct sit-ins and make rage in the newspapers. His fingernails are thick and rimmed with black. He does not tie his shoes. He is toothless, and fat has begun to round away the character of his face. But he is an ally against the BIA, the OEO and the officials of the tribe. He can say with them, "They tried to destroy us for five hundred years, and now we're destroying ourselves." Dreams of freedom and self-determination are symbolized in his dissent.

Roger Stops understands his position in the tribe. It is not what he expects of himself, but it is all he can do. "This is the only culture I know," he says. "Everything I do is trying to achieve a higher state in the Indian way. But I was brought up in war, and now I fry hamburgers for a living. I'm degraded in the eyes of my people."

IV. Captain Bligh in Love

The attraction of Neolithic societies for Rousseau was in the innocence of men without power over other men. "Man is born free; and everywhere he is in chains," but not man in that stage between savagism and civilization, not the American Indian. They conceived of power as magic, an attribute of supernatural beings, but not of men. They governed by unanimity; their leaders were those who gave more rather than those who had more. Without a concept of surplus, they lived as equals. There were exceptions, notably in Central America, Mexico and the Pacific Northwest, but in the main they lived without slaves or property. There was no need to invent writing, because there was nothing to catalogue, and without writing, the accumulation of knowledge was limited to the capabilities of memory.

It is possible to make this discomforting distinction between Neolithic and progressive societies: one is based in egalitarian awe of nature, and the other is based in greed, oppression and the desire to conquer nature. That is the radical view of Western Civilization which leads the gelatinous minds of some popular philosophers, including rock band leaders, LSD takers, anxious professors and more than a few Indians, into dreams of a return to Neolithic values. By making the proper combination of the theories of Marshall McLuhan, Theodore Roszak and Vine Deloria, Jr., one could arrive at the conclusion that paradise is a tipi furnished with a color television set. That Neolithic societies had no means for coping with surplus is of no consequence to some of these gentlemen; entropy has frightened them out of their wits.

The Indian, who is just getting up to speed to enter the endless race of Western Civilization, suffers all of the prob-

lems of the mixture of science and magic, power and equality, democracy and unanimity, conquest and harmony,
enslavement and freedom. With such conflicts to cripple
him, he has been easy to love—until now when he has come
to see his lover as a rapist and begins to resist. But resistance
is difficult; one must take power to oppose power, and the
Indian still shies away from full knowledge of the use of it.
Perhaps the shards of the shattered crystal are still potent.
Perhaps innocence is tenacious. Perhaps his once objective
view of Western Civilization has led him to think he cannot
gain enough to compensate him for his loss of innocence.
Whatever the reason, he appears to be making an effort to
blind himself to the realities of his new life, hoping power is
a trick that exists only in mirrors. And out of this pretense of
blindness comes his solution for the failures of the Bureau of
Indian Affairs: replace the white bureaucrats with Indians.
It is the answer for both militants and traditionalists; both
groups make the assumption that an Indian oppressor would
not be an oppressor because he is an Indian. The linking of
race and culture, the absurd trap baited with identity, goes
the next step and defines the essence of the individual prior
to action.

It is a pathetic hope, a hope born of desperation, and a
paradox born of the paradox of the relationship between the
Indian and the BIA: The Indian can not survive without the
BIA, which is the instrument that destroys him. Thus the
paradox is solved with another paradox. Sanity is preserved
by the defense; but the situation is perpetuated, the ignorance of power continues.

An Indian reservation is an island, and the Indian is Billy
Budd or a member of the crew of H.M.S. Bounty. The
captain of the island is the BIA superintendent. To question
his rule the Indian must appeal to God or Washington. The
analogy, though it seems overstated on first thought, is
accurate. The BIA Superintendent can have an Indian de-

clared incompetent, he may order his herds or his farm machinery to be liquidated, he has veto power over the tribal council, he can deny an Indian the help of relocation or educational programs, and he can determine who is to work and who is to go hungry on reservations where the majority of jobs are in BIA programs. The BIA official differs from the captain of a ship or the king of an island in but one major respect: he is not restrained by the possibility of mutiny or revolution.

As one would expect, there are both good and bad superintendents, but Lord Acton's maxim is generally proved true. The Indian, without a concept of power and now powerless, does not believe the maxim, nor can he accept the history of man, the progress from power to writing to the accumulation of knowledge. He must believe Indians are exempted from the weaknesses of men, though he has evidence to the contrary. While asking that the BIA be made acceptable through staffing it with Indians, he complains against the current commissioner of Indian Affairs as he did against his predecessor, and both of them are Indians.

The explanation given for the inconsistency is that these men are not really Indians, but men of Indian descent who have always lived in the white man's world. If they had been real Indians, they would have been different. The link between race and culture suddenly becomes selective, convenient. A people being driven to alcoholism and suicide by despair are willing to sacrifice reason to gain hope.

Sitting Bull was killed by Sergeant Red Tomahawk and Lieutenant Bull Head of the Indian Police, and Geronimo was hunted down by Apaches. That is the reality of Indians working for the Federal Government. The solution to the problem of the Bureau of Indian Affairs cannot come in the corruption of a few more Indians. It is more likely to be found in the strengthening of all Indians.

7 AND POVERTY SAID . . .

"I DIDN'T KNOW I was poor until I left the reservation."

It is a joke told by Indian traditionalists to demonstrate the difference between white and Indian conceptions of poverty, an attempt to prove that the cash economy is still an alien form to Indians, an attack upon the lovers who impose their own forms upon conquered societies. But the joke is made in white society, and it is made by well-fed, English-speaking Indians, the fatted militants who appear in newspaper articles. On the reservations it is not so easy to make jokes about poverty.

The statistics are well known; Indian poverty is an annual feature story in magazines and newspapers edited by men of good intention, churches solicit funds for their missions among the Indians, and there are advertisements and television commercials picturing poor Indian children and soliciting funds with which to alleviate their suffering. It is not surprising to read that the median family income on the Fort Apache and Papago reservations is between $500 and $999, and that the average family on those reservations is composed of six or seven people.

Nor is it surprising to find that state and federal assistance programs are not reaching the Indian poor, because the Indian poor are unaware that assistance programs exist, or cannot get to the offices that administer welfare programs, or lose their benefits in one way or another through their fail-

ure to understand how such programs work. The welfare
programs themselves are the product of a continuing struggle between the state and federal governments to see which
of them can do less, a contest that arises out of a perverse
sense of fairness in which both the BIA and the states keep
their payments at the lowest level to save Indians from
suffering the disappointment of false expectations. As a
result, malnutrition and disease are common, substandard
housing (by both white and Indian standards) is almost
universal, and death caused by starvation, as in Biafra during the siege, is not unknown—the symptoms are the same
as those reported from Biafra: the belly swells, the hair turns
red, irreparable damage to the central nervous system takes
place, the child is eventually unable to accept whatever
nourishment is provided and dies.

There are several explanations of the causes of Indian
poverty, in addition to the obvious problem of the diminish-
ing land base. The strangest of them is offered by Vine
Deloria, Jr., who claims that the Sioux have given up farm-
ing and raising chickens because anthropologists have
caused them to spend their summers in endless rounds of
Indian dances. Mr. Deloria is of course right about the destruction caused by anthropologists, but the reservation to
which he refers specifically is Pine Ridge, and the Oglala
Sioux of Pine Ridge suffer from other causes.

In the spring, the grass at Pine Ridge is thick, and along
the tributaries of the White River, the cottonwoods are
clouds of dark green. The grazing cattle are taking on fat. It
is good land, much of it, grassland that has survived the
dustbowl, the Great Plains that put beef and bread into the
bellies of millions, and the Indians who own the land have
none of it.

A piece of grazing land is of no use to a man who doesn't
own a cow, and a good cow costs $220, twice the annual rent
the BIA has negotiated for a hundred acres of Indian land.

There is no place for the Indian to begin to take back his land. Terms on loans are short and repayment plans are not flexible enough to accommodate the vagaries of agriculture and husbandry. The Indians lost their herds through defaulted loans and BIA liquidations a long time ago. On the section of the reservation called White Clay, there is not a full blood Indian who owns the cattle that fatten on his grass. There are men on that part of the reservation who have been unemployed for as long as they can remember.

The small moccasin factory in the town of Pine Ridge, where a few women worked, went bankrupt without meeting its last payroll. The supermarket, built with tribal money, is leased out to a white storekeeper. The water in White Clay Creek is polluted because four steers owned by a white rancher lie bloated and rotting upriver where they died. Whites are hired to drive the machines that infrequently and ineffectively grade the roads. The teachers at the Lone Man School are whites, while Indians with degrees in education live in the area and work part time or are unemployed. The employees of the BIA and the Public Health Service live in neat cottages and gaudy housetrailers, and the Indians live in ammunition huts abandoned by the Army and log houses without running water, sewage pipes, gas or electricity. An Indian does not need to leave the Pine Ridge Reservation to learn that he is poor; there are more than enough middle-class whites in the area to give him a lesson in economics.

There are worse places than Pine Ridge. Pheasant and antelope are plentiful in the area, and the Sioux are still good hunters; no Indians will starve there. But there are reservations where the game is gone and work has never come, where people starve on a diet of fry bread and water, though that is impossible in America.

The curious feed upon the spirit; the lovers, as in Christian ritual, consume the body as well. At Fort Belknap, where the whites pushed the Assiniboin Sioux and the Gros Ventres into a union that destroyed the languages of both, the vegetable farms are gone, the cattle belong to whites who lease the land, and the water in the creeks is no longer fit to drink. "Farm," said the lover, "and you will be as I am. Here is the seed, here is the life-style—take them and prosper." The Indians said yes to that first wave of lovers and planted the seed. Then another wave came, so loving that they gave the Indians even greater knowledge in the form of instructions: "Do not plant here. For better crops you must plant there. Let this be grass to conserve the soil. Plant potatoes here, not corn. Plant corn there." And still the Indians said yes, bearing the burden of love for the sake of their wives and children.

But there was no end to love, and there was seemingly no way to please the lovers. "You have too many cattle. You have too few cattle. You must have a ton of hay for every head to get through the winter. You may not sell these calves. You must sell those calves. Plant more potatoes, less corn. Move the turnips to this land. Plant beans there. You have not paid your loan in time; the cattle must be liquidated; we will arrange for someone to lease your land; we will sell it to a white man because he has an Indian wife."

Yes was not sufficient for the lovers, who came from agricultural schools to teach the men who rode with Crazy Horse, the Oglala Sioux, how to handle horses. *Yes* did not please the lovers who came to Fort Belknap to civilize the Gros Ventres and Assiniboins. To have enough money to survive, the Indian cattleman did not brand some of his calves, and secretly sold the "slicks" to white ranchers at a third of the market price. He had no choice; the lovers had told him he could not sell the calves.

The herds dwindled, the farms disappeared, the loved ones surrendered; it is better to be passive than to fail in every act. "Build roads across my land, send me bills for irrigation ditches I do not want, lease my land to the white man, but let me alone. I will hire out my body to the white man and buy whiskey at exorbitant prices to quell my mind, but do not tell me again that I have failed. I do not understand conservation; the water in the creek was clear when I was born, and the grass was endless; my horses ate the bark of trees in winter, there were more cherries than I could carry; what have I done to the land?"

There is regret among Indians at their failure to understand the white man's economics early enough to have taken advantage of the land as it was assigned to them before the Allotment Act of 1887 was passed and ninety million acres, two-thirds of their tribal land, was taken from them in an unceasing erosion that was finally slowed in 1934 by the Indian Reorganization Act. The regret is expressed in a story told by the Sioux: "My grandfather (or great-grandfather) was at the Custer fight on the Little Big Horn, but he was too young to fight, and they gave him some gold coins to play with while he was up there. My grandfather says the coins came from a wagon train that was attacked by our people before it got to Custer. He and his friends stayed up there on the mountain, watching the fight and playing with the coins, dropping them down into a crack in the mountain. You see, they didn't know what it was. It was just yellow metal to them. He's gone back there twice now, looking for those coins, but it was so long ago, he can't find the place."

The story in all of its versions is apocryphal: there are no mountains close enough to the Custer battlefield to provide the view they describe, and the Sioux knew very well how valuable the "yellow metal" was; it was to hunt for gold that the whites broke the Black Hills Treaty and started the war that culminated in the Indian victory over Custer. The story is a lie, fiction if not myth, and like all such lies it is expressive of deeper truths. The various people who tell the story—it occurs in three generations among the Sioux, and

the Apaches and some California Indians have similar tales—
are telling their version of the conquest, bemoaning it: the
gold is the land lost, improperly used and valued in comparison to the white man's use of it, and the failed search is their
recognition of the value of the land in the white man's terms
now when they can no longer find the land to make use of it.

The story is an expression of hopelessness, of men made
strangers in their own country by powerful alien invaders. In
it, too, is an expression of cultural surrender, acceptance of
the white man's values as symbolized by the yellow metal,
which had no value to Neolithic man. The Black Hills were
holy to the Indians, while the white man shouted, "There's
gold in them thar hills." But now the Indian, who suffers the
health problems of people of underdeveloped nations and
earns less than one fourth as much money as the average
white, sees a new magic, having been driven to that view by
generations of poverty.

But the statistics on Indian poverty are distortions, say the
young traditionalists. Indians are not so poor as they seem—
they just don't use cash. With the weaving of blankets and
the selling of wool from his sheep, an Indian can get all the
cash he needs, according to Herbert Blatchford, former
executive director of the National Indian Youth Council and
president of the Red Rock Chapter of the Navaho Tribe, and
now director of the Gallup Indian Community Center. "The
whole economic system is based upon keeping people in a
state of anxiety so they'll buy more things. To us, anxiety is
taboo."

On the subject of life expectancy, Blatchford says, "It is
only the infant mortality rate. When an Indian is healthy
enough to survive his childhood, he lives to be a very old
man, if he lives in the Indian way. The oldest people in
America are Indians. Go on the reservation and look at the
people of eighty and ninety years and more. No, our life
expectancy is not forty-four years. The statistics distort the

truth about the longevity of our people. Show me a man in
the dominant society who is eighty or ninety years old and
still works on a ranch or a farm."

It is pride in defense of spirit rather than foolish pride
that causes Blatchford and the other activists to take that
stance. They know the poverty of the Indian; most of them
have lived it. But the admission of poverty is the admission
of the failure of the traditional life, an attack upon one's
roots, and the roots are now so fragile.

It is better to tell the Navaho story about Poverty, which
was a great rock found in the Third World by the Hero
Twins. The Twins attacked it, chipping it away until Poverty was almost completely destroyed. Then Poverty said to
the Twins, "Please do not destroy me, for when I am gone,
what will you have left to fight?" The Twins allowed Poverty to survive, which is why it exists in the world today.

Industry is coming to the Indians now. They sew underwear and polish diamonds and assemble electronic equipment. Gas and oil and uranium come out of their land. The
people who call the Earth their Mother have strip mines to
look at. Indian tribes own sawmills. They are institutionaliz-
ing the tourist business by building resort facilities. Some
Indians go to college, though the drop-out rate hovers
around 90 per cent. Everything would seem to be getting
better, but most of their money comes from the land, which
remains stable in area while the birth rate soars. The BIA
has little talent for statistics, but it claims that half of all the
Indians in its care now are seventeen years old or younger.

The growth of the Navahos Tribe has been spectacular. In
1868 when the Navaho made the Long Walk back to the
area that is now their reservation, there were perhaps fifteen
thousand people in the tribe. There are now over one hundred twenty thousand, and attempts at birth control programs
have so far been fruitless. Milton Bluehouse described his
experience in trying to convince a man with eight children

that he should have no more. He said the man refused to
speak to him at first, telling him that he was not old enough to
have had a pet dog. Bluehouse then told the man how he had
herded sheep in the worst weather, with his feet wrapped in
rags and tears freezing on his cheeks. It was sufficient to get
the man to listen to his ideas about birth control. Bluehouse
told the man that having more children would make him even
poorer than he was. The man laughed. "You see this shirt,"
he said. "It is the only shirt I have. And this is my only hat
and my only pair of boots. I have no pants but the ones I'm
wearing. If I have another child, it can only make me
richer." To a people who say of an old woman, "She has a
child to raise to keep her happy," birth control makes no
sense at all. To one faction among the Hopis, a group that
has tried to tear up telephone and sewage lines because they
do not want their way of life disturbed, modern measures of
economic well-being seem unimportant.

In popular magazines and newspapers, there are references to the mud and log huts, the hogans, of the Navaho as
an index of their poverty. It is for love of the Indian that
such stories are written and printed, that men of good conscience would like to help the Navahos get rid of his hogan of
mud and logs. But it is typical of the lover not to know that a
Navaho who lived in a castle would build a hogan beside it,
for Navaho religious ceremonies cannot be held in a castle,
only in a hogan.

An economic solution within the traditional life-style of
the Indian is utterly impossible on the reservations. Off the
reservations, the change in life-style sometimes makes living
impossible. People raised under the rule of the BIA and
living in the nineteenth century, are suddenly relocated into
Los Angeles, San Francisco, Denver or Chicago. Some survive, but for others the shock is devastating. The trip from
the extended family on the reservation to the impersonality
of city life is analogous to the trauma of birth: there is a

chill air of prejudice, the sights and sounds dizzy the senses, but there is liquor to drink to recreate the lost warmth internally, and the slums of the city provide a cradle.

Herbert Blatchford tells of a Navaho in California who became lost. He spoke no English, and no one recognized his language as Navaho. After a time, the Indian stopped speaking altogether. It was decided that he was insane, and he was committed to a mental hospital. He had passed years in silence when a man who spoke Navaho came to the institution, recognized the Indian as Navaho, and spoke to him in his own language. Soon the man regained the ability to communicate, and he returned to the reservation.

An Indian dressed in Levi's, a work shirt and a western hat, walking in the streets of a major American city, stopping for a drink, looking with curiosity at the chaos around him, is apparently the object of police suspicion; one Indian leader has been arrested six times on suspicion, though he has never been charged with a crime.

In the cities it is possible for an Indian to hide in the slums or to slip into white society, abandoning forever his Indian identity, but in the towns near Indian reservations the prejudice against Indians is intense. In Gallup, New Mexico, at the edge of the Navaho and Zuni reservations, Indians are not permitted to use the toilets in most public places. In Rapid City, South Dakota, Indians are afraid to go into restaurants. Everywhere that Indians live the whites speak of them as lazy, living off the Federal Government, drinking up their dole. It is essentially the same view of the Indian that prevailed in the seventeenth century. As long as the Indian does not live according to Locke's conception of labor and land, so long will the aspirant gods have failed to make him their brother, and so long will his captors withhold human justice.

8 CRAZY HORSE IS ALIVE IN SAN FRANCISCO

IN THE MONTH of July, 1810, William Henry Harrison, governor of the Indiana Territory, and a Shawnee warrior met on the riverbank at Fort Knox to debate the course of American Indian policy. They had agreed to meet in some privacy. Harrison appeared with the entire Supreme Court of the territory, their ladies, a military escort and a gallery of spectators; the Indian arrived with a flotilla of eighty canoes manned by four hundred warriors.

The Indian was Tecumseh, a brilliant soldier, orator and political visionary, who had traveled North America from Canada to the Gulf of Mexico in an effort to unite all the tribes into an Indian state. His chief adversary was Harrison, who had had enormous success in dealing with individual tribes, separating them out of Tecumseh's proposed union by his manipulation.

At the meeting, Harrison spoke of peace between whites and Indians, and Tecumseh answered:

> . . . You try to keep the tribes apart, and make distinctions among them. You wish to prevent the Indians from uniting and looking upon their lands as common property. You take tribes aside, and advise them not to come into this union. Since I have lived at Tippecanoe, we have tried to do away with all tribal distinctions, and take away power from the town chiefs who have done us mischief by signing away our land; it is they

who have sold it to the Americans; and it is our wish that our affairs shall be managed by the warriors.

I am not alone in this; it is the determination of all the warriors and red people who listen to me. I now wish you to listen to me. If you do not, it will appear that you wished me to kill all the chiefs who sold you the land. I tell you so because I am authorized by all the tribes to do so. I am head of them all; I am a warrior; and all the warriors will meet together in two or three moons from this one; then I shall call for those chiefs who sold you the land, and shall know what to do with them.

A little more than a year after Tecumseh's speech, Harrison attacked Tippecanoe. Tecumseh was not there. The outnumbered Indians, led by Tecumseh's brother, The Prophet, were defeated. Tecumseh continued his work, joining the British in the War of 1812, until Harrison's Kentucky riflemen ended the dream at the battle of the Thames in 1813. Outnumbered and plagued with a neurotic British commander, Tecumseh's Indians were defeated, and the Shawnee leader, though he is said to have "fought like a tiger," was killed.

The faith of Deganawidah that his Iroquois League would become a world order extended to the admission of the Tuscaroras to the League in 1715, and no further, though there is speculation that the form of government devised by Deganawidah and spread by Hiawatha had some influence on the United States Constitution.

At the close of the three hundred years of war between the Indians and their white conquerors, a Paiute named Wilson, who called himself Wovoka, had a vision. It took place, perhaps during an eclipse of the sun, at the Walker River Reservation in central Nevada. Within a few months, Wovoka became the Indian Messiah. His vision was acted out in the Ghost Dance, and new hope was felt by Indians from twenty different tribes. Wovoka's prophecy promised that all dead Indians would return, as would the buffalo, at which time the whites would leave Indian lands.

The quick dissemination of the prophecy was facilitated by the Indians' growing use of a common language. Letters, like the following example quoted by James Mooney, were sent from tribe to tribe. This one was given to Mooney by the Cheyenne. He remarks that it is written in Carlisle English, a bitter comment on the quality of Indian education, and one that would be almost as accurate now, for recent graduates of BIA secondary schools are still refused employment because they are unable to read or write.

The Messiah Letter

When you get home you have to make dance. You must dance four nights and one day time. You will take bath in the morning before you go to yours homes, for every body, and give you all the same as this. Jackson Wilson likes you all, he is glad to get good many things. His heart satting fully of gladness, after you get home, I will give you a good cloud and give you chance to make you feel good. I give you a good spirit, and give you all good paint, I want you people to come here again, want them in three months any tribs of you from there. There will be a good deal snow this year. Some time rains, in fall this year some rain, never give you any thing like that, grandfather, said, when they were die never cry, no hurt any body, do any harm for it, not to fight. Be a good behave always. It will give a satisfaction in your life. This young man is a good father and mother. Do not tell the white people about this, Jesus is on the ground, he just like cloud. Every body is a live again. I don't know when he will be here, may be will be this fall or in spring. When it happen it may be this. There will be no sickness and return to young again. Do not refuse to work for white man or do not make any trouble with them until you leave them. When the earth shakes do not be afraid it will not hurt you. I want you to make dance for six weeks. Eat and wash good clean yourselves.*

The last few lines of the letter given to Mooney were erased. He believes they were an admonition not to show the letter to whites. Mooney brought this letter and an Arapaho version to Washington in an effort to demonstrate the peaceful nature of the Ghost Dance religion and to avoid a repetition of the massacre at Wounded Knee, for it was the Ghost Dance that panicked the whites at Pine Ridge Agency into committing the atrocity. But Mooney need not have been so concerned; Wounded Knee was enough for the Indians, the Ghost Dance religion quickly died out, and the pan-Indian dream lay dormant for three quarters of a century.

Of all the pan-Indian movements, the only one that has survived is the Native American Church, which is neither entirely Indian in its philosophy, nor political beyond its efforts to maintain the legal status of peyote. The basic problem of any pan-Indian movement is that it must encompass a host of "nations," many of which are traditional enemies. Moreover, almost every Indian tribe uses a language that is unintelligible to other tribes, and has traditions which are nothing less than anathema to its neighbors. For example, the Pueblos, who believe that no man should raise his head above the others, could hardly be comfortable at a potlatch. And how will the Navahos and the Hopis settle whether this is the third world or the fourth world? Can the egalitarian tribes of the Plains merge with the Natchez and their caste system of Suns, Nobles and Stinkards?

The Navaho culture is eclectic, and the anthropologist George Devereux has put forward a theory of areal culture among the Plains Indians, but on the whole every Indian's

* Mooney, James: "The Ghost-Dance Religion" in Annual Reports of U.S. Bureau of American Ethnology, Smithsonian Institution, Vol. 14, Pt. 2, p. 781.

concept of Indian identity devolves from the distinct culture of his own tribe. The possibilities of Indian unity then must come not from within, but from a definition of possibilities which has been provided by whites; only a lumpen aboriginal population is available to the Indian activist to be organized into a pan-Indian movement. It is another paradox of the American Indian: if the Indians can only save their traditions by combining their diverse cultures into a single Indian tradition, they will have to abandon their unique cultures to perpetuate them.

Indian activists do not deal much with the philosophical problems of being activists. Perhaps the paradox is an acceptable situation in the world-view from which they claim to operate, though a mediator like the raven or the coyote is not apparent in the structure. Perhaps it is only that the Indians are without the stimulation of working with diverse allies. It is not possible for them to unite with the blacks, for the Indians want to retain a culture and the blacks are seeking to create one. Besides, blacks and whites have always seemed of one culture to the Indians; most Indian languages use the word for *white man* joined with the word for the color *black* to designate the American Negro, and both the Sioux and the Navahos have suffered terrible massacres at the hands of black cavalry as well as white. It is no less easy for the Indian to find an ally in the white radical; there is no room in Marxism for people who revere nature and call the Earth their Mother. Nor can the Indians become revolutionaries; their aim is not to change the dominant society—they want only to avoid being devoured by it.

"Why should I join the dominant society," asks Milton Bluehouse, "when people who were born in it are dropping out?"

But "returning to the Blanket" is not possible, either. Gerald Brown, a law student at UCLA and former secretary of the National Indian Youth Council, listed what he and many young Indians consider the three possibilities for Indians:

"You can go to school until you can't take it any more, then drop out in the seventh or eighth grade.

"Or you can go through and sacrifice whatever is necessary. You think maybe Indians aren't so good because you don't read about them in books. When kids come back from school, they're different, they aren't Indians any more. As an Indian you soon realize that the BIA is it, a foreign aid station in a police state; they cause everything to happen. By the time you get to college, you've bastardized yourself in order to get that far.

"The third alternative is to try to accept what you are and fit the new tools into that context. We can be doctors, engineers and lawyers and make all the money we want, but not join the country club, be what we are. I can't explain it. Maybe you have to be an Indian to understand it."

Brown had just returned from a student confrontation with the administration at UCLA. He watched newsreel film of the crowds on a color television set. His little daughter made pancakes out of plastic at a table in front of the receiver. His brother-in-law, who was then recovering from a wound received in Vietnam, watched without comment. He preferred ministering to a five-week-old puppy out on a narrow, cluttered balcony to talking about politics.

"The speakers at the confrontation kept saying that it was serious, really serious. If you're an Indian, nobody has to tell you that it's serious," Brown said. "I talked to SDS, and all I got was a lot of mottoes. I hear them ask for a socialistic, totalitarian kind of state, and here I am sitting down at the bottom, and I'm going to get shit on, no matter what. I don't trust SDS or any white radical, because they may wake up one morning and decide they want to join the mechanical society."

Traditional Indian life is impossible for Brown. He breaks

down his ancestry as one fourth Flathead, one fourth Sioux, and half white. He is a Catholic, born and raised on a reservation where there are more assimilated Indians than traditionalists. His wife, Anita, is a Navaho. She speaks the language and follows the old religion. Gerald says his daughter is Navaho.

Anita Brown is the secretary of the United American Indian Council of Los Angeles. She is a delicate woman, with exquisite cheekbones and secret eyes, but she is strong. Her husband makes jokes about her "tearing apart" people who disappoint him. When a gaudy neighbor woman suddenly injects herself into their apartment to talk about a dance, Mrs. Brown listens, apparently interested, then replies with feminine coolness that she and other women from the Many Tribes Club are taking their children to the Ice Capades on that night.

As a child Anita Brown sometimes stayed with her grandmother and herded sheep. The leap to the rotting little Los Angeles suburb of Venice is not easy for her. "When we first came here," she said, "we went out in the car to find some open country where we could breathe. We drove for a long time, but we couldn't find a place. It was so disappointing, we haven't tried it again."

They are activists, they say, by which they mean they are "trying to assure the people that they are valid." Gerald was secretary of the National Indian Youth Council—which he described as a spirit more than a formal organization—when he went to the Seattle Fish-In with the NIYC, and he led an unofficial delegation from Montana to the Poor People's March.

The Browns are mild in their criticisms compared to Lehman Brightman, a graduate student at Berkeley and one of the founders of United Native Americans. Brightman wants action now. "Get those white asses off the reservations," he tells Indian audiences. He sees a union of all the

Indians of the Americas. He sees and shouts and curses, but always about general subjects, say other Indians; when it comes time to do the specific work, Brightman has made his speech and gone.

It is apparently a proclivity of all activists, including Indians, to engage in internecine warfare, with calumny as their chief weapon, and Brightman has become a choice victim. It has made him hysterical. He claims that his phone is bugged and that he is constantly being asked if he is a communist. When he went to Washington to testify against the appointment of Secretary Hickel, he said there were rumors that he was an ex-convict allied with communist student radical groups. To this charge he replies that he is a registered Democrat who was wounded fighting for his country. He calls other Indian leaders clowns and embezzlers, and says that people are trying to steal his organization from him—an organization which is either small or the most powerful Indian organization in America, depending on which of his tirades one believes.

He screams obscenities about the Indians as well as whites. He claims the press pays no attention to Indians' problems, that he can't get press coverage—and then he damns the press for misquoting him. He baits whites, saying "I never saw a white man yet who was worth the powder it took to blow him to hell." But it is all the sound of air, a release from the pressure of attempting leadership, and somehow he is not a villain, but a man who can't get his thesis done in time because he was busy making speeches in towns where the people think he might be some sort of communist, a man who is lean for money and fat with enemies, getting tired before he makes his run for power.

The Cheyenne River Reservation is his home, but he is no longer welcome there; the people are afraid that just knowing him will cause trouble for them. He wants to see Indian tradition survive. His son is named Crazy Horse. "That's his American name," says Brightman; "his Indian name is Tash-unka Witco." Brightman's parents are Sioux and Creek, his wife is Sioux. He wants the Sioux tradition, but it is elusive for him; he has to learn it. His wife has taught him what he knows of the language, and this has caused him some embarrassment. On his first visit to the Sioux Club in Oakland, he joined a group of men and began speaking with them in the Lakota dialect. They responded with laughter. "Boy," they said, "you've been in the city too long." Brightman had learned to speak in precise imitation of his wife; he used the verb forms of the feminine speaker. Yet, there are moments, in a meeting hall in Rapid City or in a high school in Susanville, California, when he is able to make Indians feel proud. His anger gives them hope.

Dr. Jack Forbes, head of the Far West Laboratory for Educational Research and Development, is another prominent member of United Native Americans. He rejected an offer to head a department of American Indian Studies at the University of California because he thought the appropriation for the department was too small. But Brightman, who did not have the large grants from the Department of Health, Education and Welfare and other government agencies that Forbes had, took the job. Forbes is the author of several books and numerous papers about the American Indians. In his works—which suffer from Dr. Forbes' interest in cross-indexing himself through quotations from and references to his published and unpublished writings—Forbes calls for "A community responsive, multicultural approach to Indian education," and for an American Indian College with an Indian board of trustees.

According to Dr. Forbes, who is a Powhatan, "It would not make any difference if virtually all of the traits of the Powhatan were of non-Powhatan origin, so long as the

Powhatan people maintained themselves as a viable, distinct socio-political group with a 'history' (largely internalized) of their own."

The suggestion that Indians can retain their identity by internalizing history is the most interesting of Dr. Forbes' many theories, since the structural anthropologists have developed a textbook definition of the difference between the two kinds of societies using the internalization of history as the salient characteristic of Western Civilization. In his research, a part of which was carried out under a grant from the Guggenheim Foundation, Dr. Forbes has apparently found even more unique information than that which gave him reason to think the internalization of history is an Indian characteristic—he implies a definite link between race and culture. According to Dr. Forbes, acculturation is not possible; if Indians behave like non-Indians, it is not that they have forsaken one culture for another—they have simply made the non-Indian life and language into the Indian life and language.

While Dr. Forbes offers a practical, if irrational, view of the possibility of saving something, his concept is not what most activists mean by Indianness. Sun Bear, the editor and publisher of *Many Smokes Magazine,* and probably the wiliest man in America, wants to retain Indian traditions while building a viable economy on the reservations. "You've got to use your *keppeleh,*" he says, pointing to his head to explain the Yiddish word. It is an astounding performance: a tall, dark Chippewa Indian with big shoulders, dressed in turquoise and buckskin, dropping Yiddish and show-business expressions into his conversation. The comedy is so perfect and so disarming that Sun Bear, while chuckling over his own act, is able to win concessions from Nevada legislators and huge loans from insurance companies.

He is, for some totally unexplained reason, the former president of a large Democratic political club in the Mexican-American section of Los Angeles, and the actor who was chosen to play a bearded Jew in the movie *Spartacus*. *Oy!* as Sun Bear might say, how did a man who spent his first twenty years hunting and trapping on the White Earth Indian Reservation become such a *macher?*

Sun Bear was born just in time for the Depression, which the Chippewas endured with little change in their economic situation, except that Sun Bear remembers white people bringing gifts of used clothing to the reservation, "and waiting around for someone to thank them." He shakes his head over the white notion of generosity: "Among the Chippewa gifts for the poor are left on the doorstep at night, so the donor remains anonymous. Then it is as if the gift came from the Great Spirit. If I went hunting and I had extra meat, I would just leave a piece at the door of a poor family." He stayed in school through the eighth grade, although he was often told, "Chippewa and French are good languages; English is a bastard's language." For the next few years he hunted and trapped, living with nature, learning the ways of the Bear Medicine clan, particularly the herbalist cures, which he still practices. "The Medicine Lodge is often called the Bear Lodge," he said, "because Indians know the bear is the only animal that heals itself. When a bear is hurt, it makes a poultice of mud to cover the wound, or if it's sick, a bear eats the right plants to cure itself. And only the bear makes the long sleep."

Although he believes "the Earth is our Mother, and you cannot sell your mother," Sun Bear left the reservation when he was twenty years old to go into the real estate business in North Dakota.

During the Korean War, he refused to fight: "I told them that my people had been prisoners of war for three hundred years and I didn't intend to fight any Koreans as long as I was a prisoner of war." He said his lawyer did a good job of defending him, "but I did seven and a half months at

Lompoc." Then he laughs, "Some of the shrewdest crooks in the world were there; I caught their show." But the laughter is not comfortable. It is one of the few times that he allows his anger to come near the surface, betraying the source of his comedy.

He married a Jewish girl from Brooklyn, and went home with her to be introduced to her mother. Sun Bear does the mother's accent in falsetto. " 'Oy!' she said. 'He's not a Jew, and he's not a *goy*. It's an Eendyan! I tawt dey vos so ogly, bot dis von's not bad looking!' " They stayed together only a few years. His second wife, Annie, is not Indian either. He explains the conflict between his traditionalism and his non-Indian wives with yet another joke, "It's one way to take back the country."

The show-business style and language come from his years in Hollywood, working as an actor and technical advisor. Sun Bear knows actors and directors, and he is glad to drop a little gossip about them. He knows, for example, of John Ford's liking for the Navahos, which explains why the Cheyenne warriors in *Cheyenne Autumn* are Navahos singing their own Winter Ceremony songs.

Some Indians are critical of Sun Bear, saying that he is "too sophisticated in white man's ways," or that he plays the clown too often. But he gets results. When he thought the houses on one reservation needed to be painted, he promoted the paint through a television program, and got juvenile delinquents to do the painting. "It took us two and a half months to paint all the houses," he said. "I had to paint too. You can't be a leader and sit in the shade; you have to be the first one to pick up a paint brush."

To give a group of young Paiutes an idea of business management, he started them in the only business he could think of that needed a capital investment of less than a hundred dollars—a worm farm. "Once I got a bunch of Indian artists together to start an art school," he said. "I can't draw a line, but I'm a good coffeemaker."

Most of his activities are not so colorful; the red tape of an OEO grant or a small business development loan is just trying of one's patience, but to Sun Bear, who has made the four-day fast, and who builds sweathouses in the desert and rubs himself with sage, it is his medicine work. "I don't do this work because I'm good," he said. "I do it because I enjoy it." And he laughs. The only time he does not laugh is when he talks about his religion. His wife teases him about his "toys": bear claws, a gourd rattle, and the stone pipe in which he smokes *kinnikinnik*. But the teasing elicits no laughter. Nor does his loquaciousness extend to his medicine. "If you tell the secrets of your medicine," he said, "you lose the power of it."

Sun Bear said there was a church on the White Earth reservation, but he had never been inside it. At the Isleta Pueblo in New Mexico the church was for a time more successful. While maintaining their own religion in secret ceremonies, the Isleta Pueblos also attended the Catholic Church. It was a pleasant relationship, according to Clarence Acoya, a Pueblo from Laguna and a director of the National Congress of American Indians, until Monsignor Stadtmueller demanded that the Indians become completely Catholic. "At Christmas," said Acoya, "they used to dance in front of the church because they couldn't give any other worship to Christ than the dance. But the Monsignor said they had to be either Christians or heathen. So, to discourage them he placed concrete on the area where they danced. The Indians can only dance on Mother Earth.

"In the summer of 1964, the governor of the Pueblo asked the Monsignor to leave. He asked the Archbishop for a replacement, but the Archbishop wouldn't send one. Finally Andy Abeita went into the church, handcuffed the Monsignor and walked him off the Pueblo lands. The church remains closed at Isleta Pueblo."

Like many Indians, Acoya believes that "Christianity has not been the answer for the American Indian; the missionaries did more damage than the soldiers. The mainstream of American life is not a full life for Indians without their own Indian life and religion." Though he is proud to be a Pueblo and anxious to see Indians take control of their own affairs, Acoya is thought to be conservative by many young Indians. But he says, "The real radicals are trying to find identity. Many of them have not lived on reservations. All of a sudden there's an improvement of the image and they suddenly come back."

Clarence Acoya is but one of the Indian activists in Albuquerque, a squat, dusty town where the grass is for the rich and rain is not expected soon. In Albuquerque, where Indians are loved as local color and despised as people, every Indian seems to be a movement unto himself. Shirley Witt, who says she is "Mohawk and Jesuit," wears shift dresses of vaguely Indian design and works on her Ph.D. in anthropology at the University of New Mexico while caring for her children and trying to create some alliance between the Indians and Mexican-American radicals in the state. The Indians refused to support Reies Tijerina when he was a candidate for governor, though he made overtures to them to supply him with a candidate for lieutenant governor. The refusal was polite, but Indians are privately more skeptical. One man said of Tijerina: "He always says that we have an Indian mother and a Spanish father, and you know who gets screwed in that deal."

Standing in front of his Alianza Headquarters leaning on a car, Tijerina, dressed in a ruffled shirt, pants with a gold stripe, and a sheriff's hat, looks like a small-time Mexican politician. He is an extraordinarily handsome man, who preens himself in the way of men who believe success is overdue. He stands on the street because someone has threatened to bomb his headquarters again, and he needs to show his people that he is not afraid. "No. I didn't ask any Indians to run with me," he said. Then an old man put a knobby hand on Tijerina's shoulder and turned his face up to him. "But Reies," the old man said, "you did." So Tijerina attacked the Federal Government and the press briefly, and went back to greeting his friends, who were arriving for the dance that was to be held in the Alianza Headquarters that evening.

Mrs. Witt, who is said to have conducted the negotiations with the Indians for Tijerina, made excuses for the little deceit, saying that it had been a very difficult day for Tijerina. It is a part of her character to make such excuses, as if she thought forgiveness were a part of hospitality. She does not like the BIA, and she does not like the Texans, as she calls them, who treat Indians and Mexican-Americans badly, but she is, like many intellectuals, a radical without rage.

She is a traditionalist, which is to say a radical among Indians, but she is also a divorced woman with two blonde adolescents to care for, enduring the financial and emotional struggles of getting a Ph.D. As a member of the National Indian Youth Council during its formative period, she must have been less womanly, less a believer in working at the "grass roots" and more hopeful of overnight solutions.

If Mrs. Witt is an Indian, however, anyone can become an Indian; her manner is that of an NYU graduate student in the bohemian days of Greenwich Village—the bookbound analytical mother tilted to the left. She is one of the few Indians in America who are best described as *gemütlich,* and she suffers the usual ambivalences of radicalism generated by restrained tears of compassion: she complains against the liberal whites who do not live in the *barrio,* who are not with the people, but she sends her son to the town's exclusive and nearly all-white private high school.

Since the founding of the National Indian Youth Council in 1961, Mrs. Witt has worked closely with Herbert Blatchford, who was executive director of NIYC for four years, and now operates the Gallup, New Mexico, Indian Community Center. Blatchford, who looks like an Indian version of Oscar Levant, is said to have been NIYC's intellectual. He is an easy, likable man, who manifests his strengths reluctantly. He is a survivor of oppression, but that has not turned him into an anxious runner; he is the antithesis of Brightman's hysteria. "Harmony and peace is my purpose," he said. "I have it now. I just want to live as long as I can." Though he leads Indian people in youth movements, is head of the Community Center, and was for a time president of one of the chapters of the Navaho Tribe, his view of leadership is an Indian view: "As I grew up," he said, "people kept coming to me and asking me questions, and I always tried to answer them as best I could. That was apparently what the tribe wanted of me, so I got myself ready to do it as best I could. They've been watching me since I was a kid; they decided what I could do, and I'm doing it."

Blatchford didn't get to the University of New Mexico until 1953, when he was 28 years old. Before that he had been a soldier, a cook in a BIA school, and a construction manager for the Navaho Tribe. "The war broke down the barriers," he said. "The last time most Navahos saw Albuquerque before the war was when they were coming back from captivity. They didn't want to go back. At the University, Indians from different tribes didn't speak to each other, because of the BIA policy of keeping people separate at boarding schools, where students from different tribes were kept in separate areas. So when they got to the University and mixed with students from other tribes, they couldn't speak their own language. And since they couldn't speak English well, they really couldn't talk to teach other at all. But with the help and the prompting of W. W. Hill of the anthropology department, we started the Kiva Club, the first intertribal student organization."

Blatchford has a degree in education and a year of law school. He was helped through school by the BIA: "It took me three years and cost six hundred dollars to get a BIA loan, not a scholarship, to go to school. In 1956 I got it—a hundred and fifty dollars." Now he helps other Indian students to negotiate loans, grants and scholarships, though few of them complete more than a semester or two before dropping out. Blatchford is not disturbed by the drop-out rate, which runs close to 90 per cent. "If I can get one girl to go for one semester," he said, "maybe her children will go for four years. The wisdom of my people is that you live a long time; you look at the long term."

He is one of the few Indian activists who is comfortable talking about the difference between white and Indian ways. "We have a world view," he said, "oriental rather than occidental. We're all born from one Mother Earth. We look upon the Great Spirit as the manifestation of all organic things. We're as interested in the tangibles as the intangibles. We have an organic existence in contrast with the Europeans who want to control everything to improve on nature. We call the animals our brothers. Indian people are interested in the how, but not in the why. We take care of the subjective, while the European ignores the subjective." It is disconcerting to ride with him in his air-conditioned shiny blue car, even though it is a Pontiac, after listening to him talk about his "organic" life.

During the summers, Blatchford and Mrs. Witt conduct a "workshop for leadership" at the Indian Center in Gallup. "We keep the kids together for six weeks," said Blatchford, "giving them $10 a week for food. They have to live together to make that money work. We try to teach them Indian history, to build up confidence in their identity. During this six weeks, they begin to learn by themselves to work together toward a consensus solution to problems. Social pressure, usually by the more traditional, tends to help them to find this consensus." It is a peculiarly Indian definition of consensus that he teaches. Though it is not the unanimity of the Iroquois League or of the Sioux of Sitting Bull's time, it is not a consensus which permits dissent. Blatchford is teaching tribal rather than democratic political structure. As an example, he uses Black Elk's experience at the Ghost Dance. When Black Elk disagreed with the idea of the group, he withdrew from the council instead of remaining as a dissenter. Later, he rejoined the group, but only after he was able to think in harmony with them.

"Most of them in the workshop are college students who go back to school ready to try a litttle harder," said Blatchford. "Some are near dropouts who stay in after the workshop."

When Blatchford took over the Gallup Indian Community Center, it was in debt and ready to close. Without it, Indians in Gallup would have had no place to wash or change clothes, nor would there have been a toilet for them to use after the long drive in from the reservation. Blatchford rented rooms, held dances, sold candy, got a little money from the Navaho Tribe and a little from the United Fund; he was willing to do almost anything to maintain a sanctuary for Indians in that grim, hostile town crawling along the railroad tracks. He has kept the Center open somehow, but his activism causes the people of the town to become increasingly hostile to him. The debts have not been paid off, and he must fight for every contribution.

It is a tiring fight, one that appears to be consuming more and more of his life. At night, he sits in his office on the west end of the low flat building, waiting until midnight when he

closes the center. He keeps a single lamp burning above his
desk, the rest of the room in darkness. It is his home now, as
well as his office. There is a bed folded in the corner, his
clothes are there. He waits for a visit from his son or a telephone call from Shirley Witt, or perhaps someone will need
him before he locks the door at midnight.

In the dramatic darkness of the room, his mysticism seems
to grow. He talks about bringing to the surface the underlying cohesion that unites all Indians, pretending that there
has always been that cohesion, forgetting the old wars,
thinking perhaps that the Iroquois have consumed so many
Hurons as to be forever allied with them, saying that it does
not matter whether the Hopis or the Navahos were the first to
come up out of the underworld. He speaks of the possibility
of a compromise tradition. He says that tribalism is a valid
way to look at an Indian organization, then says that the
Sioux were never more than seven different groups, that they
could never get together.

He speaks, too, of the Navaho clans, recalling the history
of their failure to operate as a cohesive unit and the battles
with the whites that resulted. From his files he produces a
copy of his genealogy, showing him to be a direct descendant of Manuelito, a war leader of the Navahos who also
became the first commander of the Navahos police. The
genealogy reveals that Blatchford's father was not a Navaho,
but a white man who built bridges and ran the sawmill on
the reservation. "He was a man who worked hard and didn't
say much. He provided for his children, but that's about all.
My mother raised us in the Navaho way. He didn't interfere."

The office is filled with files, the success of the activist.
Blatchford finds a poem in a yellowing newspaper, a clip-
ping, an article. He produces an essay he has written, explaining that his friend, Stan Steiner, is arranging for its
publication. The essay is a nicely said plea for recognition of

Indian values, sometimes angry, histrionic in places, not anything that has not been said before. He is not a writer; the work is less than the man.

It is winter, and there are long mounds of gray ice in the shadows of the building, the dreariness of the high plateau in its nakedness. Trains pass, long rows of freight. Cars move on the highway, staying at the maximum speed. There is nothing to see: bars and curio stores, hardware stores, cafés serving up plastic water glasses only slightly blue and losing their transparency to scratches, raw turquoise, a gallery of gas stations, trays of beads, the Zuni and the Navaho degraded, a street with one side. The venereal disease rate in Gallup, New Mexico, is fifteen times the national average. Pickup trucks and paresis fill the streets. "It is not promiscuity," says Blatchford. "Our people live according to the Beauty Way."

In San Francisco Bay, Alcatraz has been taken over by the Indians. Blatchford reads about it in the newspapers. People send him letters. He says he was the one who first planned the takeover. He calls the people on Alcatraz "the warrior society," using that phrase to explain why they are so different from reservation people, and from Herbert Blatchford, who is one of the "medicine people," though he is not a medicine man.

He is a believer in Indian medicine, he says, but when his personal problems caused him to have severe blackouts lasting several hours or more, he did not go to a medicine man to have the problem cured. "I was afraid it would get around," he said, "and the people of the chapter would think they were the cause of it." And there is already trouble in the chapter. He has missed several meetings in a row; the people may want someone else to be their president. Blatchford is not too concerned: if that is what the people want, he has done all he can for them. Perhaps it is time to find a man from their midst to lead them, perhaps he has brought them that far.

There was little that he could do for the people of Red Rock Chapter. It is a checkerboard area where the land was allotted, and much of it sold to whites. The people are poor, neglected by the tribe, neglected by the state, neglected by everyone but Blatchford. He tried to sell the rugs they produce, hoping to get $15 for a two by three foot rug that takes fifty or sixty hours of spinning, dying and weaving to complete. The going price to them is three or four dollars. Blatchford says that it is the Goldwater trading operation that depresses the market, because the Goldwater traders buy at low prices (rugs by the pound) from Indians in financial trouble, then undercut the market whenever Indians try to get better prices for their work.

Though he contends that Indians don't need much cash, giving as an example a medicine man from Red Rock Chapter who has three wives and twenty-four children to support on livestock or goods he is paid for practicing the nine-day Arrow Way Ceremony, and contending that the man, his wives and his children are happy and well-fed, Blatchford is a consultant to the Southwest Indian Foundation, which is trying to build roads and dig wells and supply such things as carfare to Indians. There are few activists more Indian in their outlook than Herbert Blatchford, but even he cannot accept the harshness of the impoverished remnant of the old Indian life-style as the lot of his people.

It is a conflict suffered by all Indians who long to maintain their identity through tradition, but it is most clear in one of the factions of the Hopis. Thomas Banyacya, who calls himself a spokesman for the traditional Hopis, travels around the country acting as a missionary, telling of the Hopi prophecies for this, the fourth and penultimate world. Atomic war, he says, will destroy the world. Nothing will be

spared beside the land of the Hopis. It will be a war, says
Banyacya, caused by materialism and spiritual conflict. For
the Hopis represented by Banyacya, science will destroy this
world as the other weaknesses of man have brought about
the destruction of other works of Sótuknang, who made the
physical universe at the command of the Creator.

The philosophy of Thomas Banyacya, missionary from
Oraibi, the baked mud pueblo on an Arizona mesa that is the
oldest continuously inhabited place in the United States, is
also the philosophy of Janet McCloud, the great-great-grand-
daughter of Chief Seattle, who lived as she does amidst
verdure that must be inconceivable to the Hopis.

"I realize that I'm a brainwashed Indian," said Mrs. Mc-
Cloud, "and that I have to learn. I adopt the chickadee
philosophy when I'm with my own people, because the
chickadee is the smallest bird, and just listens and watches
and learns." Mrs. McCloud doesn't look like a chickadee,
and she doesn't sound like a chickadee. She has a strong
voice, marked by a low trilling, and when she wants to make
a point, her vehemence can be counted in decibels. She and
her husband are short, thick people, with such gentle beauty
in their round, open faces, that they seem almost unreal, their
dimples and tiny noses out of fairy tales.

Don McCloud was a fisherman until the Indians were prohibited from fishing on what remained to them of their ancestral grounds. "Two years before I was born," he said,
"they took my father to jail for fishing with a gill net." The
crux of the fishing dispute is the use of these nets, which are
designed to catch fish by the gills and strangle them. The
authorities say it is a modern method, one which is not allowed in the treaty made with the Indians. But the Mc-
Clouds have pictures of gill nets made by Indians and used
before the treaties were signed. They hold that the pictures
of nets in the Smithsonian Institution are all the proof they

need to win the legal battle. On those grounds, McCloud and twelve other Indian fishermen staged the first fish-in six years ago. Since then, there have been mass fish-ins and demonstrations.

In 1964, non-Indian sympathizers, ranging from Marlon Brando to Kay Boyle and Dick Gregory, joined the National Indian Youth Council and the Nisqually River fishermen in a mass fish-in. When it was over, the whites and blacks were gone, and the Indians were left to carry on the demonstrations, face the fines and jail sentences, and have their fishing gear and the motors for their boats confiscated by the authorities. An organization called Survival of American Indians was formed in 1964 to get money, publicity and financial support for the fishermen, but many of the Indians dropped out of the organization when its leaders made a foray into radical politics, forming short-lived alliances with SDS and the Black Panthers.

Hank Adams, executive director of Survival of American Indians, said, "The fish-in issues remain unresolved." He does not accept the failure of the demonstrations, but the lack of resolution is not felt by the Fish and Game Department, which continues to arrest Indians who fish with nets. Nor is there any lack of resolution for Don McCloud, who is descended from a thousand generations of fishermen; he now works as a lineman for the local power company.

Mrs. McCloud has taken up the role of activist since her husband went to work for the power company to support them and their eight children. She was instrumental in the founding of a Native American Free University, an informal local school for the teaching of Indian culture to young boys, and she also helped in the founding of a cultural organization for girls, which includes a choir and classes in sign language, Indian legends and the Chinook language. Unfortunately, the Chinook they teach is a trader's jargon and not the original Salish language. Mrs. McCloud shrugs off the teaching of a bastardized language, saying, "The core of Indian culture was the religion."

But she does not practice the religion of the Pacific Northwest, though she and her husband still go to potlatches and other remnants of that culture which grew out of an affluence provided by nature. "I learned from the Hopis," she said. "They're the core of this spiritual movement."

Janet McCloud travels around the country, organizing, making speeches, carrying the message of "the People of Peace," but she does not consider herself a leader. "Indians have no leaders," she said: "We are followers. But Indians don't follow a man. We follow a way of life, and if you find this harmonious path of life, you can find inward peace."

Whether Mrs. McCloud has found inward peace through the Hopi way is dubious. When she talks about the BIA, or the school principal who cut her son's hair, or her former associates in Survival of American Indians, or the "termination" policies of Sen. Jackson of Washington, or the relocation policies that "put Indians into city ghettoes and make industrial slaves of them," she is furious. "If the spirit grows strong within us," she says, "we'll survive." Then her voice rises to oratorical pitch: "We will survive. We were here for twenty thousand years, at least. We were given this land by the Great Spirit. If we can endure all that we've endured, and still be here, we'll be here in the future."

The McClouds live in a world somewhere between the city and the reservation. Their little green house is surrounded by trees. There is a boat in the front yard. Don McCloud still hunts, claiming that he can "feel" a deer looking at him. They are far from reservation life, but they are close to nature. In the cities, where 250,000 Indians live, the problem of maintaining any Indian identity beyond an incapacitating affinity for liquor is more critical. "I know people who've been down-and-out drunks on Madison Street who have been helped back to respectability by the Indian Center," said Jess Sixkiller, who ran American Indians United out of a tiny windowless office in an abandoned Masonic Temple in Chicago. More than one drunken Indian has been picked up by Sixkiller himself, some to be saved, some to be thrown into the drunk tank. After eight years as a Chicago cop, he took a leave of absence to "firm up American Indians United, to make it a force in society."

Sixkiller is a detective by trade, an interrogator. He deals in confidential information and tight-lipped answers. When he tries to negotiate a loan for a group of Indians in Cleveland, he uses the mixture of aggressiveness and obsequiousness that he learned in a police interrogation room: "Would you explain that, please, sir?" He leans back in his chair, sips at a cup of spice tea, listens again, turning the airless office into a squad room by his manner. Then the chair jerks upright, and he attacks: "What do you mean? Why are the standards for Indians different?" The man on the other end backs down, and Sixkiller tells him, "Yes, sir, I'll get the letter in the mail to you immediately. Yes, sir."

He has worked as a bodyguard for Mayor Daley, but he says, "If I thought that demonstrating or hell-raising was necessary, I'd do it." And he is not avoiding the issue, but stating the conditions. He points to the Seattle fish-in, asking, "What good did it do?" Sixkiller is hardly the man to make alliances with the Black Panthers and other urban radical groups, but he takes a radical Indian position about American society. "Our value system is not based on the American dollar; it's based on humane things, things that are much more substantial."

When he and a representative of the BIA met in Tempe, Arizona in a public meeting, Sixkiller questioned the man unmercifully. It was a kind of confrontation the Arizona Indians had never seen before: a Cherokee Indian who was born in Oklahoma and educated in BIA schools dominating a BIA man. Sixkiller became a hero.

The aggressiveness is part cop and part Cherokee. The tribe that learned to read within six months after Sequoyah invented the first written language for Indians does not produce passive men. It is said by other Indians that if ever there is to be another Indian uprising, the Cherokees will lead it. Perhaps this is because they have a special bitterness, for the Cherokees fought in the courts against the removal policies and they won, only to have President Andrew Jackson ignore the United States Supreme Court decision and send them on the "Trail of Tears." Four thousand people, almost a fourth of the entire tribe, died on that trail.

The result of Sixkiller's aggressiveness has been the formation of a national organization of urban Indians, financed by a $90,000 Ford Foundation Grant. American Indians United is composed of fifty urban Indian groups, and it may become the first taste of political power for urban Indians. The future of the organization is hardly certain; urban Indians tend to melt into the general population. Without tribal or geographic ties, they are united only by poverty and a tragic community of disorientation. The organization may be no more effective than the National Congress of American Indians, its counterpart for reservation Indians, which considers its major accomplishment for 1968 the suppression of a television series celebrating Col. Custer.

There are no "Red Muslims" any more, if ever there were "Red Muslims." There is really no "Red Power" movement; an Indian has only to look at twenty-two million powerless blacks to know that six hundred thousand Indians aren't going to have much power. Half a dozen kids in Chicago call themselves Red Panthers, and Hank Adams once flirted with SDS; the Passamoquoddies are suing the State of Massachusetts for two hundred million dollars, and Lehman

Brightman has developed the rhetoric of rage, but the real movement among Indians is to save themselves from cultural extinction while trying to rise up out of brutalizing poverty. In the cities, they are looking for a viable self, and on the reservations they are seeking the strength to become free men rather than wards of the Federal Government. As people of the land in a time of technology, their problems seem almost insurmountable.

But their strengths are surprising. Mrs. Muriel Waukazoo, who has several teeth, a stiff right knee, a husband with "a drinking problem," and both children and grandchildren to care for, recently defeated the U.S. Public Health Service in Rapid City. She had help from Sixkiller in Chicago, and from Mel Thom's Coalition of American Indians in Nevada, but the victory belongs to Mrs. Waukazoo, who threatened to lead the Sioux in a march on the Public Health Service hospital unless her demands, including a preventive medicine plan and the hiring of a staff member fluent in the Sioux language, were met.

Her social activism was generated by her own poverty—she said she once considered breaking into a grocery store to get food for her family—and through social activism she has found a new vision of herself, and passed it on to her children. "For a while there, my children and I didn't want to be Indian," she said. "They always tried to hide it on their record in school. We were so pushed down I was afraid to come into a restaurant because of my color, because I'm Indian." She smiled, showing her several teeth, and glanced around at the restaurant in which she was sitting. It was tolerable, but she made it quite clear that she had been to better places. "Now," she said, "we want to be all Indian."

9 THE SAVAGE HOPIS

IT IS NOT NECESSARY for butchers to be the pioneers of Western Civilization; destruction may begin with the caress of a lover, a people may be smothered in the blood of Christ or the tears of liberalism. The sword is quicker, but its service to the conqueror is brief: love is the long death, the most civilized assassination. And no people have been more truly and more purely loved than the Hopis. They are the ones chosen by their conquerors to be the noble savages, the objects of a love that has penetrated their civilization to distort it until it conforms to the fantasy of the conqueror.

The three mesas in northern Arizona are Atlantis and Athens, Eden on the high plateau. "*Hopi* means peace," say the lovers; "the Hopi Independent Nation has not engaged in warfare in over a thousand years." And another fantastic lover writes: "The Hopi People are by religious conviction non-violent." So the unreal Hopi is created. The anthropologists say he is completely passive. Frank Waters writes *The Book of the Hopi,* documenting fantasy. Mu, Atlantis and Hobbits abound in the minds of the lovers, and the Hopis live on Spam and donations.

There is a deep split in the tribe. Both factions call themselves traditionalists, but one is public and the other private; one is fantastic, the other real; one is radical and the other seeks survival; one is the reflection of the conqueror's fantasy and the other seeks to contain the conqueror inside the web of Hopi order. Thomas Banyacya is the spokesman for one faction; Emory Sekaquaptewa, Jr., Peter Nuvamsa, Viets Lomaheftewa, Farrell Sekakuku, Abbott Sekaquaptewa, and dozens more speak for the other faction. Thomas Banyacya was raised as a Christian and speaks for the radical orthodox faction, while the others, all of them initiated into the Hopi religion, speak for some rapprochement that will allow them to maintain their religion in the face of the inexorable encroachment of science upon the magic of the Hopi world.

Banyacya, the only Hopi who operates regularly in the public places of white society, became a radical during World War II when he served several consecutive prison terms as a conscientious objector. Though his opposition to war was undoubtedly sincere, he could not prove his sincerity to the government, for he was not a member of a Christian church that opposed war, nor was he a member of a Hopi religious order. His case, based upon the fantasy that *Hopi* means peace, was hopeless.

After his prison terms, Banyacya returned to the reservation, bitter, radicalized, opposed to the government that had treated him so unfairly. In his anger, he went to the old clan leaders, trying to organize resistance to all things that are part of the white world. Hotevilla, which had split off from Oraibi and the rest of the tribe in 1906, was the most receptive of the villages. The people there considered themselves the orthodox practitioners of Hopi religion, even though they did not hold the quadrennial initiation ceremonies. They had defined orthodoxy as opposition to the Federal Government when they split away from Oraibi in 1906 and founded the village.

The old men at Hotevilla and a few other clan leaders joined Banyacya in opposing the installation of sewage lines and electricity. They boycotted the tribal council, demanding that the people return to the old ways. Banyacya enlisted the aid of CORE and a group of whites in Los Angeles who call themselves the Committee for Traditional Indian

Land and Life. He began touring the country, representing himself as a missionary and the spokesman for all traditional Hopis. He invited Indians of other tribes and whites into the kivas, giving away the secrecy of the underground chambers in which the Hopis hold their religious services.

It is a strange orthodoxy that Banyacya and his allies practice. More Hopis go to college from Hotevilla than from any other village. Banyacya himself has children in college, owns two cars, and has no visible means of support beside the fees he earns by lecturing to white audiences. He tells his Hopi critics that the two cars and the education of his children are the work of his wife, reminding them of the supremacy of the Hopi woman in all things that relate to the home.

In his relations with people outside the tribe, he sends the following message to explain himself and his missionary work:

My name is Thomas Banyacya. I've been interpreting for my people for a number of years, since 1948 when, in Shungopavi village, Hopi leaders, Chiefs and Religious men met for four days and went into many of the Hopi prophesies and knowledge that was kept within the religious societies ever since we came here many, many centuries ago. Since 1948 I have been putting all of my time and effort into helping my people to explain their position, their religious lives, their traditions, their warnings and their prophesies, for they tell that this is the time of world events and troubles. Things that had been prophesied are now being fulfilled, and they felt that it is time that this knowledge be brought out to all people, not only the Hopis, not only the other Indian People in this land, but to all people who are here on the continents called North and South America. Because, we are facing a severe day where severe punishment may be meted out for some of us who have not been following the instructions of the Great Spirit.

The Hotevilla People have the sacred stone tablets, the Oraibi people have the sacred stone tablets, and the Shungopavi people on another mesa have their religious order still functioning as it was from the beginning. The village of Mishongnovi and the first mesa people are still exercising and carrying on their sacred ritual ceremonies. They are all holding on to the life of the Great Spirit and of the people here in this land, so that this land will never be destroyed like it happened in another world.

The main reason they are now bringing this out and sending us to different areas is to tell the people, to warn the people, to explain this to them, to compare our knowledge, to compare our languages and to compare our religious things, so that through that religion we are going to find each other—we, who are searching for the right way of living the truth and the peaceful way of harmony with each other and with nature all around, the clouds, the rain, the animals and the plant life. We are all a part of it, we cannot break away from that. We are going to have to understand this so that we can look at each other. We are just like the trees out there—all different people with different languages, different colors and different ways of expression. We are just like any other part of nature that is around us. This, we must understand.

The Hopi stands on the religious and spiritual grounds that our old people have kept in their religious societies. Each one has his own special duty, and this is like in any animal, bird, fruit of all kind and the flowers. Everything has its own gift to give to the world, to share and to give to others. So, each one of us and each of the religious men also has that duty, whether he is a small person or a young man. We are all looking and searching for peace, harmony and better understanding amongst ourselves, so that we can face that day which Hopi call Purification Day, some say Judgement Day, some say Last Day. The Hopi were given that religion or belief and understanding of life in order to stand there to prove to the Great Spirit when we face him again that we will still be speaking the Hopi language and standing on our own path. The others were given their knowledge also, and you must stand on that path.

But, together we must share with each other, come together and live in peace until we get there, so that when the Great Spirit stands up we will not be afraid. Because, the Great Spirit also provided that there will be a Purifier who will stand there to weed out the bad ones from among us. It will be done with power and might. We cannot change that, we cannot stop it, and we cannot add anything to it to change it. That's the way it's laid out, and these leaders know this. So, the basic thing now is for these leaders to explain this standard of life, so that we may get a better understanding of it.

It is an irresistible message, delivered in the time of the Vietnam War by a man out of the past, charming, the fantasy of the lover whispered back to the lover. It is also a surrender to the dominant civilization, a surrender much deeper than the acceptance of electricity or sewage, for the letter panders to an alien theology. The Hopis have no concept of "The Great Spirit." God to them is ineffable. To answer the plague of Christian and Mormon missionaries, they have developed two descriptions of a purely spiritual being: "the one who walks unseen" and "the man without blood," but at the apex of their pantheon is something much closer to the idea of the unmoved mover.

Banyacya stands between two lovers, the enemy of one, the ally of the other, and the victim of both. His chief ally, the Committee for Traditional Indian Land and Life, is the most neurotic of lovers, a group of whites whose only actions are to interfere in the lives of the people they claim they are saving from outside interference. Among the material distributed by the Committee are pamphlets printed by the Minute Men and the Black Panthers. They supported the invasion of the Hopi Reservation by hippies, but they do nothing to help provide food or clothing for the Hopi poor. They know very little about the history, culture or political organization of the Hopis, but they are most willing to support dissension in the tribe. Thomas Banyacya is their man; he tells them what they want to hear, and they tell him of his importance. They grow fat together, feeding on the reciprocity of outcasts, while the tribe grows thin with the tension of internecine war.

There have been other times when Hopis fought each other; the legends are filled with rivalries between brothers, and in historical times the Hopis committed a terrible massacre of their own people: after the Spaniards left the village of Awatovi, having converted a large part of the population, the other Hopis destroyed the village, and killed everyone but a few of the women and children. That was not the only exception to the myth of the passive Hopis. They conducted raids against the Navahos, showed more than passive resistance to the Spanish priests, and even designated one of their clans as defenders of the people.

To Emory Sekaquaptewa, Jr., who has been initiated into the Hopi religion and holds office in a Katchina society, the general misinformation about the Hopis is infuriating. When Frank Waters' *Book of the Hopi* came to the attention of the tribe, Emory Sekaquaptewa, Jr. was the spokesman for the Second Mesa delegation during a meeting which resulted in the tribe trying to get Waters to "either give up his rights to the book so the Hopis could have its publication stopped, or make an addition with the statement that the material in the book should be questionable since it did not come from the right sources." Oswald White Bear Fredericks, who provided the source material for the book, was chastised by the tribe and made to promise that he would never again give out such misinformation. But Fredericks was also forgiven; he is from a Christian family and he is married to a white woman; he had done something that could be expected of such a man.

Some parts of the book are particularly irritating to the Hopis because they are wrong about the most basic concepts in Hopi theology. Waters confused Taiowa (the Sun) and the Creator, seeing them as the same. According to Sekaquaptewa, "The Sun is a creation; it is not the Creator. I can even describe the Sun by its manly attributes. The Sun is not a cause, but an instrument. The Sun was created by the Hopi people through divine power. Their next creation was the Moon."

Another of the notions that bothers Sekaquaptewa and other Hopis is the translation of *Hopi* into "people of peace." He says it is a concession to whites, a simple way of defining the Hopis for them. "*Hopi* means the one who follows the path. *Hopi* means to be good. It involves peace in the same way Christianity involves peace. It has been one of the big factors in the Hopi reluctance to fit into the modern society. Under the Hopi system no person has power over another. You have to live in peace with him." Nor does he see the Hopis as pacifists: "In my family, we are protectors, bound to be exposed to the enemy first. The Eagle Clan were given their lands on the perimeter because they were the first line of defense. In prehistoric days Hopis were very much involved in wars with Navahos, Apaches, and Utes, but always defensively."

Whether all of the wars were defensive is questionable, but one does not enter into disputes about the Hopis with Emory Sekaquaptewa; he is a believer. In his fortieth year, after having been a governor of his village, a delegate to the tribal council, an associate judge of the tribal court, a soldier in the United States Army and a teacher in a BIA school, he is completing his last year of law school at the University of Arizona. "I'm in law school," he said, "for the purpose of trying to reinstate the Hopi values. I want to learn the law and how it affects the Indian to learn how to reinstate these values without taking away from Indians themselves. The Indian people have abandoned their values because they did not bring about material gains. Now they find, after achieving material values, that they want their own values, but they keep making the gap between themselves and their own culture wider and wider."

He is a small man, delicate but not effeminate; the sun has lined his face, but it has not coarsened him; his eyes are sharp and opaque, but his eyelids are as delicate as insect wings. He is a priest who has built his own house. "I put in my own plumbing, dug a ditch a quarter of a mile by hand in order to have running water. I know what it costs, what sacrifices have to be made.

"A man looks at the Indian situation in his own terms and says it is tragic, but if an Indian looks at his problem, he comes to a different conclusion. The Indian needs to have as much of the conveniences of life as the affluent society can offer, but it means nothing to him if electricity is just given to him. It's no progress for him, if he takes it strictly as a gift and not as an achievement. Everybody's talking about how much money to give the Indians, but nobody ever talks about what the Indians must do.

"We have electricity all over the reservation, but many people don't have it in their homes for economic reasons. They're not ready to accept that responsibility. What if they can't pay the bill?"

The toughness that seems so unexpected in the "passive Hopi" goes even deeper. "It is the plan of the Creator," he said, "that people should live their life to the ultimate, what-

ever that may be. If we do not step from the straight and
narrow, we will be the only people who have fulfilled God's
wishes, and we will lead people into the next world. But
Hopi tradition does not send people out as missionaries. We
have our own way; what do we care about the others! The
Hopi view of the white man is that he is less than human,
that he has no qualms about exploiting his own brother,
mother and father. He's something like a mule or a bastard.
He's nobody in terms of not belonging to a clan. He has no
spiritual role, therefore he's a nobody."

He does not deliver his opinions casually: everything that
is Hopi is certain and unyielding, and everything that is
from the outside world must be qualified. He asks for admin-
istrative discretion within the structure of the Bureau of
Indian Affairs, an Indian point of view instead of a white
middle-class orientation to time and money. He seeks self-
determination for his people, yet, he says, "I'm not sure that
if I had been the Secretary over all these years that I would
have done any better. You have to take into consideration
the historical pressures in the development of the United
States."

The radicals, Lehman Brightman and others, have been to
visit Emory Sekaquaptewa, but to little avail. "Radicals may
have a purpose or role in our time," he says, "but what their
objectives are, I'm not sure. As we say in Hopi, 'People are
very heavy; you can't just move them around as you will.' I
disagree with Lehman Brightman, but what he's doing will
be helpful for off-reservation Indians."

The differences between the general society and the Hopi
society for him are in the sense of time, its value and the
value of material goods. He questions whether there can
ever be a union of the two societies. "The kind of leadership
envisioned in a democratic society has no place in the Hopi
society. People become leaders because of sacrifices they
make, whether anyone takes note or no. People like myself

find it very difficult to compete in this world. I don't know whether I want to go home because I'm afraid of this society or because I want to be there."

He has come to law school to find out "whether the white man's methods of reaching a just conclusion can be applied to Hopi justice." He wants some union between the two societies, but he is not certain that it can work. "If modern methods can strengthen the Hopi principles, that's what I'll do. If not, I'll find something else."

There is no alternative to the acceptance of modern methods. He knows that is the case, but he cannot bring himself to say it. Perhaps there are political reasons for his reluctance. People outside the tribe who know its problems say that Emory Sekaquaptewa himself is the answer to the dissension within the tribe, that the lawyer-priest is one of the few people who may possibly bring the factions together. He cannot comment on his own possibilities: "There's no such thing as individual fame among Hopis. One is supposed to be humble. If his deeds are recognized, it's okay, but he can't promote himself."

The crisis of acculturation is clearest to him in the problems of language. He blames the misinformation about Hopis on inadequate translations, explaining that Hopis will often agree to any English equivalent to a Hopi word because it makes no difference to them. He tells the complications of translating the name Sekaquaptewa. It is his father's name, not his; he and his brothers have taken the name to keep the family together. Sekaquaptewa translates literally as The Yellow Spot on the Neck of the Coyote, but its implication is that the coyote is better-looking because of the spot. And even that is not the full meaning of the name, for it is involved with the clan and has meaning within the clan structure. To find a simple English equivalent seems hopeless to him. He said he once thought there were no English equivalents for many Hopi concepts, but he finds that to be less true as he learns more English. Then he asks himself aloud, "Or is it because I'm compromising Hopi concepts?"

It is no easier to be a Hopi on the reservation. A highway passes the villages on the three mesas, bringing tourists, hippies, missionaries, anthropologists and journalists, serving the BIA as well as the Hopis, conveying the lovers to their work. The men who are building the Hopi Cultural Center wear hard hats and drive heavy machinery. The offices of the tribal chairman and the Community Action Program are housed in trailers placed on cement foundations. There are copying machines and carpets. The lunch hour is clearly defined. Photographs of Honani and Lololma, Hopi leaders at the end of the eighteenth and beginning of the nineteenth centuries, decorate the walls of a house built of cement block. A woman of Shungopovi said, "We opposed the right of way for the railroad tracks because a Hopi woman is always free to leave, and we were afraid she would go too far. Now we have the highway and the young women hitchhike."

It is not difficult to understand why a young woman would want to leave the Hopi Reservation. There is not enough work, and there is not enough rain, and there is not enough land any more. The Navaho Reservation surrounds the Hopi land, squeezing the Hopis, who arrived in the area at least several thousand years before the Navahos. But there are 120,000 Navahos, and they too suffer from an inadequate land base. The two tribes bicker incessantly over their property rights. The youth of the world is ended in northern Arizona.

The placement in time of the beginning of youth is less clear. Oraibi is the oldest continually inhabited place in the United States, having been established during the twelfth century A.D. But the people of Shungopovi point out that the Bear Clan, who they say were the first people to emerge from the underworld, established the village of Shungopovi at the foot of the mesas long before people moved up to Oraibi on Third Mesa. Theirs would have been the oldest village if they had not been forced to move to the top of Second Mesa during the sixteenth century. The rivalry between villages is not new. The Hopis were organized as independent villages before the Indian Reorganization Act; tribalism as a form of political and social organization is new to them. That concept was forced upon the Indians by whites, though it has now been taken up by some Indians and their lovers as a panacea handed down from the noble savage.

The history of most tribes, with the exception of the Iroquois who had begun a more complex organization under the influence of Deganawidah, indicates that tribalism is a highly unstable political and social form. Tribes had a common culture, and occasionally acted in concert (though the Hopis say that some villages, for example, united with the Utes to attack other Hopi villages), but the tribes were in a constant process of fractionalization. The evidence of that process is easily seen in a chart of Native American languages. There are more than thirty different Ute-Aztecan languages, including those of the Hopis and their enemies, the Utes, as well as those of the Comanches, Pimas, Papagos, Yaquis and Aztecs. Obviously there was a root language and a root tribe. Unless the multiple migration theory proves to be true to some extraordinary degree, the fractionalization can be even more clearly demonstrated by the total number of mutually unintelligible languages that existed in the Americas prior to the conquest: the estimates are questionable, but it would appear that at least two thousand languages were developed in about twenty thousand years. Any expectation that tribalism will prove to be the panacea uniting all men would seem to be denied by the linguistic evidence.

The first attempt to make the Hopis into a single social and political unit came with the Indian Reorganization Act

of 1934. A tribal government was set up with the aid of
experts supplied by the government, delegates were elected,
and the council began some preliminary functions. It had
not been in existence for ten years when Peter Nuvamsa,
then chairman of the council, determined that the function
of the tribe should not replace the function of the elders in
the Hopi theocracy. He walked out, resigning his position
and closing the council. For more than a decade afterward,
the council did not function. In 1953 it was reorganized and
again recognized by the Federal Government. Peter Nuvamsa is now nearly eighty years old, though he is not sure
of his age because years were not counted by the Hopis
when he was born. He is, however, the oldest living member
of the Bear Clan of Shungopovi, and thus holds the position
of ceremonial spokesman. One would expect his age, his
position in the clan, and his stand against the tribal council
when he was chairman to put him in Thomas Banyacya's
faction, but he has taken the opposite position. "The advan-
tages do not harm our background at all," he said. "Everything that is Hopi is spiritual, and has nothing to do with
politics."

He is, of course, aware that acculturation is taking place.
He knows the encroachments of Christianity and Mormon-
ism; from his vantage point of eighty years he can see the
changes in himself and his village. He wants the Hopi way
to be preserved, but he is too thoroughly a Hopi to put
anything above the welfare of the people of his village.

His hands are very old, abrasive to the touch, with the big
curling thumbs and heavy nails that come of seventy years
of work. The form of his skull is evident under his aged skin.
He wears bluejeans, a plaid shirt and desert boots. His hair
is graying, long, falling below his ears at the sides, gathered
at the back and wound with white cord. Around his temples
he wears a black shiny headband tied at the side with a flat

knot. He is a small man; the set of his shoulders is worn, but he is not stooped. His English is almost as good as his health, which is magnificent.

For the most part, Peter Nuvamsa earns his living by hauling water. He and his "partner" have a battered red pickup truck which they drive between Shungopovi and a well powered by a windmill. They fill several iron containers with water, then drive six miles back to the village to distribute it.

Shortly before Christmas of 1969, Nuvamsa and several other men were completing the digging of a well in the village. Snow was predicted along with a hard freeze, so the men worked all night to complete the well. The next day Nuvamsa was tired as he went about his work of hauling water, one of his last days of work before the well in the village could be used. But he was pleased about the well, talking of the number of gallons per hour that could be expected and how they would soon lay pipes to all the houses to provide them with running water.

Did he realize that when the well began to function he would no longer be able to earn his living by hauling water?

"Yes."

Then why did he work so hard to bring in the well?

"It's for the good of the people," he said, smiling at the interlocutor, indulging a fool.

And did he know that in the dominant society men who acted as unselfishly as Peter Nuvamsa were thought to be saints?

"I don't like those Mormons," he answered. "They say theirs is the only true religion, and I tell them we must all worship the Supreme Being in our own way. When I pray, I pray for all men."

He is generally unimpressed with the society that was imported from Europe. "To begin with," he said, "the society has good meanings to it, but those meanings get changed." It is also possible that the Hopi meanings get changed, though he does not admit of such possibilities in his own life. He has talked with anthropologists from every part of the world. Those who come from as far as France and Germany have impressed him least, because they speak English poorly; it is a foreign language for him too, and he feels justified in being disdainful of their lack of fluency.

Perhaps it is this long contact with curious strangers that has caused him to develop a simplistic explanation of Hopi theology, or perhaps he merely tells them what they want to hear in order to quickly have done with it. "*Hopi* means one who walks in the right direction," he said. "If you follow the path, you have everlasting life, your grand and glory. If you don't, you go to Hell. You become a fire eater.

"There is a law of just or divine retribution. If you do wrong, it won't happen to you in daylight. Maybe you'll get sick or something. The wisest people have planned—the world unrolls like a roll of paper. If everything is so corrupted, the world will end. We will know when there is no respect for one another, when everyone thinks only of good times and not of the good of man. It may be a fire, a flood, a rain of arrows or stumbling (turning over and over) that will answer our wickedness. This place where we are now is where we're supposed to prepare ourselves."

He tires quickly of talking of Hopi theology; what difference can it make to a white man? He prefers to walk through the village, pointing out a community building paid for by the Save the Children Federation, explaining that he is the village coördinator for the Federation, and that he asks the children to bring him receipts for the money they spend so he can be sure it is not wasted or used for liquor. He talks of Banyacya again, saying that he (Banyacya) opposes the Federation and tells the people the white man will one day come and demand that they give the money back. Peter Nuvamsa shakes his head: "We would like to have an adjustment with the Hotevilla people."

It is a small village, set between the highway and the great escarpment that was the main defense of the Hopis, a dry, dusty place on uneven ground. The dirt road that leads from the highway loses its definition at the entrance to the village, and the houses and kivas appear without apparent pattern. Most of the structures are of native stone. A few of the newer buildings are made of cement block. Peter Nuvamsa points to a stone house under construction. He is the stonemason. "I built eight of the stone houses in the village," he said. "These new ones, cement block, are easier to put up, but they don't fit in with the land."

The house of his niece is one of the new ones. It is a small building, deadly gray, made of sharp corners. There is a single large room and a kitchen alcove inside. At midday, the family gathers around the dining table at the west end of the room: Peter Nuvamsa, his niece and her husband, an adolescent boy and girl, and a baby who reeks of the need to have his diaper changed. The meal is composed of fried Spam, soaked corn kernels, fry bread, coffee and prepared breakfast pastries served in the blue carboard and plastic package.

Nuvamsa's niece is a rotund woman, bespectacled. She hides her sentiments in the perfectly round jovial mask of her face. Her speech is clipped, giving the impression that she talks very rapidly. Her husband is a big man, dressed like a white collar worker on vacation; he speaks very little. Neither do the adolescent children talk much. It is near Christmas, and they are home from boarding school. The girl giggles. The boy, sixteen years old, has not been initiated into the Hopi religion, and the time has passed. He is no longer "young in mind." He is a fragile boy, graceful, but it is not the masculine grace of his great-uncle; the sinew is lacking.

During the meal, Peter Nuvamsa uses the presence of a white guest to talk about Hopi religion, directing his remarks to the guest, though they are really meant for the two adolescents, who do not give him the courtesy of their attention. "Whenever a student is attending boarding school," he says, "when it's time for him to be initiated, he can be brought back." There is no response from the boy. "When a child leaves too early," Nuvamsa adds, "and is raised around outside people, they're not much of Hopi."

"A man can't be a Hopi unless he is initiated," he says, still speaking to the boy, though not looking at him. "You can't learn from books or talk, you have to be there to have the emotional experience, the risk. After your initiation you can walk as an honest man with any class of citizen." He talks of the "making of the man" ceremony. Though it is secret and should not be spoken of before those who are not initiated, he wants to reach the boy. He speaks again and again of the risk, telling of being doused with icy water from a spring and being made to walk wet and naked in the cold. He recalls ceremonies where some of the boys could not make the long climb up the escarpment, and tells how their fellows carried them on their backs.

There is no response from the boy. Finally, Nuvamsa turns to him to deliver what he considers to be the core of the Hopi way: "Be spiritual and humble and concentrate your mind on your given instruction. And do everything you can for your children."

The girl and her father leave the table and begin putting up Christmas decorations. "This is also part of Hopi culture," says Nuvamsa. He laughs, perhaps for relief of the bitterness that was in his joke. Then he goes on: "Our prayer-feather ceremonies are like Christmas. We pass out blue eagle feathers to all the people. When we send our prayer feathers to our friends, they treasure that. They deliver the prayer feathers to their shrine, and pray every day for four days. But in this other way, we give toys to the children and the next day they step all over them."

Then the boy too leaves to help with the Christmas decorations. Nuvamsa's niece begins to clear the dishes from the table. Only the old man and his white guest are left at the table. He points to a photograph of Honani, his clan uncle, and talks of how he predicted automobiles and airplanes long before such things had been seen by a Hopi. He and his niece carry on a brief conversation about a man of Shungopovi who gave away ceremonial secrets to a man of another village. Then, quite suddenly, he says, "People do things that are against nature; they kill it. They cut down trees to have grass. But all of these things have a purpose: deer, salt, turkeys, logs, grass, trees, everything; they are a comfort to the earth. And when people do these things that are contrary, then . . ." He claps his hands—the end of the world.

The baby is frightened by the clap of his hands, and begins to cry. Nuvamsa takes a long drink of his coffee, emerging from the drink with a sigh, acquiescing to his tiredness, his age. "We tell our boundaries by designs (pictographs) that are on the rocks, but the area where we want to go is public domain. Why don't they let us kill deer that are used in ceremonies without being penalized? Let us cut logs, dig roots. We don't have those things here."

Outside the house, walking through the village again, he stops to knock at the door of his nephew, the silversmith, but there is no answer. His "partner" is waiting for him; the well is not yet completed, there is more water to be hauled. A young boy passes, shouting to him, "Peter, your partner is looking for you."

Peter Nuvamsa smiles and nods. He is going. He is going. What is the use in being old now? What is the use in knowing? He has known how to read and write for seventy years. That is what brought it all to a closing, to dying. Everything can be written, even the name of God, everyone can know. There is no place for old men any more, even for those who would marry magic with science, even for those who are wise beyond their long years. The counting of time has begun at Shungopovi.

10 THE DEFEAT OF THE RODEO

ON THE FIRST MORNING of the Sun Dance, the Cowboy* was flat broke and still drunk. The cornea of his left eye was red with blood, the cheekbone below it was fractured, and his left arm was covered with scabs and shiny scar tissue. Three days before, he had come out of the chute on a saddle bronc, the horse had bucked wildly, the Cowboy had missed his timing on one of the bucks, and in falling, had pulled the horse over on top of him. He had managed to come away from the rodeo with a few hundred dollars in prize money, but a girl had rolled him for it in a little off-reservation whiskey town called Whiteclay, where he had gone to celebrate his return home to Pine Ridge, and to ease the pain of his newest wounds.

It was a few moments before sunrise; though the light was beginning, the night chill was still in the air. Indian men in mackinaws and women wrapped in shawls and blankets were making coffee in the tents surrounding the sacred Sun-Dance grounds. Streamers hung from the cottonwood tree that had been chopped down by a virgin, carried to the grounds and erected there the night before—black, white, red and yellow, representing the four cardinal directions. There was a problem with the public address system. The man with the change box had not yet arrived at the ticket booth. The Sun Dance was to begin at dawn, and it was late.

* "The Cowboy" is a pseudonym.

The Cowboy bummed the price of a cup of coffee, by-passed the admission booth, and went inside the barbed wire fence to stand behind another barbed wire fence that enclosed the sacred ground. "Lord-a-mercy-goddammit, it's cold," he said. He looked for someone to talk to, but not many people at Pine Ridge have a lot to say to the Cowboy. His relationship to "Chief" Charles Red Cloud gives him some status, but he is a troublemaker, perhaps a little crazy from falling off too many horses. Most people stay away from him.

In the announcer's booth, Robert Mousseau, secretary of the Oglala Sioux Tribal Council and chairman of the Sun Dance, busied himself with the problem of the public address system. He had planned a different kind of Sun Dance this year, assuring the tribal council that it would not lose money: a carnival had been allowed to set up rides and games a few hundred yards away from the sacred grounds, and Richard Wilson had been put in charge of a rodeo to be held in connection with the Sun Dance.

· Outside the sacred ground, west of the spectator area, three medicine men prepared the participants for the dancing. Lame Deer, a tall, straight, compellingly handsome man, was to be the director of the dance. Fools Crow, wearing spectacles and without his costume, which he had sold for $235 while touring with a group of Sioux dancers, would supervise the dancers directly and do the piercing of the flesh on the fourth and final morning of the Sun Dance. Catches, a younger medicine man, was to be the lead dancer. Of the seven dancers, five were old men, one of them blind; one was the child whose parents had promised he would dance if Fools Crow could save his life after the Public Health Service doctors had pronounced him a terminal case; and one was a young law student, recently returned from Vietnam where he had flown a hundred and five missions as a fighter pilot, and laughed at the missiles and anti-aircraft guns because he was protected by a necklace given to him by Fools Crow.

The dancers had just returned from the small sweat-lodge next to the canvas tipi in which they were being prepared. The sun had come up. They were late, but the Red Cloud Singers, the old men who sang in the traditional way, were also late. The public address system was still not working, but the ticket booth had opened. Admission was $1.50 each day. There was a $5 charge for permission to use a still camera or a tape recorder, and a $20 charge for the use of a movie camera. A small group of people moved in through the gate. Their hands were stamped so they might come and go without paying again, and they were given receipts for their camera and tape recorder fees, along with an admonition to keep the receipts because the Indian police would ask for them.

It was not yet 6 A.M. when the sun rose. The dancers did not enter the sacred ground until after 8 A.M. They came in a file, blowing eagle-bone whistles with downy white feathers on the ends, barefoot, dancing easily to the singing and drumming of the Red Cloud Singers. They wore garlands of leaves in their hair, and long blankets, like skirts, around their waists. There were bracelets of leaves at their wrists and ankles and red marks were painted on their bare chests. Their faces were marked with paint. Catches, who had affixed feathers to his arms by passing hooks through his skin, carried a buffalo skull.

The dancers circled the grounds several times, then stopped in a row at the west side, where Catches added the skull to a simple altar; then they turned to the east, raised up on their toes, lifted their arms to the sun and blew on their whistles. All but Catches and the former pilot were fat, the small boy was confused, there were arc lights on poles behind them, cameras were clicking on every side, the public address system suffered regular bursts of whining feedback, and Fools Crow was dressed like a cowboy mystic; but it was a moment for the Sioux, a fleeting reviviscence of the time before their crystalline world had been shattered and ground into sand.

The Cowboy watched for a while, finding the sun more uncomfortable than the cold. He accosted a tourist, offered him some information about the ceremony ("They are praying to God"), then asked him for a dollar. "I'll pay you back tonight," he said. "My grandma's holding some money for me." The tourist looked up at the battered Indian, seeing the exaggerated flatness and high cheekbones that conspired in the Cowboy's face, causing him to look anachronistic, fierce. There was a moment's hesitation. The Cowboy pulled his straw sheriff's hat lower over his eyes and dug the toe of his boot into the grass, more cowboy than Indian. "C'mon," he said, "I'll pay you back. I promise." Still the tourist hesitated. "Lord-a-mercy-goddamit, it's only a dollar." The tourist gave him the money.

After another cup of coffee, the Cowboy went out to the parking area east of the Sun Dance grounds, across a dirt road that was already throwing up clouds of dust behind each passing car. He hitched a ride with a man and his son who were on their way into Pine Ridge. "You like to ride horses?" he asked the boy. To the expected answer, he replied, "C'mon out to my place and I'll let you ride on one of my horses." They went through Pine Ridge, off the paved road onto a gravel road and off the gravel road onto a pair of deep ruts that led to a small house. The Cowboy calmed the dogs that greeted the car, and tried without success to rouse his brother, who was asleep inside the house. "The saddles are all inside," he said. "It's just a pony; the boy can ride without a saddle." He crawled through the barbed wire fence around the pasture, and held the strands apart for the boy to follow him. They went out into the pasture where a Shetland pony stood, interrupted in its lackadaisical grazing.

He lifted the boy onto the horse, which walked a few yards before it bucked him off. The Cowboy laughed, slapping his knee with his hat, and shouted encouragement to the boy. After being bucked off three more times, the boy gave up. The Cowboy rubbed the boy's head. "You think that pony is mean; Lord-a-mercy, you ought to try big Red there."

He led the boy over to the fence, where a bay stallion was feeding. "Don't stand too close to him," he cautioned the boy. "He'll kick you or bite you for sure." Then he walked close to the horse and stroked it, talking softly to the animal. When the horse was calm, he reached his hand over its neck, grabbed its ear, and put his other hand on the horse's nose, pushing down. They wrestled for several minutes before the Cowboy was able to work the horse's head into a position that gave him enough leverage to bring it down. He lay on the horse for a moment after it fell, his hat knocked over to one side and his face shiny with sweat. "You see," he told the boy, "you got to push down hard on the nose."

After he let the horse get up, he wiped his face with a red and white handkerchief, patted the horse once or twice, and grabbed it again. They fought for only a minute before the horse went down. When they were both standing again, the horse moved over close to him, as if asking for one more fall. He slapped the horse on the rump, "I'm too tired, Red." To the boy, who now looked at him with adoration, he said, "You come to the Sun Dance tomorrow, and I'll saddle up that pony and bring him over so you can ride him all day."

At the Sun Dance grounds, Robert Mousseau had announced that there would be no dancing in the afternoons during the rodeo, which was to be held on the second, third and fourth days of the Sun Dance. There had also been an altercation at the gate. Two old Indians had been barred from the spectator area because they did not have the price of admission. The case was brought to Mousseau, who ruled that everyone but the singers and dancers had to pay; the tribe needed the money. There was grumbling on both counts: the rodeo had not been a popular idea with many of the older people, and the prohibition of dancing in the afternoons to support the rodeo had angered them, but to bar two Indians from the Sun Dance because they could not pay the price of admission was infuriating.

In the tribal courthouse, Amos Bad Heart Bull defended a man accused of one of the minor crimes the tribe is allowed to judge. The maximum sentence a tribal court may give is six months in jail and a $500 fine, but there is no rule against consecutive sentences for various counts, and there is no procedure for appeal of a judgment by a tribal court. Amos Bad Heart Bull calls himself a "twenty-five-cent lawyer" because most of the cases in which he participates would be classed as misdemeanors and his fees are often small. On the other hand, he argues before a judge whose opinions are as final as those of the United States Supreme Court, and his fee in some cases is said to be as high as seven hundred dollars.

He is a man of vast bulk, a full blood, the great-grandson of Bad Heart Bull who kept the winter count for the Oglala Sioux when they were led by Crazy Horse and Red Cloud. The ancestral occupation is important to him, and he has begun to write what he calls a history of the Oglala tribe, basing the work upon his interpretation of picture writing left by his ancestors and legends that are told by people on his part of the reservation. He writes the history in the Sioux language, then translates it into English. But it is not a history in the Western sense. In the portion of the work he has completed there are no dates, and there is no sense of real time. It is a history within the sacred hoop, obliged to the form of the circle in which time is conceived by the Indian. There is no progress; nothing is permanent but the form, which is unchanging. Drawings on a buffalo hide can mark the glory of a man, but a man is a passing thing; like the buffalo, his bones will fertilize the grass, and the circle will go on without interruption. At the end of the completed portion of his history, he calls for a rejuvenation of the Sioux, but it is an enfeebled requisite of his own time, an admission of objectivity, out of tune with the words that have come before.

Amos Bad Heart Bull's work was begun as independent study at Black Hills College, where he is working toward a master's degree in sociology, taking a few courses in the summers, too pressured now with responsibilities to go to school full time. Much of it is material that has already been recorded by anthropologists, but in the few thousand words he has translated into English there are some astonishing ideas. The Sioux, who were called cutthroats in the sign language of the plains (a finger drawn across the throat) are commonly thought to be a people dedicated to war. They are described in the literature as something akin to the early psychologist Bard's cats after they were lobotomized into continual rage. But Amos Bad Heart Bull has written: "*Wicapa waksa oyate na wolakota kage sa oyate hecel cage iklatapi,*" which he translates as "We were called cutthroats, but we prefer to call ourselves the people who prefer peace over war."

It is undoubtedly true, as Peter Farb has suggested, that the Sioux became warlike when the French armed the Ojibways, who then used their superior weaponry to push the Sioux westward onto the plains, where they in turn had to displace other tribes. Lowie's theory that "The objective (of plains warfare) was never to acquire new lands" is simply wrong. Rousseau's vision of the "youth of the world" is proved again; it was the invasion by the whites that brought about the concept of property (in this case, tribal lands), which leads to strife; the Sioux culture was corrupted by Europeans before there was physical contact between the two cultures. The failure of anthropologists like Lowie to grasp the cause of the warlike attitudes of the Sioux is easily understandable; the change had taken place before any ethnographic data were collected. The horse is often given as the reason for the cultural change among the Sioux and other Plains Indians, but its importance pales before the power of the concept of property, which works a basic change in human societies, one that cannot be shrugged off with references to "The Territorial Imperative." Property and territory are not synonymous: Rousseau made that quite clear when he described a man choosing to find another source of food rather than fight over food that had been taken from him. The notion of territory allows that alternative; property allows no alternative—it is after Eden.

The old ideas are so strong in Amos Bad Heart Bull that he cannot fully accept the tribal structure imposed upon the Oglalas by the Bureau of Indian Affairs. He speaks of *tios'pa* (tĭ-ōsh-pä), kindred, and the areas occupied by them (*tios' paye*) as the real social structure of the Oglalas. His theory is borne out by Charles Red Cloud. The old man, sitting with his wife in front of their tent on a hill overlooking the Sun Dance grounds, surrounded by the tents of his relatives, all of them come to the Sun Dance, is the leader of one of the *tios'pa* of Pine Ridge, but not a leader of the tribe. His patriarchy does not extend beyond his kin, though he is treated with respect by all the Sioux because of his great age. He and his relatives have little use for Amos Bad Heart Bull, recalling his tenure on the tribal council with a distaste that has its origin in the dispute between the people from Porcupine and those from White Clay,* and there is apparently no social need of sufficient power to break down the old antipathies between the bands.

* White Clay refers to the area around White Clay Creek, not to Whiteclay, Neb., the whiskey town just off the southern boundary of the reservation.

When Amos Bad Heart Bull and his group were voted out of office, they were replaced by Enos Poor Bear and his followers. A second conflict within the tribe is in evidence in that election: Poor Bear represents the mixed bloods, for the most part, while Bad Heart Bull was more closely allied with the full bloods. There is some softening of the distinction now that the number of full bloods has become so small and those remaining have gained new esteem through the cultural nationalism that has touched a few of the younger people on the reservation, but for many years the full bloods suffered the problems of acculturation most directly: they were called "blues" by the mixed bloods (a reference to their skin color), and they were the least likely to speak English and understand the complexities of the managed life, causing them to become the poorest of the poor.

The plight of the poor, represented by the two people who had been barred from the spectator area at the Sun Dance because of their inability to pay the price of admission, had been occupying the minds of the Sioux during the entire afternoon. A few people had danced, and most of the singing groups were there, but it was desultory dancing. Most of the people milled around the area between the dancing and the circle of tents and makeshift counters that served the vendors. There was conversation about the Catholic priest who had raised thirty thousand dollars to finance a search for the bones of Crazy Horse. A young Indian, who was working on a doctoral degree in education, passed out leaflets in English and Sioux, urging people to keep their children in school.

Rodeos and basketball games occupied some of the younger men's thoughts. A woman sat on the ground under the bower of pine boughs that shaded the spectators; her legs were crossed and she leaned against a pole; wrapped in a great dark shawl with her, like a secret, was her suckling child. In front of the largest tent, a group of Hawaiians, missionaries of the Mormon Church, stood beside a poster that asked whether the Indians were the lost tribe of Israel. The following afternoon, they attempted to charm the Sioux into their church with Hawaiian songs and the plunking of ukuleles.

Water trucks patrolled the roads, converting the dust to mud, which soon dried and became dust again. An Indian policeman directed traffic. The ferris wheel turned, ignored by the Sioux. Wild turnip and corn soup did not sell as well as hot dogs or hamburgers. The owner of a portable popcorn and candy stand called "Custer's Last Stand" readied his wares for the expected bonanza of the night crowd. On the public address system there were announcements about the rodeo. The dancers of the morning had retired before noon; those who replaced them wore buckskin, feathers and bells. The temperature reached ninety-five degrees before the afternoon waned.

The dancing ended at five o'clock. It was presumed that the people would return to their tents or their homes, have dinner and come back at seven-thirty to begin dancing again. The singing groups, called drums, were advised of the starting time. The amplifiers were turned off, the coffee and the popcorn cooled. A wind of evening came up, blowing dust and papers over the nearly deserted grounds.

At the Moccasin Drive-in, Amos Bad Heart Bull and Gerald One Feather told a white visitor about Crazy Horse. They leaned on the fender of One Feather's pickup truck, their coffee cups balanced on the hood, both men of great bulk, slow in their speech and movements. They were often called, "The laziest men on the reservation," but it was meant mostly as teasing. The two full bloods were better known for their shrewdness. Bad Heart Bull, the lawyer, could be depended upon by a man in trouble, and One Feather, a young activist grown to manhood, had worked around the country in OEO programs for Indians. He had married the former Miss Indian America, and he was the reform candidate for the office of tribal chairman. Their conversation slipped up and back from English to Sioux, recalling the history of the man who had led "the greatest light cavalry in history." Gerald One Feather puffed on a cigar, using it as punctuation. They spoke easily in Sioux, slowly in English, describing the seven powers of Crazy Horse, attempting to translate magic into the language of science.

At precisely seven-thirty, Robert Mousseau mounted the steps to the announcer's stand, waited for an assistant to assure him that the microphone was turned on, called out numbers to test the equipment, then officially opened the dancing for the evening. Not one singer appeared, and there was but one dancer, a white man dressed in Indian beads and moccasins. Mousseau called for singers and dancers, knowing that the loudspeakers carried his message to the tents that had been set up around the Sun Dance grounds and to the cars parked along the road. The Indians waited. They sat in their cars, listening to the radio, chatting, tending to their children. In the tents the people dawdled over dinner.

People began to come into the spectator area: anthropologists, reporters, curiosity seekers, missionaries, BIA employees, vendors, an itinerant Frenchman, but no Indians. Mousseau continued to call for singers and dancers. By eight o'clock the lights had been turned on and the temperature had dropped below seventy degrees. The wind had cleaned the ground of papers. A red dusk was coloring the sky, muted by blown dust. The whites who had come to see the dancing stood quietly, asking each other what had happened, some of them making jokes about Indian time, others understanding that some sort of boycott was taking place. At eight-thirty, Mousseau offered five dollars to the first drum that arrived at the announcer's stand. "Hoka-hey," he called, then recited the names of the various drums: "Red Cloud Singers, Porcupine Drum, Sons of the Oglala." In the tents and in the cars the Indians waited, some of them in full dancing regalia, eagle plumes on the seats of Chevrolets.

There had been no formal negotiations between Mousseau and those who boycotted his Sun Dance, nor had there been any organization in the formal sense. There were no hand-bills and no mass meetings. The banning of afternoon dancing in favor of the rodeo was one problem, but the crux of the matter was the two poor Indians. Before the conquest, it was always said that the helpless ones were to be protected; the helpless are now the ones without money. The people had been moved by their distaste for this manifestation of the dominant culture. It made them Indian again, defending the helpless, preferring the Sun Dance to the rodeo, denying that any man may have power over another. Robert Mousseau was the representative of the tribe, and the people were in opposition to the tribe. The Sioux are addicted to gossip and argument, but the boycott had been achieved by arriving at a consensus almost silently.

Mousseau remained at the announcer's station, calling out his offer. He did not talk to a delegation or even to a representative of the people who were boycotting the dancing. Perhaps there was no one to talk to. Some said it was Charles Red Cloud who had started the boycott; others said they "just knew." The only explanation everyone could agree on was the "moccasin telegraph." At eight forty-five, Mousseau announced that there would be dancing the following afternoon at two o'clock. The first group of singers appeared immediately, a crowd of dancers gathered at the entrance to the Sun-Dance grounds, and the two Indians who could not pay the price of admission walked through the gate into the spectator area.

Across the road, perhaps a quarter of a mile to the east of the Sun-Dance grounds, Richard Wilson was working on his rodeo. The portable chutes, which had been rented at great cost, were brought in at the last possible moment, and the job of setting them up had gone through the day and into the darkness. There were no floodlights. The men worked in the semi-darkness of moonlight and the headlamps of cars. The Cowboy worked with them; the whiskey and the hangover were gone, and he had been promised the twenty-dollar entry fee for the saddle bronc competition in return for his labor.

They tested the chutes by running horses out of them, bursting into the moonlit arena, making silvery puffs of dust, sweating in the cold, cursing, slapping the horses, worried about running them too hard in the cold. They practiced roping and bulldogging, chasing the terrified calves blindly; all to be ready, all to have the chance. For the Cowboy it may have been more important than for the others. "My dad was an RCA (Rodeo Cowboy Association) cowboy," he said, "We got the trophies at home. I'm not that good. I won a few trophies though. But I pawned 'em. My dad was really good. I don't have the timing. Saddle broncs is the only thing I ride now. I don't enter what I can't win. And I can sure use that prize money; that girl rolled me. Lord-a-mercy-god-dammit, didn't even leave my wallet."

The dancing stopped when Mousseau announced that two members of the tribe had been injured in an automobile accident. A collection was taken up for them. The money was counted, and the total was announced to some applause. After that, the drums stopped and the people went home. They contributed generously, and they went quietly. Indians know about automobile wrecks; the bad roads, poorly maintained old automobiles, and the liquor laws that force people to drink too much too far from home have put them all in jeopardy. Every Indian knows someone who has died in an automobile wreck; it is the expected death.

The Sun Dancers were late on the second morning too. They danced for two hours, retiring before two members of the local American Legion post raised the flag. Fat men, wearing the blue and gold overseas caps of the American Legion at a rakish tilt, their navels peeking from the missed connection of their bright colored shirts and sagging trousers, they saluted while the Sioux national anthem was sung. A peace-pipe ceremony followed; most of the people invited to the announcer's stand to puff on the pipe were whites. The Frenchman, who said he had come to South Dakota to write a book about Sitting Bull, made a brief speech.

By mid-afternoon a conflict had developed between an NBC television crew and the tribal council. Enos Poor Bear, chairman of the council, had made an agreement between the tribe and Casey Tibbs, a rodeo performer and producer of movies about rodeos, giving Tibbs exclusive film rights to the Sun Dance. It was rumored that Tibbs would pay six buffalo skins, one live buffalo and fifteen hundred dollars to the tribe as his part of the bargain. Tibbs had even brought along Joel McCrea, an actor who played Buffalo Bill in the movies, to add luster to his documentary. In addition to calling out, "How! Red Cloud," before the old man emerged on cue from a canvas tipi, McCrea was to lead the rodeo parade. Poor Bear was also to present a pair of beaded moccasins to Tibbs at the opening ceremonies of the rodeo, a sign of eternal friendship between the Oglalas and Tibbs. The NBC crew had no intention of paying either Poor Bear or the tribe for the right to make a documentary film. Said the producer in charge of the crew: "We don't do that kind of journalism."

On Poor Bear's orders, the Indian police harassed the NBC crew, keeping them away from the action, forcing them to set up their cameras in the spectator area. The NBC producer was peeved by the lack of respect for the power of the network; the Sioux appeared to think of them as nothing more than tourists with fancy cameras. Casey Tibbs, on the other hand, was known on the rodeo circuit, and he had a movie star with him. A series of discussions between NBC and the tribal council ended with Poor Bear holding firm to his agreement with Tibbs, and threatening to have his police confiscate the NBC cameras if they violated his orders. But the blow that ultimately destroyed the morale of the NBC crew came on the third day of the Sun Dance.

A member of the crew confronted an elderly Indian in the spectator area. "How, how," said the Indian, amused by the sight of whites carrying loads of equipment that any Indian would have put on a horse or in the back of a pickup truck.

The man from the network introduced himself. "We'd like to take your picture," he said.

"Where you from?" asked the Indian.

"We're from the NBC television network."

"What's that?"

The man from NBC stepped back, reeling as if he had been struck with a club. He could not speak.

The Indian, who was perhaps sixty years old, spoke excellent English, and knew very well what the NBC television network was, but he saw the opportunity to amuse himself at the expense of a white man, and a haughty white man at that.

At two o'clock there was dancing at the Sun Dance grounds while other Indians roped calves and rode bulls inside the makeshift arena across the road. There were no stands, so the Indians parked their cars around the fence, pointing in at the arena, and sat there in the sun, listening to their radios and watching the contests, sipping soft drinks and coffee, and keeping their car windows closed against the wind that blew great waves of gritty dust across the hot ground.

The riding and roping were mediocre and without much excitement. The bronc riding, that classic of the rodeo, was to come the following day. A moment of excitement came before a young man was to try to ride the buffalo in an exhibition designed to amuse the spectators: the buffalo had been let into the pen with the horses, where it waited quietly until someone poked a stick through the fence and into the buffalo's hindquarters. The animal suddenly became enraged, charging the horses, attempting to gore them with its short, thick horns. Using whips and poles, some of them climbing over the fence into the pen, the Indians managed to cut the buffalo out of the herd of horses before it did much physical damage. But the horses were upset by the dust and screaming and the fearful sweat, which may have contributed to the lackluster performances in the First Annual Oglala Sioux All-Indian Rodeo.

The second night of dancing was more spirited. Amos Bad Heart Bull, who sings with the Sons of the Oglalas, arrived late, having gone to Rushville, Nebraska, south of the reservation, to have dinner in what he called "a decent restaurant." Gerald One Feather and Amos's eight-year-old daughter had been with him. The conversation had been about politics; the problems created for Poor Bear by Mousseau's and White's mistakes in organizing the Sun Dance and rodeo had vastly improved the chances of the young reformers who were led by One Feather. After dinner, Amos and his daughter went to the Sun Dance, but One Feather made no appearance. The politics worked out neatly: Amos sat with the Sons of the Oglalas, smiling at the dancers as they passed, nodding and chatting with every influential man in the tribe, the reminder of reform; but One Feather stayed away, avoiding any involvement in the dispute.

Amos explained his late arrival: "I had to go home to feed my fish," but none of the other singers were concerned; Amos was generally late. And he had an excuse beyond that of most of the men. He was divorced, and had custody of his eight-year-old daughter, a shy, pretty girl, who spent much of her time with her face buried in her father's chest.

Next to Amos sat Calvin Jumping Bull, a thin, quiet man, who said he identified with the full bloods even though he was one fourth German. Calvin has a degree in education, but he cannot find work in the local schools as a teacher. The best job offered to him was that of part-time librarian at the Pine Ridge School. He spends most of his days there, gentle with the children, coaching them in the techniques of basketball when the trailer-classroom which houses the library is locked. He is disturbed by the paucity of books on Indian history in his library, but he is in no position to change the situation. He is a cautious member of the reform group, more given to smiles than anger.

Calvin is among the best of the singers and dancers. His costume is magnificent, but he is not entirely pleased with it: "The beaded harness is modern, but even so, there's only one woman on the reservation who makes them now, and she charges sixty-five dollars for a harness like mine. The whites who come to dance have the best costumes; they can afford to buy the quillwork and the breastplates." He points to a young white man who is dressed in long underwear, quillwork, a long breastplate of horizontal rows of matched bones, bells and feathers. "That's a really authentic costume from around the time of Crazy Horse. Even the eagle-bone whistle. If he blows that three times, it means he likes the song, and we keep singing."

Though he is quick to talk of his descent from Short Bull, one of the leaders of the Brulé band during the time of the Ghost Dance, Calvin is sometimes astonished at the holdovers from that period. In 1968, he was called upon to participate in a ceremony held over a captured Viet Cong flag. "We got four virgins," he said. "I had to find the girls. Then we put the flag on the floor and had a ceremony, and everybody counted coup on it." He shrugs away the astonishment which has returned at the thought of the ceremony. It is not his way to question such things. He will go no further in his questioning of people's actions than to join in the laughter of his fellow singers when a white woman, her hair braided and her skin darkened to look like an Indian, dances by. She is fifty years old, perhaps more, frenetic and clumsy. The Sons of the Oglalas have named her Cochise.

The elasticity of Calvin Jumping Bull is not shared by all of the Indians. He is mildly amused by the white dancers, commenting on their abilities as if they were Boy Scouts learning Americana under his tutelage. But the use of the eagle-bone whistle in particular upsets some of the other Indians. "He shouldn't do that," said a young Cheyenne. "You have to earn the right to blow that whistle. Somebody ought to kick his ass." The resentment over the white dancers made its way up to the announcer's stand, where Mousseau translated the mutterings into a speech.

"Some people are saying there are more whites than Indians dancing here tonight. And with all respect to our many white friends, I'd like to see if that's so. You know, our good white friends say, 'The only good Indian is a dead Indian'; and we say, 'A good white man has yet to be born.' But we're all good friends. Now in this next dance, if our white friends would just stay to one side, let's see how many Indians are dancing here tonight."

The whites stepped out of the center of the circle, conspicuous and slow moving. They comprised perhaps a third of the dancers. Most of them wore beautiful costumes and imitated the style of Indians so well that only an expert or an Indian would have realized that they were imposters. When the next dance began, the whites stood along the barbed wire fence, looking at the ground, Leatherstocking exposed, suddenly guilty for his attempt at savage nobility, the man of the machine expelled from Eden. The history of the frontier is momentarily recreated, the old idea of savagism hangs over the arena, the shame of men fleeing their own civilization is fleetingly exposed. But that is not enough; for the next dance Mousseau asks the Indians to step aside and allow the whites to dance. It is a victory for the Indians; the scrutiny acts as a hobble. Even the best of the white dancers were unable to find the excitement of the music. The Indians did not laugh, but smiled their indulgence. In the next dance no distinctions were made between whites and Indians; they danced together without apparent discomfort, the stress of the moment of revelation having passed.

The Cowboy had hitchhiked from his brother's house to the Sun-Dance grounds. He watched the rodeo in the afternoon, ate dinner with the Red Cloud family up on the hill, then watched the beginning of the dancing. His thoughts, however, were on the rodeo; the office closed at ten o'clock, and he had not yet paid his entry fee in the saddle-bronc riding contest. There had been that promise of a free entry from Richard Wilson in return for his work in setting up the portable chutes. But it was too vague for him to count on it. He needed twenty dollars or the assurance of twenty dollars being available before he went to the rodeo office. He found his white friends of the previous day, chatted with them, lifted the boy onto his shoulders to give him a better view of the dancing, then asked them for a ride into town. "I got to get to the office before they close the entries," he said. "I can use that prize money. You know I was rolled by this girl. She even took my wallet."

On the way into town they drove with the windows closed to keep out the dust that alternated with sloughs of mud where the water truck had stopped too long. The Cowboy kept his arm around the boy's shoulders, calling him "Little Cowboy," and telling of his own adventures in Pine Ridge. "I used to be a deputy sheriff here," he said, "but I got fired for letting too many people off. Now, there's a deputy here who's after me. You see, one night I was riding my horse in town, raisin' hell, when he drove up in his car and asked me did I have any liquor. 'Yep,' I said, and I took this half pint out of my boot and showed it to him. He said he would have to confiscate the liquor and arrest me, but I took off. I rode that horse everywhere with him chasin' me in the car. He was close to catchin' me when I took off across the crick. He couldn't follow me there, but he's had it in for me ever since." He laughed over his victory and the predicament it had caused for him. The boy laughed too, having found a hero in the Indian turned cowboy, the reversed Leather-stocking.

The rodeo office had been set up in a vacant store. There were two people behind a counter in one corner, and three Indians sitting on imitation leather and chrome chairs along one wall. A cigarette machine and a soft drink machine, one empty and the other out of order, completed the furnishings. The man and his son waited in the car while the Cowboy went inside to register for the bronc riding. He made con-versation with the people behind the counter for a moment, told one of the men sitting in the chairs that he was sorry to hear his wife was in the hospital, and then he asked if Richard Wilson had left word that he was to be given a free entry in the saddle-bronc riding. An inspection of the entry book and the shelves under the counter did not turn up a note from Wilson. They told the Cowboy they were sorry.

He rushed out to the car where the man and the boy waited. "Did we get here in time?" the boy asked. The Cowboy got in the car and slammed the door shut. "You got to help me," he said. "They didn't get the message about my free entry. I got to have twenty dollars right now." He was near to weeping.

The man said nothing. "Please," the Cowboy said. "I'll give the money back to you soon as I find Dick Wilson. I did the work, honest. They promised me. I won't have to win to get the money back. Honest, you can trust me. I'll give the money back."

The man still did not answer. "Please," the Cowboy asked again. "I'll give the money back to you. I said I would. Don't you believe me? Lord-a-mercy-Goddammit, it's only twenty dollars."

The boy began to cry. "Please give him the money," he said. "You believe the Cowboy, don't you?"

"Okay," the man said, wiping away his son's tears. He gave twenty dollars to the Cowboy who then leaped out of the car and ran into the office. The man told his son, "You shouldn't have done that. You shouldn't have said anything."

"Won't he pay back the money?"

"No, I don't think he will."

The Cowboy came out quickly and got into the car. "Here's a pass for tomorrow," he said, handing a piece of paper to the man. "It's worth two-fifty." He put his arm around the boy. "You come and watch me, huh? It'll be about three o'clock, maybe three-thirty tomorrow."

It was a hot, windy afternoon. The arena had not been watered down, and the dust kicked up by the horses did not dissipate between the rides. A hundred people waited in line at the vendor's wagon. The man and the boy were there to watch the Cowboy ride. The boy had found some Indian playmates in the morning, and he passed the time riding around the perimeter of the arena with them on an old Shetland pony. They rode the animal everywhere, even sitting on it through the long line to the vendor's wagon.

The first of the saddle broncs came out of the chute at three o'clock. It bucked twice, then settled down to a slow walk around the arena. The announcer said the cowboy would be given another mount. The second horse bucked off its rider as it came out of the chute. There was speculation among the onlookers over the effect of the attack of the buffalo the previous day. "Spooked," some said. Others talked about the erratic nature of bucking horses, and still others complained that the tribe had been cheated, paying far too much to rent such erratic animals.

The fourth rider was the Cowboy. His name was called three times. The fourth time there was an ultimatum. Then he was disqualified. "Probably drunk," someone said. "He can't ride anyway," said someone else. The boy turned to Olivia Jumping Bull, who was sitting behind him on the Shetland. "Do you know the Cowboy?" he asked. She nodded. "Let's go for another ride." she said. The boy turned the horse away from the fence, shook the reins, kicked it, cajoled it, and kicked it again before the old Shetland began to walk.

On the final morning of the Sun Dance a rope had been attached to the tree for each of the dancers. Fools Crow carried his steel suitcase out to the tree, and one by one the dancers lay down beside the tree and allowed him to insert a piece of wood into the skin of their chests. He rubbed an ointment on them before he inserted the skewer, then rubbed dirt over the torn skin after he attached the skewer to one of the ropes. The old men of the Red Cloud Singers drummed and sang during the piercing, and afterwards when the dancers moved back from the pole, stretching their skin with the ropes, leaning, dancing slowly backwards, blowing on the eagle-bone whistles, waiting for the skin to tear and loose them from the tree.

Fools Crow placed the skewers carefully, very shallowly, so there was not much bleeding. The first dancer broke free within two minutes after he had been pierced. Catches danced back from the tree, the last to be pierced, blowing fiercely on his whistle. He reached that point where the rope was taut, tested it once by leaning back, then spun away from the tree, wrenching the skewer out of his skin so that the rope made a popping sound. The crowd gasped at the act. The young medicine man had produced the one thrill of the Sun Dance, a moment of atavistic bravado, the reason for their coming. The popping of the rope as his flesh was torn was an affirmation; the victories of Red Cloud, the seven powers of Crazy Horse, the magic of the Uwipi, the existence of Wakan-tanka were all real, *they* were real. It was not yet the end of the world.

It was the penultimate act of the Sun Dance. The final act did not come for half a year. Shortly before the tribal elections, Robert Mousseau and Richard Wilson were indicted by a federal grand jury. Mousseau was indicted on four counts of "embezzling and converting funds belonging to the Sun Dance to his own use," and Mousseau and Wilson were both indicted for "unlawfully converting tribal funds to the use of another individual." The charges against Wilson were later dismissed, and Mousseau was convicted on only one count, but with two members of his opponent's council under indictment, the election of Gerald One Feather was assured.

11 WELCOME TO THE PROLETARIAT

On a reservation in New Mexico or Montana the land dominates; mountains are the boundaries of the imagination, worlds must be constructed inside horizons. In those places the season is written in the grass, and time is marked by the angle of the sun. Determinism is the calf crop and the rain. The most significant works of man are his dreams. It is more cruel than romantic now that the boundaries are so narrow and the dreams have been sabotaged by science, but it is clear, a life made of immutable rhythms. Once, in that lost eon of fecundity, it was enough.

Now the Indians are coming to the cities to live in the long, encrusted strings that are the slums of the West; to squabble with the blacks, Chicanos, Chinese, Filipinos and poor whites for the urban crumbs; to be lost, befouled with vermin and garbage, breathless, powerless and afraid; to meet savagery in the streets of the slums and the employment offices; and finally to die alone and unmourned, as if in dying they disappeared.

They are the least sophisticated of the poor. The city was their expectation; after it there are no more dreams. Their young are angry, but their anger is everywhere tempered by the memory of Injun Charley, the glorious killer. They tremble at the thought of rebellion; they are so few: twenty thousand in Los Angeles, twenty thousand in the San Francisco area, a few thousand in Denver, Chicago, Minneapolis, Seattle. And the BIA is watching them. What hope have they? The city is sand, they are atoms, drunk, comic, cheated, hungry, sharing, committed to history for the last rag of dignity with which to cover the darkness of their skin and the accent of their words. They walk the mazes of concrete and asphalt, jolted by the hardness of the surface, made weary, but they walk, recalling landmarks and directions, bemused by buses and subways; they walk because they do not have carfare or because they are afraid to lose face by having to ask directions. And everywhere they go they submit. The landlady, the foreman, the teacher, the welfare worker, the bartender, the cop, the BIA caseworker, the state caseworker and the city caseworker ask nothing more of them than submission. They have no future. They are limited to contemplation of the past.

"Sometimes I lay awake at night," said Mary McDaniel, "and I think of Crazy Horse and of the little stones that walk to the water." Her reveries are disturbed by a drunken man pounding on the thin wall of the rooming house or her concern about paying the rent—eighteen dollars—or the hunger pains that come after getting through a day on coffee made thick with sugar. The daughter of Silas Afraid of Enemy, twelve times a grandmother, lives in one room without cooking facilities. She is alternately coy and angry, full of winks and guffaws. Her face is dark and wide, almost square. She has a chipped tooth, and brown eyes long ago melted, hardened, and forever melted. Her figure is gone, she is no longer pretty, though she recalls the time when she walked along straight lines to make her legs and body straight, and she remembers the boy who was expelled from school for lifting up her dress—so shameful to lift up the dress of the daughter of a Presbyterian!

"They thought I was going to be a boy so I had to be born among my people at Pine Ridge. My father is Hunkpapa and my mother is Oglala. My father had three brothers who were killed at Wounded Knee; they were the grandsons of

Big Foot. My other great-grandfather was Chief Gall. You know that one time around the war, the Uwipi were going to bring Hitler over, but they needed a lot of money to do it, and Roosevelt wouldn't give the ten thousand.

"After I was born, we went back up to Cheyenne River. I'm enrolled there. My number is 3872. I don't know about that enrollment. The craziest thing happened: my children were all enrolled at Fort Yates, and they had a per capita payment. Then they told my children they were never registered. I have some land up there—I don't know how many acres. I get $17 a year for it. There's buffalo grass on it, but alkali water; the water is no good. When my grandmother died, they took her land to pay back her old-age assistance she had been paid. They held the lease checks for fourteen years to pay that back. The BIA does that. We're just a bunch of dumb animals to them.

"When I was a little girl at Cheyenne River, my grandmother used to part my hair in the middle and color the part yellow and put on a white plume so I wouldn't be struck by lightning. We used to have to go down to the creek every morning. My grandmother talked to the water. Before we washed, she would tell it how beautiful it was and thank it for cleansing her. She used to tell me to listen to the water, and then she would sing a song to it. You know the sound water makes? When she sang, it sounded just like the water.

"One day we were with my grandmother and there were coyotes whining. She went out and fed them because that's what Great Spirit said to do, to take care of the herd.

"You know I used to play in the fields and eat those little yellow flowers.

"We lived in a big log house. But we used a tipi in the summertime to be cool. When you feel sick, you hear the wind in the top of the tipi and it makes you well again. I used to help with the work, carry water, and cook. But when an Indian woman's part of the month comes around, she can't touch food, and she's supposed to stay out of the tent.

"We kept ourselves clean; I don't know why they call us dirty Indians. Once I was running away from my daughter's father, and I went through a herd of coyotes and a herd of wild horses, but they didn't bother me, because I had no body odor, nothing but natural. We used to use oil and an herb for scent, and mud to make our skin smooth.

"We had a lot of things like that. To learn what herbs to use, you followed a wounded animal to see what he eats. And when my grandmother pulled a medicine root out of the ground, she used to shove tobacco in the hole to pay back Great Spirit. But like salt, you never sell salt or even trade for it. We used to use a leaf, like marijuana, too, and smoke the animals with it to calm them, but only the medicine man could use it. The secrets died with them, because they knew the white man would brainwash us. We had birth control too; you could drink the tea of a tall weed and you wouldn't have children.

"In the thirties, we moved back to Pine Ridge. You should have seen the people when they first got their commodities; they threw all the flour away, they didn't know what to do with it. But we never went hungry. My mother's father, Joe Wounded Horse, was chief of police and a scout during the Indian Wars, and my father was an agriculturist. There was a picture of our log house in the BIA office, and a sign under it that said, 'The house that corn built.' My father worked all summer, and when he harvested, they all came and he gave away whatever he didn't need. He used to kill elk too, and pass it out to old-age people. He used to say, 'This is what you used to eat, and I know you're still hungry for it.' They voted him to be chairman of the Pine Ridge Council, but he was a Canadian Sioux, so he couldn't hold office. He was a Republican. He said anybody can be a Democrat, but to be a Republican you have to keep your feet on the ground and never cheat. I'm a Republican too.

"I went to boarding school. You were punished there if you talked Indian. After you got used to it, it wasn't bad.

"They called us full bloods 'blues' at the boarding school, because we were so dark. The mixed bloods were real light. They used to point at us in the shower, and the matron punished us more than she punished the mixed bloods. I was proud to be a full blood, but in my own mind. I didn't express it out loud, because it was no use.

"Our English teacher called us idiots. But I always studied my spelling. If I missed a word, I'd write that word a hundred times. Now I do crossword puzzles. That's why I buy the paper. I learned it from my father.

"They were like Nazis at the boarding school. A———— and B————, they whipped them so hard, they killed them. Miss C———— called Mr. D———— and they took A———— out of there, and next morning he was dead. They split his liver. Mr. E———— was the one who did it.* I think it was about 1930. Before that, he and F———— beat up my aunt Hazel, and afterward they had to put her to bed. After all that, they didn't touch an Indian child, because the Indians raised particular heck. They said, 'We just talk to them, why do you have to hit them?'

"One of the Indian girls became pregnant by one of the teachers and had to get married, and down at the church there was a girl who was raped by a priest, and she's crippled to this day. There was one time too when four Indian girls were stolen from the school and taken to Kansas to be in a

---

* While the author does not doubt the veracity of Mrs. McDaniel's recounting of the murder, the names must be deleted for legal reasons. The information is corroborated by another former student at the BIA school, but both Mrs. McDaniel and the other former student claim that the case was "hushed up" by the BIA, which would account for the lack of information in newspapers of the time.

house of prostitution, but they just cried all the time, so a man heard them and called the police, and they got sent back, except for one; we never saw her again.

"I finished the eleventh grade before I ran off and got married. My father wouldn't give me twenty dollars, so the next Friday night I eloped, and got married on their wedding day. I married Daniel McMasters—he was part Mexican. I didn't want to marry an Indian man, because they don't carry their paycheck home; they quit their jobs. Also, I promised myself to marry a white man so my children wouldn't be as dark as me. I almost married a Mormon, but I couldn't stand it; I'm too jealous to have 'sisters.'

"A Sioux woman don't care nothing for her husband anyway. But my children are my flesh and blood. I live for my children. The whites say the father is the keeper of the kids and the mother is just a bag. But we don't think that way. A Sioux man always walks ahead of his woman; in case there's danger ahead, he'll be the first one to meet it. Even so, we always put a baby facing out so he'll get to know the world. He better, because his mother won't live forever.

"I wasn't in love with Daniel McMasters. My mother told me, 'When you're in love, it's always like you're at a lake with nice cool water and green trees.' It wasn't like that with Daniel McMasters. I regretted it from the day it started. It must have been infatuation, because it sure wore off fast. But I stuck it out for four years until my father died, because my father didn't believe in divorce. I had two children.

"After I got divorced, I moved to Custer, and never went back to the reservation no more. At Custer I worked in civil service in the factory there, cuttin' mica for the airplanes. I met my second husband there. He was working at the planing factory, finishing lumber. He was French and Russian.

"We moved to Oakland in '54, and he started drinking. We used to sing and play guitar in the bars. My husband played rhythm and I played the chords, and we sang Western. We made money, enough to keep up our bills. When my husband's mother died, he took her to Miles (funeral home). They were too expensive, twelve hundred dollars. He should have gone where the Indians go; it's only six hundred dollars. Because he went to Miles, I had to go to the BIA and get a loan. We got divorced in '58. He beat me up and broke my jaw so I couldn't eat, and I had tuberculosis. The judge put my children in a foster home until I got well.

"I got married again in 1960. He passed away in 1965. I had three husbands; when I get to heaven, I won't be lonely.

"I got a wedding ring on my finger now from a man who wanted to marry me. I kept house for him, so I could take care of my kids, but he was too old-fashioned, so I didn't marry him.

"I don't owe nobody now, but I have my rent, eighteen dollars a week. I'm so worried, I don't know what to do. When you're here, you're like in a rat race, wondering what's going to happen. There on the reservation people are happy to see you. Here the people are happy to see you too, but you wonder what they want. Our word for the white man is *was'ichu,* the one who takes everything, the greedy one.* I don't know what to do about my rent; that place is no good anyway. I have some beadwork out, but they haven't paid me. I sew for people too. It takes about a day and a half to make a headband. I make medallions too, with the peace sign, or your initials. I made a lot of those medallions with matching earrings. The medallions sold, but the earrings didn't do too well. It takes a long time to do that work. First, you got to pick your beads, and right now, beads are hard to get. I think it must be the Russians in Czechoslovakia; they make the best beads there. You get the clay beads and get them wet, they melt. The glass beads, the water washes the

* Literally: Takes-the-fat, a combination of was'i (fat) and ichu (takes).

color right off. Now I have mostly black and white beads and a little drawer of red and yellow, but I need blue."

She smokes long cigarettes and often fingers a thick piece of root, which she says is a tranquilizer. When she thinks of her age, she slips away into remembering the weight of her history book and the night she dressed as a ghost to frighten the other girls in the dormitory of the boarding school. The thickening of age has blurred her face, and her hair is washed into old straw. Her vigor is belied by the occasional ruminating motion of her jaw. It has been a long time since Sioux Eagle Robe, the great-granddaughter of Chief Gall of the Hunkpapa band of the Teton Lakota, ate flowers and sang to the waters.

But she will not be without a man. There is one waiting for her at the top of the twisted stairs of a two-story tenement. He is standing behind the often enameled door, waiting with her daughter and son-in-law. His face is freshly shaved at noon. He is Mary's man, this dapper, pallid gentleman from Iceland, who drinks to pass the time until a certain large sum of money arrives from Reykjavik. And while he waits, he would like to sell a beautiful pair of beaded moccasins that Mary has made. If he could just find them. Mary has a habit of putting things away. She must have been packing. They were getting ready to move to a better place, all packed up, just waiting for his money to arrive from the sale of his estate in Iceland.

Mary survives on female energies and memories, recreating around her that time when women were the keepers of the race. She is before the infant mortality rate was controlled with drugs and incubators. Hers has always been the first work; she will not let the image of it be stolen from her by science. The worst moment of her life came when they took her children from her, eliminating her purpose. And even though it passes, and she says, "My grandchildren nearly give me a nervous breakdown; I just don't understand them," she was formed in the ancient role of woman, and the form withstands Oakland and Iceland. The defeat will be on her children.

The sinew of the old forms was not given to Lois Taylor. She is Hoopa, Yakima and Sioux, born on the Hoopa reservation, but raised in the city. Her husband, Dennis, is a Navaho from Chinle. They lived for a long time in a condemned house on the edge of Oakland's vast black ghetto. It was, perhaps, the worst house in California, but the rent was only seventy-five dollars a month. They put off moving, hoping for another place at the same rent, mostly doing nothing, waiting, asking another month and another month with the plaster falling and the ventpipe of the gas heater disconnected.

For Mrs. Taylor the world was never whole. "The white man made me an Indian," she said. "I never felt like an Indian until I came to Oakland. Then when I came of age, everywhere I went for a job I was sent to Intertribal Friendship House. Once I went to the employment office, and they called up a man, and said, 'I got a girl here. She's Indian. She speaks good English for an Indian, and she's pretty clean.'" She speaks in rapid spurts. Though she is overweight, shapeless in a dress of black and white vertical stripes, seemingly lethargic, stroking the baby girl lying in her lap, the tension flings the words out of her, mixing thoughts and times, squeezing her.

She is not a pretty woman; her forehead bulges and her jaw is underslung, but she is made attractive by her generosity; her hospitality is so complete it has made her poor. "My husband makes nine thousand dollars a year—he's an aircraft mechanic at Alameda Naval Air Base. People ask what we do with our money. But when we find a family that has no money, we give them some. We're Indians. That's how we are."

They are barely able to survive on nine thousand dollars a

year. She puts newspapers in the cracks of the windows in winter. She worries over the health of her baby, and she knows that her husband's job may soon be over. "If they lay off people at Alameda, my husband's supervisor will get laid off, and he'll take my husband's job. But my husband can't kick a man out and take his job. That's how Dennis is. He's made a career at Alameda. He gets there an hour before his job starts. He's funny about time." She looks down at the baby in her lap, strokes it, then raises her head with a jerk. "I hate Nixon. My husband works for the government, but I fight the government. I'm writing a book. Its main characters are going to be Robert Kennedy and Belva Cottier and Stella Leech and other people who are helping. I want to be a social worker like Belva. I went to a trial in San Jose. An Indian kid from Alaska had a public defender. I heard his own lawyer make fun of him. But I wrote it down, every word that was said, the way they treated that boy.

"We don't know what to do, the Indian people. When I go to Kaiser Hospital, they say what religion am I, and I say American Indian, and they say American Indians never had no religion. My daughter, she's eight, sees this junk on television, and she's afraid to go to the reservation because she thinks those Indians are wild. Then her teacher asks her why she doesn't go out on Alcatraz and live with the other Indians. I went to PTA, but they just sit and stare at you, so I don't participate in Jefferson School any more. I send my money, but I don't go.

"We have trouble all the time with the teacher, all because we're Indians. We taught my daughter to love flowers and nature. And one day she picked a flower to bring to her teacher. She brought it to school and she was three minutes late. The teacher took the flower and crushed it in her hand.

"I'm afraid when my daughter goes to school because of the colored kids. I try to take her or send her in a cab. She's been beat up in the park by colored kids. And the teen-age girls who babysit for me say they get beat up by colored gangs in school and they beg their mothers to go back to the reservation. I don't know what to do. Sometimes I get so uptight about things I can't express myself. A social worker told me to go to a psychiatrist. A lady now is telling me to take a pill when I get worried about my children.

"My baby's had pneumonia three times. I took her to Kaiser and they said she had an earache and she would outgrow it. Then she got a high fever in the night and we took her there in a cab and they put her in. They gave her shots, and I can't stand to see my baby get needles. Our people don't believe in sticking needles into themselves. It made me so sad. I didn't ever want to go and visit her. Then I saw this one nurse and I knew she was an Indian, one of my people. Take care of my baby, I asked her. Keep an eye on her. And she understood."

She sits facing two television sets, a bulky floor model that is dark, and on top of it a small receiver that flickers and drones while she talks. She paid $500 for the floor model, even though it was secondhand. The salesman told her that after three months, if she made the payments regularly, she could turn it in for a new color set. When the three months had passed, she called the salesman to order her new color set, but the store had gone out of business. Soon afterward, the large set stopped working. A repairman said it wasn't worth fixing. The loan contract had been sold to a collection agency, which demanded the money but refused to honor the rest of the contract. When she refused to pay the loan, they threatened to call her husband's employer. She sends the money every month, while the defunct machine sits before her, the largest and most impressive piece of furniture in her house.

Like many Indians, she is preoccupied with death. It is in her conversation, but it is more in her eyes. She is staring at Injun Charley, who is riding toward her, the universal exe-

cutioner, impervious to the eyes that follow him. She has
become resigned to fear, waiting, bovine, responding to the
smell of death ahead. "My husband's mother died of starvation," she said. "They found him nursing on his mother after
she had been dead for five days. His father had gone out for
food. It's proof a woman can give milk after she's dead. And
here in Oakland a Navaho baby died of malnutrition on
Thanksgiving Day. The nurse at Kaiser told me. She said
'They deserve it.' She was a Navaho herself, but she was an
educated one, she's made it."

There is a crib in the room and one chair. The overhead
light is bare, as are the kitchen light and the bedroom light.
There is no use in fixing them; the building is condemned. It
has been condemned for a long time, and now the city
demands that the Taylors move out. The city said nothing
when they lived there for three years without heat, nor did
the city care that the ceiling was falling in. Nor does anyone
care that her husband is an artist and she is a writer. No one
has read her work, and the only one who cared for her
husband's painting was the man whose picture decorates
several of the walls of her house, Bobby Kennedy. "I met
him," she said, "and I gave him the painting my husband
made of him. It's in the Kennedy Museum now. Bobby
Kennedy is the only man I ever met for two minutes who
made me cry. He united us. He was a prophet. We all knew
that. There was one blind old woman who heard he was
coming, and she said she just wanted to touch him. They
carried her to the hall and helped her up all those stairs, and
then she just touched him, that was all she wanted. Now,
he's dead." Always the dead: murders, suicides, car wrecks,
disease, starvation. "A lot of Indians turn up dead in this
town. The BIA doesn't tell you anything about them. It's not
in the papers."

Lois Taylor and her husband tried to get out once, to buy
a house of their own. She went to the Bureau of Indian

Affairs to ask for a loan. The application asked the most personal questions: How much did she spend on cosmetics? What was her food budget? How much did she spend on drugs, entertainment, clothing, carfare? She filled it out and sent it back to them; a house was worth it. Her loan application was turned down because her husband made too much money for the low-income houses and too little to buy a house without that subsidy from the state.

There is trouble in her marriage. Belva Cottier, a field worker for the Oakland American Indian Association, has spent long nights with Lois and Dennis Taylor, hoping to solve the world for them, explaining to Lois that she must forget her worries when her husband comes home, that he wants a good meal and smiles. "That's the way an Indian woman treats her man," says Mrs. Cottier. And Lois Taylor answers, "I had a Hoopa hat and a Sioux belt and a Yakima basket that were given to my husband when we got married. They represent the tribes that are in me. One time, when we needed money, I pawned them for thirty-five dollars. And now I can't get them back; the man won't sell them to me. I have to have them back. My luck won't be any good until they're in my house again."

When at last the Taylors were evicted from their house, they had still found no place to go. Mrs. Taylor called Belva Cottier. She got the expected response. A few days later, the Taylors and their three children moved in with Mrs. Cottier. In her house they could live with laughter, barking dogs, and a grassy suburban yard. They would not be the first family to move in with Belva Cottier, for she is, judged by the rules, the world's worst social worker. Perhaps it is because she is an Indian, or perhaps her lack of objectivity is due to her lack of formal training; whatever the cause, Mrs. Cottier more often finds herself a source of aid than an intermediary between her client and the institutional source.

Belva is a short, strong woman who paints eyebrows of

surprise halfway up her forehead and marks the rest of her face with makeup that in its lack of subtlety would be sufficient for a ballerina playing to the largest hall. Her face snaps from deep laughter to concern, the shadings of emotion lost in the makeup. She is always in a hurry, though she walks slowly. She is dieting, but she will, if invited, eat a dinner of steak and potatoes immediately after her dieter's feast of cottage cheese and dark crackers.

Her position with the Oakland American Indian Association is ill-defined. She is a field worker, supposedly limited to ferrying confused or destitute Indians from one part of the city to another. And she is paid accordingly, four hundred dollars a month and her car expenses. But she cannot avoid responding to desperation, and desperation confronts her daily: "This Indian boy came up to the office and asked if we could help him to get a meal. We gave him money for that, then I asked him where he was living. 'On Broadway,' he said. I knew what he meant. He was just walking up and down Broadway. He didn't have any place to stay. We got him into one of those places run by the churches; but they're no good, because they just let them stay there for a day or two. Those boys need a place to stay until they can get a job and get enough money together to get a place of their own."

The money she gave him was her own. The petty cash box at the Indian Association was, as usual, empty. There is nowhere else for them to go; Belva understands that. The crumpled dollars she takes out of her change purse are dollars she needs too, but she faces the question of priority and finds herself second. The rating system may have come out of her own past. She was born on the Rosebud Sioux Reservation, the child of an Indian mother and a white father who was killed in France in World War I.

"I left Rosebud when I was seven," she said, "and became what you call a reservation bum. My mother and I just went wherever she could get work. She used to cook at the Indian

Boarding School at Cheyenne Agency. Then she went to Fort Washakie, Wyoming. Then she sent me to boarding school at Pierre, South Dakota. There, they made me a test student and sent me to public school. I started out with D's and F's, and by the end of the year, I was getting A's. There was one teacher, Miss Sorenson, who used to come to the house and help me study.

"I got here in 1943. I married after I graduated, and he went into the Navy. So I just came out here with my two children and my mother to babysit for me. When I came here, I didn't know where to take my children for medical care. I was afraid to talk to people. I'd go into a restaurant and wonder if I would be served—it's that hesitant attitude you get on the reservation. But the only real problem I ran into was in the church. In the Episcopal Church in Alameda they made us sit in the back, and they made my children sit at the end of the table in Sunday School. To this day my kids don't care about going to church.

"After a while, I bought a house, because I didn't want my kids to be kicked from place to place like I was. And after the war, when relocation started, is when I got into Indian work. The people from Pine Ridge used to come out to my house for help. There were so many of them that we got worried, and we started an American Indian Council. Those people were so lost; they didn't know how to take the bus; they'd walk from 98th street all the way in to the BIA office in Alameda. They're still doing it. But the biggest problem is that at home you know what's expected of you, and here you don't."

Belva and her husband were married for twenty-eight years before they separated. "He started to drink," she said. "The pressures on a man, the pressures inside cause that. Now he lives with another woman; she's an alcoholic too." For a while after her husband left, Belva was depressed. Two of her daughters were married, but there was still one girl to care for. She had no income besides the rent she collected from the families living in the duplex at the back of her property. And she is a poor landlord. When one tenant brought a second family into their apartment, she thought she should increase the rent, but she just can't get around to doing it. She moved from a voluntary position to paid work with the Indian Association, and found another man: "A Frenchman," she says, smiling as wickedly as she can. Sometimes she describes him as an Englishman, and at other times she talks of going to dances with her daughter at a place where her son-in-law plays in the band. "I come home with my daughter too," she says, "not that I couldn't go out every night."

The enemy in Belva Cottier's world is the BIA office in Alameda, California. Many, if not most, of the people who come to her for help have been brought to the city on a BIA Relocation Program and then dropped. At the end of inadequate vocational training courses they are unable to find work. They go back to the BIA for help, but they can receive no help once the course is completed. If they are brought to the city for "direct employment" and the job evaporates after six months or a year, the BIA can give them no help. On the reservations they are urged to move to the city, and when they arrive in the city, they realize that they should have stayed on the reservation. They move from log house to slum, bounced between the economic ciphers of America, hopeless on the reservation, lost in the city, unhealthy, unhappy, the inheritors of a world that was ground to dust before they were born.

It is not that they are incapable of survival, but that the path to survival has not been defined; those who succeed do so more by chance than plan. And it is not as if no one wanted to help them. There are lovers everywhere; those who have destroyed one world beckon them into another, but the lovers fail, even when they are sincere.

The Bureau of Indian Affairs office in Alameda has been investigated several times by BIA officials out of Washington. Committees have questioned Donald Spaugy, the director of the office.* Indians have signed petitions and sent letters to their Congressmen, but nothing has come of that. There can be no close supervision of the office because the relocation program is run from Washington rather than by the area director. The Indians are at the mercy of Donald Spaugy, a veteran of twelve years of service in the BIA, a man without experience on a reservation, a man who can produce a paper full of generalizations about the Navahos by Rosalie Wax and Robert Thomas and use it as a guide in dealing with all Indians. "All Indians bow their heads and avert their eyes when meeting strangers," says Mr. Spaugy, paraphrasing the paper. "They give very weak handshakes for the same reason. And in situations of stress, they withdraw." The comedy of the generalization was revealed when a group of young Indians staged a sit-in in Mr. Spaugy's office. They filled every seat and stood against the walls, watching him, calling out questions to a girl who interviewed him and recorded his comments. It was Mr. Spaugy who wanted to withdraw at that moment; his eyes were downcast and he contorted his mouth as he spoke.

The image of an Indian drawn by Mr. Spaugy is one made by the BIA. It is man after conquest that he describes, the powerless, hungry man standing alone before his desk, tired after a long bus ride from the reservation, utterly dependent upon Mr. Spaugy and the Bureau of Indian Affairs. The man is so insensitive that he does not even realize he is a king.

On the reservation there are havens where the Indian may shed the managed life, if only temporarily; the extended family is secure and warm, and the open range is free. In the city, the new arrival is alone but for the BIA. If he is to

* Mr. Spaugy has recently resigned from his post.

survive, he will learn to run the maze of the BIA while he learns the maze of the city. It will all begin with an orientation meeting in a stuffy upstairs room in the converted Army building that houses the Alameda office of the BIA. The orientation is a chore for the BIA counselors, who take turns at it, doing their duty in five-day spurts. The families that come in are called "units," which is the beginning of a dizzying language of jargon and acronyms that the Indian has to learn.

The number of people attending an orientation meeting varies from two or three up to twenty or more. Families generally arrive in the middle of the week and single people on the first and last days, but there is no rule. On a Wednesday morning, five people came to the "orientation" given by Mrs. Donna Gudgell. There was a Paiute woman from the colony at Bishop, California, a man from Turtle Mountain, the Chippewa-Cree reservation near the Canadian border in North Dakota, two Aleuts and an Eskimo, all three of them very young, seventeen or eighteen years old at most.

Mrs. Gudgell, a thin woman, gawky now that the time of being coltish has passed for her, was nervous. A strip of white petticoat hung below the hem of her yellow dress. She moved the training aids into place with resignation, pushing and lifting them as if the weight of routine was more than she could bear. "I'm Mrs. Gudgell," she said; "I'll be your community living counselor. You'll meet your vocational training counselor later." She picked up a packet of brown folders, adjusted her blue plastic and rhinestone glasses, and began to call their names: "Mary, you're from Bishop, and you're here on AVT. And you have a family. Duane, you're from Turtle Mountain and you're here on AVT. And you have a family . . ."

It is the beginning; the father of three children finds himself without a surname. He will learn that when he wants to buy a raincoat, he will have to ask his "community living counselor" for a voucher for seventeen dollars. It will come from his "OC money," an allowance besides his regular living allowance that is to be used for clothing and other exceptional items. It is a small amount, but he is not trusted with it. He must ask for each item as his children must ask him for penny candy. During the orientation, he remained silent, answering only when asked a direct question, thinking perhaps of his father: "My dad, when he went to school, he couldn't talk but one word in English. All he could say was 'yes.' So, the first time they caught him talking Chippewa, they paddled him. Then they said, 'Are you ever going to do that again?' And he said, 'Yes.' So they paddled him again. They kept asking him and he kept on saying 'Yes,' because it was the only word he knew."

Mrs. Gudgell's voice goes on. The modulations are artificial, rote. She speaks with used words. The room is darkened to show the crudely made slides that function as training aids. Cigarette smoke floats in the beam of light. The ashtrays are old and encrusted. Too many people have sat on the couches, leaned their heads back against the wall in the escape of sleep. The room is worn out; so many dreams have fallen there.

"Singles receive $105 every two weeks," she says, pointing to a chart. "We recommend a board-and-room situation. A family of four receives $173.50 every two weeks. They will, of course, do better in an apartment.

"*We* frown on credit buying here."

"*We're* giving you money to live on."

"Of course, *I'll* be giving you money."

She is the Bureau of Indian Affairs incarnate. She warns them, threatens them, advises them, complains about the high cost of living. Even *she* suffers because of it; what will happen to them?

The training aids go by quickly: AVT, DE, OC, BIA, BART, Home Purchase Plan, medical coverage up to $4 for office calls or half the cost of house calls but not over $6. For eyeglasses and eye examination, $35. "But don't lose your glasses, because we'll only pay for them once." Most prescriptions are paid in full; physical examinations are paid in full. "It's an excellent plan. I wish there was one like it for us." The plan ends thirty days after Adult Vocational Training is completed and also thirty days after the six-month trial on Direct Employment is completed.

She warns them about drugs and alcohol. "Some of our Indian people . . ." And refers them to Planned Parenthood: "It's not only for families, but for single men and single girls, as well."

At the end of the orientation to the BIA, there is an orientation to the city. Mrs. Gudgell shows slides of zoos and parks, aerial photographs of downtown areas and suburbs. She talks of the costs of restaurants and movie tickets, advising them to look for the free entertainments. Perhaps the man from Turtle Mountain is wondering whether he should have left home: "It was too expensive at Turtle Mountain. We paid $33 a month for electricity and $38 a month for fuel oil. It was forty degrees below zero when I left, and it's dark up there a lot. That's why it costs so much for oil and electricity. And I was only making $321 a month, working as a caretaker for the government. My car is getting paid for, though, $90 a month. This bad hip I got in the Navy; it gives me $90 a month in disability. You see, the car is taken care of. That's how I came in from the motel. I know this town. You just run right down 98th to the Tube, then you follow the road out of the Tube, make a right on Central and you're here. I'll use the car to go to school, and after I get out too. Unless the company gives me a car. I'm going to business machine repair school. I hope I like it. I saw it in the book up home at the BIA office, and it sounded good."

In the orientation room he is silent, his face a mask. Outside, he is animated by the excitement of being in the city, full of laughter and stories, anxious for this confluence of life and dream to continue. It is the room and the woman who presents herself as the incarnation of a bureaucracy that frighten him; a man can be whipped for saying yes. Questions cause laughter. Degradation is in the air, like something tangible that will strike him in his soul. "Keep your mouth shut and do what you're told."

The boys from Alaska had flown to Seattle, then taken a bus to Oakland. After twenty-two hours on the bus, they had changed their clothes and come to the orientation. They slept through it. All three of them sat together on a plastic couch, nodding, then jerking their heads into wakefulness before nodding again. Their clothes, the garish finery of the poor, were still new, the bright colors not yet faded, the shoulder pads still stiff.

At the end of the orientation period, each of them is given a small envelope containing a map of the city, a mimeographed sheet reiterating everything they had heard during the orientation period, and a large folder warning them in great detail of the symptoms and dangers of venereal disease.

The cold, stringy woman, so clearly the ruler rather than the servant of the Indians, so separate from them as to be objective in her relations with them, is herself an Indian, born on the Fort Peck Assiniboin Sioux Reservation in northeastern Montana. She has worked a long time for the BIA, long enough to learn to speak to her own people as if she had just arrested them.

From the office in Alameda the young Indians will be sent to boarding houses and technical schools. The auto repair school to which they are usually sent appears to have been set up to deal with cars made before 1940. The tools and techniques are old, and the electronic equipment now used in the diagnosis of automobile engines, transmissions and brakes is conspicuously absent. The BIA sends most of its

211 WELCOME TO THE PROLETARIAT

students to this old-fashioned, ill-equipped, grim school, while a modern school, completely equipped, including an expensive diagnostic lane, has thirty-five vacancies. Many of the Indians claim that someone at the BIA office has some interest in the old-fashioned school. But the problem may be deeper than simple corruption; the modern school is owned and operated by John Folster, a Sioux Indian.

In one of the boarding houses recommended for young men, it costs $110 a month to share a barren room with a stranger and eat the unidentifiable institutional food. The woman who runs the boarding house calls herself "Mama." She would be comic if she were not real. Her gray hair is tied in a net. In the afternoon, she is dressed in a faded housecoat, carpet slippers and faded blue anklets. Her shins, marked with veins and sprouting hair, gleam defiance at all that is gentle or elegant in the world.

There is a fecal smell in the rooms, the residue of old bacteria. The beds are covered with electric blankets, purchased after their function had failed. It is a house where joy is unknown, prohibited by the shins of the owner and the brown enamel walls. No one laughs. The pace is slow, gray, like the screen of the television set that grinds through the afternoons, the evenings, seeping into the cracked plaster of the walls, sending other worlds over the chrome and plastic tables, the cracked coffee cups, the catsup and hot sauce bottles, soothing the tattooed wrecks who survive on welfare checks in this place where expectations founder.

A single pay telephone and a buzzer system connect the occupants with the outside world. Beside the telephone is a chalkboard where messages are left. Permanently affixed to the board are the Twelve Steps of Alcoholics Anonymous. The proprietress opposes drinking, speaking in her Bible Belt accent, demanding to know what is wrong with her place, while she stands on the dead carpeting, surrounded by flabby mattresses leaning against the walls. She is not embarrassed by the nakedness of the light. She has long ago lost her sensitivity to the odor of decay. Let the serene eyes of those brown-skinned boys learn to dart, she is saying; let them get the smell of grass and fresh wind out of their heads; this is the city of opportunity, the house of success where every boy knows his "Mama" loves him.

Indian community organizations are attempting to solve the urban problems, perhaps to win the relocation function away from the BIA and themselves contract the work with the Department of the Interior. In Rapid City, South Dakota, Muriel Waukazoo finds that only 12 per cent of the population is Indian, but that 67.3 per cent of all arrests in that city are of Indians. She asked for an OEO Legal Services Program, but the local Bar Association voted against it. It does not stop her. She will find the money somewhere, and when there are cases of police brutality or discrimination, she fights without money or the backing of the Bar Association.

In Oakland, Phyllis Waukazoo, her twenty-five-year-old daughter, has also become involved in Indian problems. She came to the city trembling, needing her mother to come and live with her, but the trembling has passed. Like her mother, she is big and quick to laugh, but the laughter deceives; her anger is deeper than her mother's. Where Muriel Waukazoo is sometimes politic, her daughter is almost always intemperate; calumny and rage are her tools.

She can be girlish, giggling, clutching a pink, imitation leather wallet in her hand, then suddenly attack a former tribal chairman for having cheated the people out of a factory. Of Vine Deloria, Jr., author of *Custer Died for Your Sins,* and former director of the National Congress of American Indians, she says, "His father was a preacher. He was a little boy in short pants who had everything handed to him. What does he know about Indian problems?" When Deloria, Jr. visited in the area and had an argument with the Rev. Al Elgin, who runs the Intertribal Friendship House, Phyllis and the other local Indians were furious. "He says he's going to sue Al as soon as he gets his law degree. Just let him try."

Of a self-proclaimed local Indian leader, she says, "He's light, so he passed for a long time. He said he was Portuguese until a few years ago." She finds the mixture of Marx and spirituality of the students who first occupied Alcatraz worth no more than derisive laughter. Under the toughness and the nascent feelings of power, she is but a girl, concerned with finding a man and making a life. There is a very soft smile on her mouth when she says, "A lot of Indians who were married to whites are leaving them and going back to Indians. I guess they want more full bloods."

It is only when she talks about alcoholism that her face loses its animation. "Indians drink because of the BIA," she says. "It tells you what to do, where to live. The Bureau does everything. The people can't do anything for themselves, so they get depressed and they drink. On the Rosebud, they bootleg wine and liquor. A little bottle of liquor, a pint, costs five or six dollars. That's a lot, isn't it?" She knows the problems of alcoholism well; they have plagued her father for most of his life.

In the cities, as on the reservations, the hopeless and self-hating find solace in alcohol, drinking in darkened rooms, barren places where everything is the color of mahogany, pouring down glass after glass, until the world becomes whole again in stuporous dreams, or rage is loosed and produces a knife in someone's hand. Loving and loathing his antecedents, failing the demands of two worlds, the Indian is trapped in his becoming, for the city offers no more hope than the reservation; it only compounds his suffering with loneliness and the fearful weakness of numerical inferiority. The city is the melting pot, the obliteration of cultural diversity. On choosing to come to the city, the Indian acknowledges that he no longer wants to be an Indian. In the relocation office on the reservation, it is an abstraction: identity will be traded for affluence, a Faustian bargain, but an attractive one to a hungry man. The reality is devastating; the urban Indian soon realizes that he has sold his soul for a slum. For every Mohawk who looks proudly over New York City from his perch atop the steel frame of a skyscraper, there are a hundred Navahos, Sioux, Cherokees, Paiutes, Menominees and Lummis who look into dark and broken mirrors and do not recognize the remorseful face that looks back at them.

12 A SCHOOL FOR MEDICINE MEN

THE BEST WAY to get to Rough Rock Demonstration School is by air, and then it is good to have someone to chase the horses off the dirt landing strip. The land there is like the bones of the Earth, and it is beautiful. Only a farmer could fail to understand the beauty of such land.

It is at Rough Rock that the Indians have, in a sense, chosen to make a last stand. The BIA has given a school and the usual funds for such a school over to an Indian school board. The Office of Economic Opportunity has given more than a million dollars over three years to help operate the school's experimental programs in bi-cultural education, community development, and adult education and training. And the Indians of the area have given their time and labor and enthusiasm.

At Rough Rock, where 87 per cent of the employees are Navaho, English is introduced as a second language, the first kindergarten on an Indian reservation has been established, the concept of nongraded classes has been applied with apparent success, and the community has for the first time in American Indian history taken control of a formal educational facility.

The dormitory parents at Rough Rock are Navahos from the school district. In the winter, storytellers come to the dormitories in the evenings to teach the traditional literature of the tribe. Textbooks containing Navaho legends and history are published by the Dine Corporation, which operates the school. Navaho arts and crafts are taught to adults as well as children. Some small-scale manufacturing has been begun through the school. It is an important experiment in education, though some criticisms have been offered by ortho-dox educators, and it is also an important experiment in community. But Rough Rock has deeper meanings for Indians.

The seven members of the Rough Rock School Board have among them only six years of formal education, yet they, and not the administrators of the school, have made it the core of the community. The school is theirs; power has been returned to the people of the community. The people are Indians; the school functions. And it is obvious that the school functions better than most. It is a sign that Indians are ready to begin displacing the BIA, and the BIA doesn't like it. Indian control of schools through community corpo-rations means the end of civil service in the schools, an erosion of the bureaucracy from the bottom up.

There is even further portent for the BIA in Rough Rock: if Indians can run a school, they can undoubtedly negotiate their own leases and grade their own roads and control their own welfare and agricultural programs. The example of Rough Rock could lead to the decentralization of control of Indian life, preparing Indians for freedom from BIA man-agement.

In the concept of bi-cultural education is another hope for the Indian. His language, his religion and his traditions now disappear abruptly, leaving him in a limbo between two cultures. The last basketmaker of the Tules is dead, four-fifths of the Indian languages are dead and the rest are dying, almost all Indians are baptized into one church or another, and some of them are beginning to accept the thinking of those churches. Rough Rock is a way to extend the life of Indian society and culture, and a practical method for shaping an Indian personality that may be able to with-stand the pressures of transition to membership in the general society, for the children at Rough Rock are not the children of wards of the Federal Government—their parents have the dignity of power.

At the BIA in Washington, the public relations man, who is not an Indian, asks reporters to compare Rough Rock to the BIA schools that have begun to experiment with bi-cultural curricula. He does not wish to talk about the significance of Rough Rock in the Indian's effort to mitigate his destiny. Perhaps he does not believe that Indians are ready for such responsibility. Perhaps he loves them too much to want to see them suffer the consequences of the mistakes they will make in the unfamiliar task of running their own lives. Perhaps he is a son of a bitch who wants to protect his job no matter what it costs the Indians. The motives of the BIA are of no consequence to the Indians, but the Bureau's obdurate refusal to allow Indians to determine the course of their own lives has been devastating.

Some Indians are lost, hopeless, but not all, not so many as the lovers would have us believe, not so many that only Christ or Joseph Smith can save the children from sin and destruction. People are preserved by their humanity; language and intelligence are not soft flesh, but sinew, resisting obliteration, giving resilience to the form. The people of Rough Rock are alive and upright. They laugh easily, their children can be uproarious, the disapproving eye of a white man does not cause them to tremble.

The school is not their strength; it is only a manifestation of strength, of possibility. It is the place where acculturation is seen as renewal instead of defeat. They will go slowly, carrying with them what they can, consuming their past as they go, surviving on it; the world will not be shattered, it will be transformed. So they hope, and the hope makes it so.

There are young men at Rough Rock who left school at the age of twelve to sit with the old medicine men and learn the art of the world of magic. They will study for eight years, learning the songs and rituals, perhaps to find that magic exists only in a world of magic. But it is no matter, for they will be singers and painters in sand; their art will be the justification for the school's decision to make their apprenticeship part of its curriculum.

It is a strange place, Rough Rock, the confluence of science and magic, the intersection in time when the old stories are written down for the first time. It is, at first glance, merely a progressive school—immaculate floors and smudges on the hands of the children. But underlying the laughter is the most aggressive plan for community control of education undertaken by Indians in this century. Its ally is the OEO, which provides a large part of the school's annual budget of nearly a million dollars. The enemy is the Bureau of Indian Affairs, which watches the erosion of its major area of power quietly, waiting for an error. Any justification will do: scandal, a graduating class that does poorly in high school, the failure of the school to get enough money to continue operating, a split in the community. The Bureau and the Indians cannot exist in equality; bureaucratic love does not permit it.

The power of the BIA and its opposition to local control of schools are apparent in the case of the Oyate Corporation (Oyate is the Sioux word for *people*). Oyate Corporation was modeled after the Dine (*people's*) Corporation that administers Rough Rock. It was formed by the members of the school board of the Lone Man School in the White Clay district of the Pine Ridge Indian Reservation. They call themselves "the rubber stamps" because they are appointed to the school board by the BIA and "under the Bureau anything thought up by the people ends up in the wastebasket."

After they formed the corporation, they submitted their program for a demonstration school to the BIA, and even went to Washington (an expensive trip for people who live in an area which is utterly without employment) to plead their case. "We talked to (former) Commissioner Bennett in June of 1968," said Amos Bad Heart Bull, a member of the school board and of the Oyate Corporation, "and he gave us his verbal agreement. He said he would put out a publicity release the following Monday, and we came back and told all the people. But we did not receive the news release he promised. We wrote to him about it, but he didn't answer. Meanwhile, BIA people started to spread the rumor that a demonstration school would lead to termination. The tribal leaders, who are very backward people, also spread the rumor."

Instead of sending out the news release, the BIA decided that a referendum should be held among the people of the district. The Oyate program was defeated. In an area as poor as White Clay, the thought of termination is terrifying. Moreover, the BIA was very much in control of the tribal council at Pine Ridge.

So the educational system at White Clay continues under the BIA. The first grade teacher at the Lone Man School does not speak Lakota, the language of the Oglala Sioux, though some of her students do not speak English. Less than 10 per cent of the children from the district finish high school. Commissioner Bennett did finally answer the Oyate Corporation, but only after they got a United States Congressman to prod him. In April, 1969, he sent them a letter about the referendum.

There is not much hope in the White Clay district, and though there has been some slight interest in retaining Indian culture recently, it receded with the failure of the Oyate Corporation. Zachary High Whiteman, a tall, willowy man, with a long face marked by two deep vertical lines, who remembers being beaten with a leaded piece of harness in a BIA school, said, "I am a descendant of the massacre at Wounded Knee. I'm the guy who's supposed to hate all white men. But we have to adapt ourselves. We want to live to adapt our way to the American way of life." He looked over at Calvin Jumping Bull, another member of the school board, who closed the discussion. "I think the Indian culture is all over in America," he said.

Perhaps Calvin Jumping Bull is right about Indian culture, but he is not right about the Indian people or even about the Oyate Corporation. One of Gerald One Feather's first moves after being elected chairman of the Oglala tribe was to send a delegation to the Rough Rock Demonstration School to get information on how to set up a community-controlled school at Lone Man. A Navaho-controlled high school is in operation. The BIA's flagship school at Rock Point is considering a contract operation, like Rough Rock. It is clear that a Navaho school system is beginning, emanating from Rough Rock, and that other Indian communities are realizing the possibility of locally-controlled education. The end of the BIA school is in sight. The silent classroom, the crushing of the emergent character will end. That will come quickly, and it will slow the end of magic but not prevent it.

Robert Roessel, who founded the Rough Rock Demonstration School and then turned it over to Dillon Platero, went on from there to found a Navaho Community College at Many Farms. The college is still in its infancy; the curriculum is narrow and the direction is unclear, but the college has already been much criticized for its lack of academic excellence. Many Indians feel that it is too much like a trade school, too closely attuned to immediate Navaho problems. The college is now an end to education for the Navaho, who may learn something there about agriculture or typing or business procedures, but cannot get the education necessary to move on toward graduate studies. Perhaps the college will change, or perhaps it is sufficient as an alternative to attending state or private universities. Robert Roessel founded the college, but the Navahos will decide what becomes of it.

Barney Old Coyote, a Crow, who was the coördinator of the Job Corps conservation camps and other Department of the Interior antipoverty programs under Stewart Udall, has another plan for Indian education which he hopes to see instituted at Montana State University. He advocates a "second chance" plan in which Indians are asked to perform on the same level as non-Indians to receive a degree, but are allowed seven years rather than four years to complete the requirements for graduation from Montana State. His program, which has been accepted by the administration of the University, involves the tribes in the institution, utilizing members of the tribes as counselors for Indian students and as instructors and lecturers in an Indian Education Program that he hopes to see integrated into the various departments of the University. As the tribes become a resource for the University, Old Coyote would like to see the University become a resource for the tribes, helping the tribal leaders with technical advice and assistance.

It is an ambitious plan, but Barney Old Coyote is not averse to adventure. He was the first Indian to cross the Atlantic Ocean in an airplane. He was decorated for "extraordinary heroism" during World War II, and he is one of the few Indians who has sat in on cabinet-level meetings with the President of the United States. But his most astonishing feat has been to maintain an unsullied reputation in the gossipy world of Indians while spending most of his adult life as an employee of the BIA.

Barney Old Coyote is the kind of man the Indians hope to produce out of Rough Rock and the Navaho Community College. He is an Indian, a full blood. His voice is slightly nasal, but very soft, sometimes barely audible. He is a man of enormous shoulders, walking the halls of Federal buildings with the rolling gait so common to Crow men. Although he does not think Indian culture will last "much past the next generation," his own life stands at the confluence of

THE DEATH OF THE GREAT SPIRIT

cultures. "I'm the only Grand Knight of the Knights of Columbus," he said, "who has ever run a peyote meeting." Those are his churches. He is an assistant area director of the BIA who speaks the Crow language fluently and wants one day to write down the legend of an Indian hero. He speaks with interest of aiding anthropological investigations of the Montana tribes, but he also tells of the anthropologists who identify as crude basketry a kind of snowshoe worn by the Indians to avoid making noise when sneaking up on an enemy.

The success of the man is in his ability to contain opposites. Plenty Coups, a chief of the Crows, said, "I must live up to my name." Perhaps Barney Old Coyote is only doing that:

> The trickster of American mythology has remained so far a problematic figure. Why is it that throughout North America his role is assigned practically everywhere to either coyote or raven?*
>
> . . . the trickster is a mediator. Since his mediating function occupies a position halfway between two polar terms, he must retain something of that duality . . .
>
> Claude Lévi-Strauss†

The coyote has always lived at the confluence of opposites in Indian mythology. Now the Indian seeks in his life to imitate his art. It is not impossible. Barney Old Coyote, Dillon Platero, Emory Sekaquaptewa, Jr. and others are doing it. Schools like Rough Rock will produce more men and women like them, "coyotes" who will become the ancestors of scientists.

It is a good dream, and some will be served by it. For

* Lévi-Strauss, C., *Structural Anthropology*. New York, Basic Books, 1963, p. 224.
† Ibid., p. 226.

others the conflict will be unbearable, duality will be schizo-phrenia; failing the delicate balance of the coyote, they will be destroyed. That is the risk of creating a man of two minds. The decision to take that risk was made by the lovers; the people of Rough Rock want only to save as many as they can.

13 DIALECTICAL SPIRITUALISM

THE SYSTEM OF TERRITORIES, described by Lorenz and others as quite different from the system of properties, depends upon the existence of surplus. The bird, dispossessed from one tree, moves to another; the number of trees is so much greater than the number of birds that it would be suicidal to do otherwise. It is an irony of conquest that during the process of turning territory into property, the conquerors of America should have had an anachronistic moment in which they told the Sioux that any surplus United States property could be claimed by them.

That portion of the treaty, like most treaties made with the Indians, was meaningless. There were tens of thousands of square miles of unclaimed land in America at the time of the signing of the treaty, and none of it was then thought of as surplus. The treaty, signed in 1868, was tested in 1964 when the Indians attempted to claim Alcatraz Island. The courts would not accept the treaty as cause to give the island to the Indian claimants. But the idea stayed with the Indians, and in 1969, on November 21, they invaded the island and claimed it as Indian land.

It is doubtful that the Indians really wanted to settle on Alcatraz when Richard Oakes first swam ashore. It is not a very hospitable place. There is no fresh water on the tiny island, the little bit of soil would wash away if it were plowed for planting anything other than grass or ground cover, it is generally cold and fogged in, and the remains of the abandoned Federal prison are in a depressing state of decay. The purpose of the invasion was rather to create a confrontation that would symbolize the plight of American Indians. Multiple arrests and trials of the Indian claimants were expected to create national concern and sympathy. A second invasion was planned at Ft. Lawton near Seattle, and Oakes had his eye on a piece of land in Northern California where he really did expect to start a colony of Indian activists.

The plans for confrontation with the Federal Government went awry the following Saturday. The invaders had not counted on the sympathy or the influence of William T. Davoren, coördinator for the Pacific Southwest Region of the Department of the Interior, nor did they expect that Barney Old Coyote would be consulted about the situation. As for Walter Hickel, who had recently been confirmed as Secretary of the Interior, it seemed certain that he would respond with a brutal law-and-order interpretation of the incident, much in the style of Attorney General John Mitchell, who had already revealed the Nixon administration's attitude toward dissent during the Moratorium demonstrations in Washington. The Indians were prepared to be beaten, jailed, perhaps even killed; a hypothetical synthesis of Hickel's attitude toward the Eskimos when he was Governor of Alaska and Mitchell's penchant for violence seemed to preclude other possibilities.

In early interviews with the press, the Indians were unable to attach much seriousness to their claim to the island. They said that the two white caretakers on the island would be wards of the Bureau of Caucasian Affairs, and claimed that though they would not resist arrest, the Federal marshals would be unable to find them because they were the invisible Americans. When asked about the problems of poor land, inaccessibility, lack of fresh water, electricity, and sanitation facilities, they replied that they were accustomed to these conditions since most Indian reservations suffered the same problems. It was a time of bravado. They were mostly college students in the first days of the occupation, middle-class, without the experience of direct repression; they suffered from dread only of hypothetical violence.

Their expectations were not entirely without reason. The acting United States attorney and the United States marshal wanted to take immediate action to remove the trespassers from the island. Thomas Hannon of the General Services Administration, which was responsible for the island, a man who admitted that he had never spoken with an Indian prior to the invasion of Alcatraz, persuaded the United States Attorney and the United States Marshal to wait until noon of the following day (Sunday) before arresting the Indians. His only means of persuasion was to go up through channels to the White House to have the decision on the disposition of the Indian invaders taken out of the United States Attorney's office and given to the Department of the Interior.

On Saturday afternoon three representatives of the Department of the Interior waited in William Davoren's office for confirmation by the Secretary of Davoren's recommendations. It was a difficult time for the Department. Hickel, newly confirmed as Secretary, was on a trip to Texas, and the assistant secretary was unable to reach him immediately. Besides, Hickel had been suffering from a pinched nerve in his neck. There was no way to know how the pain would affect his disposition.

In a meeting that morning with Hannon, Davoren, the acting United States Attorney and Barney Old Coyote, Richard Oakes had presented a list of the problems on Indian reservations. He had made an error in his estimation of the group: Davoren, who had been the editor of a weekly newspaper in Colorado and had once tried to ride across the country on a horse, had been interested in Indian problems since his appointment as Regional Coördinator of the Department under the Kennedy administration. Although his job as coördinator gave him only tangential contact with Indians, he had been involved in the Pyramid Lake controversy on the side of the Paiutes. The extent to which Oakes had misjudged them was revealed at the end of his speech. Barney Old Coyote, who had been moved out of Washington by the new administration and assigned to a job as assistant area director of the BIA in Sacramento, told Oakes that he didn't know what he was talking about, and proceeded to tell him what was wrong with the reservation system, explaining the multitude of interfacings the tribal chairmen had to deal with, the land management, education and health problems, etc. Oakes held his ground, refusing to ask the people to leave the island, refusing to negotiate for another piece of abandoned Federal property, but unable to attack the people who confronted him. Davoren and Old Coyote thought him ill-informed about Indian problems, and Old Coyote was suspicious of his claims about Indian religion, but both men admired his activism. For years, they had been urging Indians to take the necessary steps toward getting control of their lives. The occupation of Alcatraz was not what they had hoped for, but as Davoren said later, "It served to get the problems of the Indians on the national agenda." The invaders had by chance caused a direct confrontation not with lovers or liberals, but allies.

It was a long afternoon in Davoren's office. There was little to do other than wait and wonder how Hickel would respond. For Davoren, the situation was particularly tense; there was a good chance that he would soon be asked to resign or move to a less sensitive position. He was more interested in conservation than politics, but there was no way for Hickel to know that. It was expected that he would be replaced by a Republican.

A press release was prepared and sent back to Washington for approval. Davoren, Old Coyote and George Webber of the Bureau of Outdoor Recreation, which had been charged with preparing a report on the possible uses of Alcatraz, discussed the feasibility of the Indian demands for a cultural center and university on the island. Mostly they waited. If Hickel agreed with the acting United States attorney, there would be an unpleasant and dangerous scene the following afternoon. The Indians would undoubtedly try to hide from the marshals or run from them. There would be chases across rusted-out catwalks and decayed floors. It would be miraculous if no one was seriously injured or killed.

It was early evening when the response from Hickel finally came, relayed by his assistant in Washington. The Secretary's immediate concern was for the safety of the women and children in the party of invaders. His only instructions were to be sure that food, water and medical care were available. The island was secured. No one expected the Indians to stay beyond the time it took to negotiate a more suitable place for a cultural center and university. Most of the Federal officials thought they would ask for the old mint in San Francisco or a piece of land on one of the nearby military reservations. The Indians had won. At that point, it was probable that they could have had either place and a guarantee of money to build and staff a cultural center, if not a university. Instead, they chose to remain on the island and stand by their demand.

The first days on the island were a festival. Reporters arrived in motor boats and helicopters; a makeshift headquarters in the ill-defined Indian slum of San Francisco was deluged with food and cast-off clothing. There were donations of money and benefit performances by white and Indian musicians. Dr. Sol Tax organized a committee of scholars to support Indian demands for a cultural center. The Indians had changed from being supported by the Federal Government to being supported by private charity, a victory for the social Darwinists, if not for the Indians. The development of altruism among members of the middle class proceeded at an extraordinary pace during that period, and fire-inspectors around the country would have been delighted by the number of attics, closets and basements that were relieved of debris that could be sent to the Indians on Alcatraz. They were young Indians, caught up in the excitement of a victory; Sun Bear was not there to remind them of the "civilizing" of the White Earth Reservation: "They sent us their junk, and told us to take off our Indian clothes and put it on. Then, when we were dressed in their old clothes, they laughed at us. It was the same again during the Depression. And they always waited around for us to thank them."

Richard Oakes, 27 years old, a Mohawk married to a Pomo, a student at San Francisco State College, maintained his position of leadership among the Indians on the island by virtue of his dedication to the cause. He brought his wife and children with him to live on the island. He refused to drink a glass of beer when he was on the mainland to make a speech because alcohol was not allowed on the island and he did not want to return with the smell of beer on his breath. He made speeches, settled arguments, appointed committees, and allowed himself to be manipulated by his supporters, some of whom saw uses for the takeover of the island that had not occurred to Oakes.

At the temporary Indian Center on Sixteenth street, boxes of used clothing, books and toys were piled on tables and counters, a deluge of junk, and the Indians took it all, making vague attempts to sort it, then carting the boxes to a pier and ferrying them out to the island. The walls were decorated with posters and crude signs. A dozen people sat at desks, typing or answering telephones, and in the back room a mimeograph machine ran off the rhetoric of the invasion. A drunk asked one of the women behind the counter for a shirt, but there were none big enough for him. He

returned to his seat in the window of the storefront building,
there to commiserate with two other drunks. "Fuck, I can't
get nothing here, brother." A child of two or three years
passed by him, pulling a broken toy on a string. He reached
over and patted the child on the head, "You made out okay,
huh, brother." The trio in the window rocked with laughter,
swaying from side to side in unison, as if they had been
organized in a drunken cheer.

A tall man slumped against the counter, resting his right
elbow on the wood, holding up his right hand, which was
swollen and discolored. He was sweating, feverish. A girl
had agreed to drive him to the hospital. While he waited for
her, the sweat spread darkly under his arms and across his
chest. "I think I have pneumonia," he said. "I got to get to a
hospital. Look at my hand! Oh, Christ's sake, look at my
hand. A window fell on it, and cut the tendon. I ain't been
able to work or collect compensation or nothing. I was doing
it to help this guy fix up his place. Oh, Christ's sake, I feel
bad."

He raised the injured hand into the air, like a banner of
meat, and called to the girl, who was using one of the telephones. "Come on," he said, "let's go." The girl hung up the
phone and came to the counter, taking a position a few feet
to his left. "I don't know how to organize a rummage sale,"
she said, speaking to no one in particular. "I don't know
where to hold it. Oh, I never did anything like that before."
The man moved over to stand opposite her, holding his useless hand in her face. "I'll ask the churches," she said. "I'll
look them up in the phone book." She smiled, delighted, and
hurried away from the counter. The man stood there for a
moment, looking at his hand, turning it, inspecting it with
seeming detachment. A shudder passed over him. He stag-
gered momentarily, holding himself up with his left hand
gripping the counter. Two white reporters and a photog-

rapher stood next to him, waiting to interview the principals in the Alcatraz story. The man stared at them. He asked one of the reporters for a cigarette, and then for a match. "Look at my hand," he said. "I'm trying to get a ride to the hospital." The reporter said nothing. The man continued to stare at him, as if trying to comprehend the nature of journalists. He shuddered again, composed himself, then turned with a lurch and went out onto the street.

The organizer of the mainland office, keeper of the petty cash, operator of the mimeograph machine, and leading theoretician of the invasion was a girl of tubercular sensuality, tremblingly thin, strings and knots but for her opulent eyes and the fullness of her lower lip, which causes her to look petulant even when she laughs. The men who used their own cars to pick up donations of food and clothing had to ask her for their expense money. A thickset man with a lantern jaw ruminating over a piece of gum, his blue and yellow athletic club jacket decorated with his name, tribe, and the word ALCATRAZ, a man constructed of brutish lumps, fell into meekness before her. "I need gas money," he said, forming the words badly, the awkward jaw causing a lisp.

"How much do you need?"

"Three dollars." He looked away from her.

"How much do you need?"

"Two dollars or three. I guess three."

"You need that much?"

His head lolled forward. He tried to escape eye contact with her. "For gas," he said. "For gas money."

She went to the cash box and returned with three bills crumpled in her hand. She smiled when she put the bills in his hand, and he smiled in return. There was money enough for him, but not for her. She had come from Paris, where she was working on a degree in anthropology, for the invasion of

Alcatraz. She had slept for only three hours in two days, she did not know where she was staying the next night, and she had given her last twenty dollars to a destitute family.

In the office, she was able to remain tough-minded and efficient, but outside, sitting in a red and white plastic Italian restaurant, drinking bad wine and smoking, lighting each new cigarette with the last, too tense to eat, she relaxed into incoherence. "We don't want the white man's life," she said. "We don't want our civil rights in a society he made. We don't want pollution and the war in Vietnam. We want our own land. Alcatraz is Indian land. We want it.

"Do you know that they're going to blow up my grandmother with an atom bomb?"

"Your grandmother?"

"My grandmother, the moon," she said, suddenly shaken with sobs.

When that had passed, she began to talk about herself, life **and** dreams pouring forth in a panicked admixture of times and levels of consciousness: "My mother died when I was three months old. I'm Winnebago, but my aunt raised me. I left the reservation when I was twelve years old. We were migrant workers. One year I went to fourteen different schools.

"I smoked my first joint on Alcatraz. I'd been offered grass before, but I'd never tried it. I wanted it to be a ritual. We sat on the rocks at Alcatraz and smoked and looked at the lights. Nothing much happened. I fasted out there for three and a half days. I went three days without a cigarette, trying to purify myself, to work out an ideology. Now, I have one.

"I'm so tired. I stayed up all night last night. And then there's this guy who's in love with me. He's a nice guy, but he doesn't understand the importance of what we're doing. He hangs around the Center, half drunk at nine o'clock in the morning, asking me to go to Kay's with him. Finally, I went.

Kay's is the Indian hangout. It opens at 6 A.M. to serve our people. I asked for coffee, but they don't have it, so I had a beer. I told this guy I would never have anything to do with him, if he didn't go out to Alcatraz. I told him to give up his job, or take a day off, if he couldn't do that." She stopped, understanding what she had said of herself, that she was willing to be a whore of good conscience. "I don't care where I sleep," she said, after a moment, "but I care who I sleep with." Then she returned to the scene at Kay's: "He listened to me, but he didn't act like a white, pretending he understood. So I finished my beer and went back to the center.

"There is a guy here that I'm in love with. I smoked the grass with him. I want to go to the Navaho desert with him and purify myself as soon as I get back from Hanoi and Peking and Cuba.

"There's a need to create awareness on the reservations. The first step in a people's fight is being aware that the conditions exist. We have the objective conditions on the reservations, but not the awareness, the subjective conditions. That's why we want a radical theater, like the Farm Workers, to travel to various reservations. The theater will perform in English—the universal language among Indians. But it has to be a theater of sacrifice—no money at all. It will spread awareness of the fact that we're facing doomsday, awareness of the fact that we don't have to accept the system."

She wrote an article about the Indian takeover of Alcatraz and tried to get it printed in *Ramparts*, but the magazine did not want to see her article. "*Ramparts*," she said, disgustedly; "did they call one of us to write something on Alcatraz? No. They sent a white chick out to do it. They don't do that with the Black Panthers; they get Eldridge Cleaver. But not us, we're not black enough for them. We're the white man's burden. They'll write *about* us; they're like the BIA.

There's no self-determination for the Indians. Well, they'll see that we're the biggest trouble this country ever had, worse than the blacks. We want a multinational society."

She wept again when she spoke of Richard Oakes. "He's the greatest Indian leader since Tecumseh," she said. "He's given up everything for this." But she had her problems with him, getting him from place to place, hurrying him to speeches, preparing him, instructing him. It was the same when she talked of Herbert Blatchford: "I ought to call him and tell him to get his ass over here." Again she stopped, seeming to hear herself. "We have to get our elders to come out to the island and teach us. We have to learn to listen to our elders. I have to find my humility."

Though she quotes Che Guevara and sides with the New Left on most issues, she said she has been a Zionist since she was a college student. "And afterwards, in Paris, during the Six-Day War, I volunteered to fight with the Israelis, but there were only two El Al planes a day out of Paris and they were taking only essential people. I care about Zionism, because those people want a homeland too."

During the time of talking and drinking wine in the plastic, franchised spaghetti palace, she was visited by a fat man in a blue beret. He said his name was Patrick, but he made a great secret of his surname. Patrick is a professional radical, part-time actor, and full-time Irishman. They spoke of Stockholm Conventions, Hanoi, ways in which the labor movement could be brought into the peace movement and of the poor security measures taken by the Brown Berets. Patrick spoke at length of Wild Bill Donovan and the OSS, equating his adventures with theirs. "I like that Red Power slogan," he said.

"I don't," she said. "We should have something original, not adopted from the blacks."

He agreed with her, then changed the subject to a discussion of his participation in the security arrangements at the last rally sponsored by the "New Mobe." "Did you see how the Brown Berets let Mad Bear up there? Now, there was no prior notice to them, which there should have been, but they knew he was okay. That's the thing about security that I keep talking about; you have to train your people. You have to train them to know who's okay."

The conversation went on, dreamlike, optimistic, a mad cabal. Patrick enumerated his accomplishments: a small boy who spoke against the war in a grade school class, one local of one union that opposed the war, the radicalization of a dishwasher. He spoke in great secrecy, careful not to reveal his true role in the revolution. After lunch, he went back to his job of handing out towels to little boys at a community swimming pool.

"He's a good friend of our people," she said when he had gone, "a white brother." Other white radicals came to talk with her, the middle management of the revolution, the momentary brothers of the Indians. They spoke of secrets and futures, praising Mad Bear Anderson, the Iroquois traditionalist who had been to Cuba, dreaming of mixtures of Marx and the old Indian ways—God as history and life without history; the synthesis would be magnificent. She drank wine and smoked and wept and laughed, snaring them with her eyes and the trembling of her lower lip, coupling with them in the dream of six hundred thousand Indians delivered to the revolution.

When all of the white radical brothers had gone, she slipped off her beaded headband. "I just can't wear it," she said. "It gives me headaches."

While she exhausted her days and nights for the people on the island, a deep split was developing between Richard Oakes and his supporters and a group led by Stella Leech, a nurse who had left her work at a Well Baby Clinic to move to the island. Mrs. Leech, who alternated between hysteria and the hauteur of a supervising nurse, was accompanied by two of her sons. Whoever Mrs. Leech could not convince with rhetoric her sons convinced with bullying. The council that governed the Indians on the island was kept in constant chaos by the split. Nothing seemed to work out. The women would not cook; a professional had to be hired to run the kitchen. Decorum could not be maintained at meetings. There were accidents: a man fell and fractured his skull; then Yvonne Oakes, the 12-year-old daughter of Richard Oakes, fell down a stairwell. It was a strange accident, for it had not occurred in one of the condemned areas, but in the relatively new building that had been used to house the prison guards and their families, and the stairwell was protected by steel railings which were in good repair. There were questions asked by some of the Indians, but they said nothing to reporters or Federal authorities. The girl was brought to San Francisco General Hospital by the United States Coast Guard. Doctors said she was suffering from a critical head injury. She remained unconscious from the time of the accident until she died several days later.

Oakes was voted out on the day they buried his daughter, according to Cadillac. (That is not his real name, but the one he was using at the time.) "I had them close the casket at the funeral," he said. "I didn't want Richard's wife to see her head. And the press, I had to chase them away. They don't give you no privacy, even at a funeral. I don't know what's the matter with those guys." Cadillac shook his head; he had been with Oakes from the beginning. When Oakes left the island, Cadillac left too.

He sipped mint tea and chewed on health food cookies. His woman, wan and slack, sat beside him, hooking a rug. "It's what pioneer women did," she said. "I'm returning to that way of living." Her eight-year-old son played in the next room, pale as his mother, hesitant and wishing, the victim of too many uncles. The nervous Winnebago girl had stayed with them in the cluttered apartment. It was there that she had been overcome by hysteria. "It wasn't the first time," said Cadillac. "She's had it before. I think she went up north now, or maybe back to Paris." He grinned, his mustache spreading, a wide mouth opening to reveal the comedy of missing teeth.

Cadillac is a short man, with a long, squared off Mexican face set on wide shoulders, and all of him carried about on thin, bandy legs. "*Cara larga*," he says, pointing to the length of his face, overemphasizing the Spanish r's. "That's how I got the name Cadillac. You know every American car is named after Indians; Pontiac, Cadillac for us Mescaleros, all of them."

It is impossible to know who he is: Mexican, Indian, revolutionary, criminal, a man of enormous force who grew ulcers in his gut during eight years in San Quentin. "My mother was a blondie," he said, "but she didn't speak a word of English. My grandfather was Chief Overalls. When I was a kid, I got shipped up and back between the San Carlos Reservation and Mexico. I never went to school, except a little in Stockton, but I speak a little of every language. I got a brother there in Stockton now, he's a doctor. If I tell him I need thirty-five dollars or something, he sends it to me right away. I got another brother in the Mission. He's an alcoholic, but he's been sober four days now. His little apartment is filled with Indians sleeping on the floor, but he says that it's okay, they're all brothers. That brother, he was a lieutenant in the Navy; he speaks seventeen languages and over a hundred dialects.

"I'm an alcoholic, too. I got over a hundred and twenty-three drunk arrests. I've never been out of jail ninety days, until now. I've done time for bad checks, government bonds, illegal aliens, and now I'm on parole after eight years in San Quentin." He made a sharp gesture at his belly: "Somebody died."

He talked on about prisons, his life, while the woman

threaded rags through the mesh base of the rug and the boy played with a toy airplane. "I'm only half a man," he said, looking over at the boy, "but I want my children to be whole, all Indian." Neither the boy nor the woman responded. He returned to talking of prisons: "They're writing a book about me. I'm proof that prisons don't rehabilitate nobody. But I've been out twenty months now. I don't drink any more. Involvement, that's how I stopped. They won't take me back on parole violation now; I got the people behind me; I'm well-known."

The panacea for him is involvement. "We got one guy," he said, "killed three people. You ought to see him packing up baby clothes." He found involvement first in prison, leading a convict strike against the use of prisoners as cheap labor, and another strike against capital punishment. For the second strike he did six months in isolation. He makes no evaluation of it except to say that he is well-known and involved. It is a strangely pure revolution that attracts and maintains him. He has read Che and books about the farm workers' strike: "I heard that I was exploited," he said. "I didn't know what it meant, but I've been living it." The end of exploitation is his dream; he envisions heaven as in an operetta: "If everybody's on welfare, nobody will be on welfare." The date of the revolution, he believes, is September, 1972. If he avoids alcohol and parole violation, he will be ready.

Alcohol is the greatest danger, he thinks. "Indians are allergic to alcohol," he says. "It's biological. The people we buried when I was a trustee were always Indians. Give an Indian five years drinking, and he'll be dead. We're losing too many Indians in the Skid Rows. Drinking breaks them; drinking broke the tribes. Like when the Indians get out of jail, they're so proud, they go right away to the bar. I'll go down the street and meet convicts, and they'll say, 'Cadillac, come on.' I'm well-known. But I don't go to the bars now. I'll drink a Seven Up, that's all. Involvement keeps me sober."

He organized a parade through the predominantly Latin American Mission District of San Francisco for Robert Kennedy. "Then he died, and they wanted the parade for McCarthy, but I couldn't do it. He didn't care about us. They had the parade, but I didn't go."

Alcatraz was a failure in his opinion, but he spoke about it easily, laughter lurking behind the words, madness and sanity, improper response the only response that could make it bearable, like his life, the transformation of rage that failed when he was drunk. "Everyone was proud to come, but once they saw how Alcatraz was, they hung their heads between their legs. The Half-breed Club from Sixteenth Street would get loaded and come out and start fights. They're like motorcycle riders. I was on security because I knew my way around; I did time there. We didn't want nothing but the best for security, people who could hold their mud in case an Indian hits them. I didn't want to fight. I would rather get hit many times than hit one of my brothers. They knew that, so they let me take the bottles away.

"In the first days of occupation of Alcatraz, we didn't let no liquor on, but how many hours could we work? That was one problem. The California Indians versus everybody else was another problem. Then the Red Panthers came, two busloads, but we sent them back; they're too young. And that place is unsafe. I don't know what's going to happen there. Stella Leech is in charge now, and Grace Thorpe—the Government paid her way out here—but I think it should be a man."

That cause lost, he has returned to the Farm Workers and their strike. There must be something to believe in or he will have to say yes to the next ex-convict who invites him to have a drink, and the brief enfranchisement will be lost. It must be Indians or Mexicans, for he cannot overcome his hatred of blacks, and he must be well-known wherever he goes, as if he did not exist except as his existence is confirmed by the objective proof of recognition.

He turned to the woman, "I've got to go to my picket now. Give me thirty-five cents so I can take the bus back." They rose together. She reached into a pocket of her housecoat for the change. After the coins were in his hand, he kissed her, reaching his hand around her neck to pull her mouth down to his. "I used to want every woman," he said. "All the women were mine, all the money was mine. Now, I only want one woman." He grinned, and touched her with a possessor's familiarity. Color touched her cheeks and fled. "You mean that?" she asked, attempting to be both shy and motherly. He said, "I don't even see other women any more." A week later he had moved out.

"Never trust an Indian," said Cadillac. "An Indian will never beg, but he'll steal in a minute," he told the woman. He explained himself to her, but she doled out the quarters and the dimes as if she were deaf, holding him with pale juices and the strings of her change purse until he was forced to fulfill his prophecy and move on.

Victoria Santana met Cadillac on the island. "I don't know how it happened," she said, "but he knows Dago, a great pickpocket, who traveled with a friend of mine who's one of the Indian thieves. My friend was a kind of traveling fence in the Indian underground, and Dago is the best pickpocket in the world. He's a wonderful old man from New York who steals from the rich and gives to the poor. I don't know how many people he's put through college."

They are strange companions for the daughter of a social worker and a professor of history at the University of Puerto Rico, a girl who did the genealogies for Oscar Lewis's book, *La Vida*. Vicky went to the University of Chicago, as her parents had done before her. At twenty-five, she has the barely perceptible uptilting of the head that marks girls of the second generation of good schooling. She smokes filtered cigarettes nervously, wasting them, toying with them. Hers is a style learned in college dormitories; she does not count how many cigarettes are left.

Her parents are separated. She is a social worker, like her mother, but she does not do social work. She moves between Puerto Rico and the Blackfoot Indian Reservation in Montana, where her mother now works for the BIA and where she spent the summers of her childhood with her maternal grandmother. She wants to be one of the people, a sister and confidante to Cadillac and the man who killed three people but now packs baby clothes. The girl from the University of Chicago and the girl who went to classes taught by Lévi-Strauss in Paris both want by virtue of their genetic heritage to find unanimity with the Half-breed Club from Sixteenth Street. But it is impossible. The Winnebago girl who had come to Alcatraz from Paris fled in hysterical despair. Victoria Santana lasted longer, working to establish a routine in the office, seeking order, reaching from her own tentative strengths to touch the people with the discipline of her own life, but finally she left too to go to law school.

It was not that she could not identify with the Indians or understand them: "All Indians go through a suicidal period when they're young," she said. "I remember feeling as if my chest was torn open, exposed to every pain. Anything said by whites or Indians pained me. Hopelessness is the reason for the suicides. It's not the ones who drop out at an early age but the educated ones who commit suicide. If you go back to your reservation, the people don't trust you. If you stay in the white world, the people don't accept you. It's hopeless."

She tried to accept the confusions of old prophecies and mouthing of Baha'i slogans that dominated conversation on the island, but when it came to repeating the prophecies, she said, "I don't know why I'm talking like this; I must be getting schizophrenic or something." She wears denim pants and a GI surplus fatigue shirt, but her eyeglasses are carefully styled. She is the child of a Blackfoot woman, but she does not speak the language; she speaks English and Spanish. "I find it easier to relate to older reservation Indians than to young urban Indians," she said, which is perhaps the best indication of the distance between the professor's daughter and the eighty or ninety ragged, disenfranchised wanderers who found respite from drifting by attaching themselves to the island.

The Indians traveled up and back from Alcatraz on a crumbling gray fishing boat run by a foul-tempered black man. They clambered up its torn and rusted railings onto a barge, carrying their possessions in blanket rolls and tin suitcases, expecting paradise, and encountering two Indians huddled over an open fire in the weathered shed where prisoners and guards had once waited for the only exit from the prison that was so isolated no man could escape from it.

When the tides were wrong and the water was capricious, their bundles sometimes tumbled into the sea, and they arrived with the nakedness of the reborn to climb the long flights of wooden steps up to the guards' housing where the invaders had settled. Indian land was a great cement courtyard surrounded on three sides by abandoned buildings that bore the mark of institutional construction in their lifeless regularity. The lack of heat and electricity forced them into diurnal rhythms. They could not keep fresh meat. They ate in a mess hall, two meals a day and coffee at noon. And they stayed. They had come to occupy Indian land; there was nothing else for them to do but perform the function of the occupiers, which is to stay. They did not build or teach or learn, nor were they destroyers; they stayed. A few planned and a few argued, the council met, there were elections and petitions, but the primary occupation of their days and nights was to occupy. Like flags on the moon, they were the symbols of arrival, people as tokens.

They erected a tipi on a hill, but they were unable to work

the smoke flaps and they did not know how to dig a trench around it as a runoff for the rain. In the apartments of the guards' housing, they lived in barren rooms, cooking in the fireplaces, flushing the toilets only rarely in an attempt to conserve water.

John Trudell lived in such an apartment with his wife and daughter. He drank tea to soothe a bronchial cough and smoked, as if in opposition to that first urge while he spoke of his life on the island and before. "We accepted the fact that Yvonne Oakes died. We didn't want it to happen, but we accepted it. Indians are used to death. America is founded on Indian death, and it keeps going on—the high suicide rate, the life expectancy of forty-four years. Two of my friends on the reservation died before they were seventeen. My uncle died before he was thirty. Another uncle was shot to death in Omaha. The guy that killed my uncle got off, but my grandmother said something would happen to him, that he would be punished for it, and the guy went blind. There are more: guys I went to school with in Flandreau and at Haskell. And all these people died because of alcohol. In Flandreau, South Dakota, I knew of kids of about eleven, and they would ask me to buy booze for them.

"I started drinking at Haskell. That's why they kicked me out, although they said it was because I didn't have papers to prove I was an Indian. I started drinking regularly then, when I went back to the rez (reservation). I was fifteen, drinking cheap wine, things like that. When I left the reservation, I drank all through the Navy. Gradually, I just tapered off. I can't handle alcohol; there's too much vengeance inside me."

He is twenty-five years old, a Santee Sioux who does not speak the language or know the history or customs of his people. He was a student at Riverside Junior College when he heard about the occupation of Alcatraz and decided to join it, but his background is not unlike that of the drunks and the barely literate who comprise much of the population of the island. "I hated the service," he said, "but if I hadn't joined the Navy, I was 100 per cent penitentiary material. I remember once back on the rez we were so hungry we were going to steal a car and get caught so we would get three square meals a day."

In his time on the island, he had learned a declamatory style for any discussion of Indian problems, an easy mask to wear for the herds of reporters and photographers who visited the island. His speech began, "We have been silent too long . . ." and progressed to adjusting to the twentieth century while maintaining Indianness. It is a pathetic speech, like that of the black attempting to be African after twenty generations of separation from Africa. Trudell had not even known the remnants of the world he sought to adjust to the twentieth century. He had never been to a medicine ceremony; he wanted to investigate the Native American Church, in itself a process of acculturation, as a way back to "Indian values."

Alcatraz, he thought, would be the place to begin to revive the Indian world, and the prime tool was to be an Indian university, a place where such things as beadwork and tribal organization would be taught. He did not want to be like his father, who, he said, gave up being Indian. "He's concerned only with his family and himself."

So he protects Alcatraz, defends it, refuses to admit that there is anything but hope and harmony on the island. He coughs and considers whether he dares to flush the toilet, but he does not betray his dream. Though he has nothing of the Indian world, he sees it as hopeful. The white world offered only defeat: "They'll beat you once a day if you're good. They'll beat you twice a day if you're bad. You might as well earn it."

Maria Lavender, a Yurok cum hippie with beautiful dark eyes reduced to absurdity by makeup, who had been put in

charge of the nursery school, had lost her dream. At the end
of the school day, she stood over the disarray of finger-paint-
ings, clay, toys, papers and phonograph records that had
occupied the morning. Her own child played a phonograph
record at screeching, distorting volume. She tried to keep
her composure, asking the child to turn off the phonograph.
It didn't work. When she demanded that the child turn off
the machine, she had her way, but the child responded with
a new demand: "I want an orange."

While she prepared the orange and tried to keep her
daughter from buttering it or dipping it into the sugar bowl,
Mrs. Lavender talked about the island in high-pitched, rapid
sentences, racing to get her thoughts in between the screeching demands of her child. "The political battle on the island
is becoming too bourgeois for me," she said. "It's a sad thing
how some people's hangups overpower them. There should
be love instead of hatred, the good instead of the bad.
There's so much hatred here. People are saying that you
don't have the right to say you're from this tribe or that
tribe. I have a cousin who's leaving the island, because he
says 'why did all these people come to our state and make
trouble.'"

She was interrupted by a squat man with a twisted leg,
who came in unannounced and hobbled over to her, holding
up a nearly completed beadwork headband. "Oh, that's very
good," she said, "very beautiful. Did you make it today?"

He grinned. "There's a lot of mistakes in it," he said, "but
you can't see them. I made it in about three weeks."

"It's beautiful," she said, returning to the orange. He held
it up for another moment, then he said, "I'm going to back it
with leather and elastic." He shook the beads before her face,
grinned again, and quite suddenly tucked the beads into his
shirt pocket and went away.

Mrs. Lavender watched him leave, waiting for the click of
the door latch. Then she began another stream of words:

"To begin with, nobody cared about the nursery. Now, they say I'm not doing a good job. They accused us of not feeding the children. Well, my husband has been purchasing the food for the nursery with our own money, and he asked to be reimbursed, but they said no more reimbursements. I plan on going now, really, now that they're cutting off food supplies for the nursery. These little children can't go all day without some little snack.

"I don't know what the Indians want here in this nursery. The only thing I'm giving them is Indian song. Oh, there are so many things I'd like to start, but I've been told by several people on the island that the things I'm doing aren't Indian. You know, it only takes three people to get you off the island. This morning, I sounded off in front of some reporters, and the way Grace Thorpe looked at me, I don't know how long I'll be here.

"Indian, Indian, to me there's a block when you say Indian; my people always called themselves 'people.' Their cultural background was a very high, loving, peaceful culture. You know, I think pretty soon money's going to lose its value to myself." The child screeched again, and Mrs. Lavender spoke to her softly. She left the child for a moment to begin picking up the papers and toys the children had left on the floor. "I have eight children in the nursery," she said, "and only one mother has showed any interest. All I ask the mothers to do is drop in, learn to be a coöperative, spend twenty minutes."

Outside, on the damp cement field, a young man put aside his crutches and took up his guitar. Lorraine Parrish, a Navaho girl employed by Jack Forbes' Far West Laboratory for Education Research and Development, photographed him from half a dozen different angles. John Trudell asked him to sing something by Bob Dylan. On the other side of the yard, a man was mending a net. "Is that a fishing net?" a girl asked. He shook his head, "Volleyball." She walked away, laughing, "For a minute, I thought someone around here was going to do something practical."

Gary Leech, one of the two sons of Stella Leech who had replaced Oakes as the head of the council, walked across the cement yard. He wore a fur cap, and he had cut off his shirtsleeves at the shoulder. He put his arm around Lorraine Parrish, who indulged him for a moment, then squirmed away. A quintet of thugs marched along behind him, stopping in a line to await his next move. "I hear there's some wood doors left down in the dungeon," he said. "I think I'll get an axe and break 'em down." No one responded. The boy who had been playing the guitar picked up his crutches again and moved off. Gary Leech stood before his remaining audience, posed, his muscles tensed for them to observe. He strutted a step or two, a handsome man, the brutishness only in his boots and the tilt of his head.

He snapped his fingers at John Trudell, who had been adjusting a portable tape recorder. "Cut out that kiddie shit," he said, "and come inside. I want to talk to you." He swaggered up the steps to the guards' housing, butch but not masculine, mean as a cellblock buggerer. Trudell rose and followed him.

The island belonged to the Leeches. Only Richard Oakes had dared to oppose them. There was a council that was empowered to set policy, but the Leeches had their way. A nurse who had come to the island to help in the dispensary left after Gary Leech took drugs and a syringe from a locked cabinet and laughed at her protests. The problems in the kitchen were caused by the Leech boys giving orders and taking what they wanted. A whispered literature of vituperation grew around them, accusing them of not being Indians, making obscene references to the way in which Stella Leech "got a little Sioux in her," but no one dared to face them with complaints. In the softness of the Federal wish to help the Indians and the disunity of the occupiers of the island, the Leech boys had found a warm host in which the soul of the prison could be revived.

When Trudell came out of his meeting with Gary Leech, he and Lorraine Parrish went up the hill to the tipi to smoke, to have an Indian moment. He took out a plastic bag filled with tobacco from Mexico, rolled a few shreds in paper imported from France, and lit the cigarette with matches mass-produced in Ohio. In the ancient fashion, they invited a white man to smoke with them as a sign of friendship. The smoking was accompanied by the sound of Navaho rattles, drums, and voices, which issued from Lorraine Parrish's portable cartridge tape player.

A film crew from the French National Television Network and a bearded man dressed in oafish formality interrupted the moment of Indian culture. The smokers left the tipi to walk along the quiet pathways on the far side of the island. An earnest young man who had been accepted by the invaders to make a documentary film about the takeover of the island followed them down the path, his sound man trailing behind. When he caught up with them, he led Lorraine Parrish and John Trudell to a scenic spot on the west side of the island.

"Now, you two walk up the path, and Lorraine, you say, 'Oh, what a beautiful day.' "

He filmed the scene several times. Lorraine Parrish said her line and John Trudell managed not to cough. Flowers bloomed behind them. The photographer was careful not to step back, for he stood at the edge of the garbage dump. Behind him, the blackened cans and ashes of the garbage made by the people who wished to live again in harmony with nature still smoldered.

Indians had lived on the island before the Spaniards came to California, probably Costanoans, like the people who lived in San Francisco. The bay had been rich with salmon, bass and cod. There had been birds to provide meat and feathers for decoration. Little more is really known about them, for the destruction of the natives of California was the most thorough of the acts of conquest. It is certain, however, that they did not watch television or listen to their songs on a battery-operated tape recorder. If they did, in truth, live on the island rather than just visit, there must have been a supply of fresh water, perhaps a spring; but that, too, is lost in the irreversible time of modern man, and cannot be recovered.

14 INDIAN LOVE CALL

THE TIME OF ISLANDS is over. Insularity is now the province of madmen and doomed societies. Man, the tool maker, is being made over by his tools. And the tools are inflexible; men must adapt themselves to them. The Indian, being human, wants, and to satisfy those wants he must sacrifice himself to the tools that provide them. It is not an easy sacrifice, for it is one's uniqueness that is devoured by the machine, and the Indian is thrashing about in his soul to find a different bargain with the twentieth century.

There is no other bargain to be made. On a crowded earth one surrenders to the machines or perishes. The ripening of chokecherries and the coming of thunder are unacceptable marks of time for the machine. A language that exists in the context of the moment is not suited to the exploration of new planets. And what Indian can fail to know? The machine tells everyone everything instantaneously, without regard for truth, innocent of its own power.

In this last effort to remain an island, the Indian is a man aware of his dying. He gasps, his nerves convulse, he calls himself an activist, radical, traditionalist, Native American, possessor by right of discovery, and he is dying, slipping over into the next world of faceless machinebound existence while his tiring heart hangs in the previous world, hoping for a miracle from Wakan-tanka, Manitou, Taiowa. Any miracle from any quarter will do.

As an Indian, he is an object of the white man's creation,

bearing the white man's name, living in the white man's boundaries, watching himself in movies recreated according to the white man's vision. The museum, the zoo of the dead, awaits him. As a bi-cultural man, he is usually a schizophrenic transition, the object and the enemy of himself, one organism containing two foreign bodies, an endless process of rejection. There is only the melting pot, and after that process what will he be? Will he fare any worse than the rest of us?

It is the process that is killing. Those who fight hardest, the activists, are the ones who suffer most, prolonging in themselves the death agonies, confusedly seeking succor in a world that ceased to exist before they were born. The suffering produces the anger they turn against each other and against all Indians. A man who seeks to save Indian traditions, who claims to glory in them, makes jokes about "Indian time." An activist says confidentially, "Don't believe everything Indians tell you; Indians don't tell the truth." It does not occur to him that he has given a paradox for advice; in his frustration he has come to believe it.

At the Cook Christian Training School in Tempe, Arizona, Ernest Bighorn teaches Indian culture. He has learned the culture from books and from tape-recorded interviews with other Indians. If it has occurred to him that Christianity is not an Indian religion, he does not talk about it.

Conquered and loved, butchered and smothered, the Indian staggers into the battle for a pluralistic society; he has seen death in the melting pot. Hank Adams, born at Poverty Flat, Fort Peck Indian Reservation, raised on the Quinnalt Reservation in Washington, chain-smokes filter-tip cigarettes, punctuating the inhalations with sips of coffee and painfully composed sentences: "All the people I grew up with have either been killed or they killed themselves." He talks about the late Senator Kennedy who gave his telephone credit card to the Indians who went to the Poor People's

March so they would feel less lonely. His is another premature death in Hank Adams' life. There is an aura of that fate about him. He seems to have lived beyond his time, and he is not yet thirty years old. "When I say develop a new Indian life," he confesses, "it doesn't mean the life of a hundred years ago, or a thousand years ago. I'm not certain what it means."

A pluralistic society in the time of television? An Apache girl said she used to cheer for the soldiers when she saw movies about Indians on television. Juana Lyon, who calls herself an activist, refused to tell the name of her grandfather, because "he's always referred to as the chief of the most savage, bloodthirsty group of Indians." She was probably talking about Quanah Parker, who fought the hunters who came into Comanche lands, and later held his tribe together during the first traumatic years of reservation life. The functional history is whatever is believed about the past, and Indians are not excepted from the recreating of history in an electrified tube. They are beset with the same information and misinformation as the rest of us. How can they not respond as we do?

The success of the lovers is assured by the machinery of the society of lovers; the Indian is arriving at the point where the lovers may have complete empathy with him. He can then be freed from hunger and disease, for he will have become human, recreated at last wholly in the image of his conquerors.

There was a life that was Indian, and though it has been made dead by the freezing eye of the anthropologist and the honeyed hand of the reformer, Indians cannot let go the memory of it. In this lost life they see their power. They call for a renaissance.

And what is raised up from the past? A girl of ten, perhaps twelve, years steps onto a cement platform. She is dressed in buckskin and beads. Beside her is a canvas tipi. Her dance will open a three-day Intertribal Powwow at Hayward, California. It is a gathering of Indians, a pageant for the old way, a feast of identity. The girl assumes a position defined by Pierre Beauchamp for the Paris Opera, and begins to dance to a recording of Nelson Eddy and Jeanette MacDonald singing "Indian Love Call."

Indians! There are no Indians left now but me.

Sitting Bull 1844(?)—1890